SHARPSHOOTER
IN THE CRIMEA

SHARPSHOOTER IN THE CRIMEA

THE LETTERS OF CAPTAIN GOODLAKE, VC

Transcribed, edited and annotated

by

MICHAEL SPRINGMAN

Pen & Sword
MILITARY

First published in Great Britain in 2005 by
Pen & Sword Military
an imprint of
Pen & Sword Books Ltd
47 Church Street
Barnsley
South Yorkshire
S70 2AS

ISBN 1 84415 237 5

A CIP catalogue record for this book is
available from the British Library

Typeset in Plantin by
Phoenix Typesetting, Auldgirth, Dumfriesshire

Printed and bound in England by
CPI UK

Pen & Sword Books Ltd incorporates the Imprints of Pen & Sword
Aviation, Pen & Sword Maritime, Pen & Sword Military, Wharncliffe
Local History, Pen & Sword Select, Pen & Sword Military Classics and
Leo Cooper.

For a complete list of Pen & Sword titles please contact
PEN & SWORD BOOKS LIMITED
47 Church Street, Barnsley, South Yorkshire, S70 2AS, England
E-mail: enquiries@pen-and-sword.co.uk
Website: www.pen-and-sword.co.uk

Contents

Preface and Acknowledgements   1

Introduction   6

Chapter 1   The Origins and Reasons for the Crimean War   15

Chapter 2   The Letters-Regimental Soldiering. Malta to Varna, Bulgaria – February to August 1854   18

Chapter 3   The Development of Sharpshooting and Captain Goodlake's Victoria Cross   49

Chapter 4   The Letters – Regimental Soldering. The Landing, Inkerman and Winter. September 1854 to February 1855   66

Chapter 5   The Letters – Staff Officer – Hut Building. March to June 1855.   99

Chapter 6   The Letters – Staff Officer – Death of Lord Raglan. June to August 1855   130

Chapter 7   The Letters – Staff Officer – Capture of Sevastopol and Road Building. September 1855 to January 1856   155

Chapter 8   The Letters – Peace and The Army's Return Home. January to May 1856   171

Chapter 9   General Goodlake's Post-War Career, Retirement and Death, 1856 to 1890   186

Appendix A   Officers of the 1st Battalion Coldstream
               Guards Serving in the Crimean War   190

Appendix B   Generals and Staff Officers Coldstream
               Guards Serving in the Crimean War   196

Appendix C   Military Terms   199

Appendix D   Bibliography   214

Appendix E   1st Battalion Coldstream Guards – Strength
               and Casualties   221

Index   222

Goodlake and Fraser Family Tree

Thomas Mills Goodlake
1807–1877
m. 1828
Emilia Mary Baker

Thomas Leinster
1829–1893
m. 1855
Mary Frederica Glyn
no issue

Edward Wallace
1830–1881
m. 1859
Hon Caroline Wrottesley
d. 1860
no issue

Gerald Littlehales VC
1832–1890
m. 1870
Margaret Curwen
d. 18??
no issue

Emilia Jane
1826–1889
m. 1857
Frederick Webb
of Newstead Abbey
1829–1899

Olivia Elizabeth
18??–18??
m. 1878
The Marquis
de Lasteyrie

Wilfred
b. 1861–1862

Algernon Frederick
1865–1884

Roderick Beauclerk
1867–1916
m. 1889
Lily Theresa Wilson

Augusta Zelia
1858–1925
m. 1889
Philip Afleck
Fraser
1845–1918

Geraldine Katherine
1859–1910
m. Lt. Gen. Sir
Herbert Chermside
No issue
b. 1850

Mabel Cecilia
1864–1891

Ethel Mary
1862–1915

Violet Mabel
1892–1947
m. 1913
Major Robert Carnegie

Phyllis May
b. 1890
m. 1936
Mr Topham
No issue

Son
1915–1915

Charles Ian Fraser
1903–1963
m. 1929
Mary Charity Campbell Preston

Malcolm Robert
b. 1930

James Patrick
b. 1932

Margaret
b. 1938

Jean
b. 1941

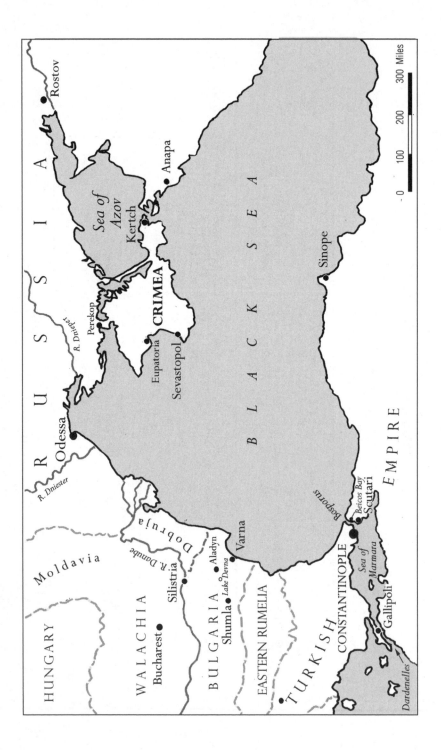

HUNGARY

Moldavia

R. Dniester

WALACHIA

Bucharest •

Silistria •

BULGARIA

Shumla • Aladyn
Lake Derna

EASTERN RUMELIA

TURKISH

CONSTANTINOPLE

Sea of
Marmara

Gallipoli •

Dardenelles

EMPIRE

R U S S I A

Rostov •

R. Dniester

Odessa •

Perekop

R. Dnieper

Sea of
Azov

Anapa •

Kertch

CRIMEA

Eupatoria •
Sevastopol •

Sinope •

B L A C K   S E A

Bosporus

Beicos Bay
Scutari

Varna •

R. Danube

Dobruja

0   100   200   300 Miles

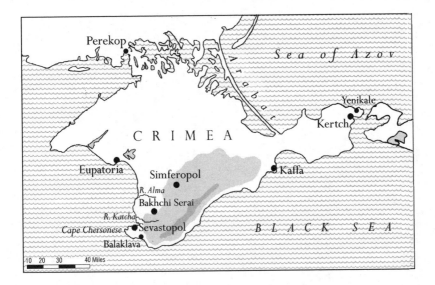

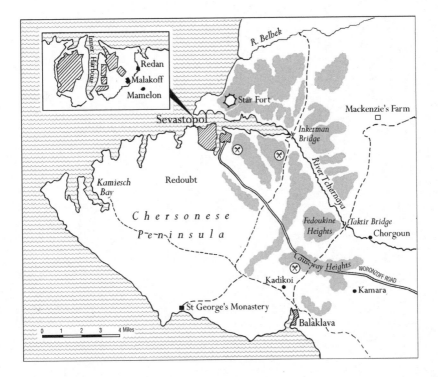

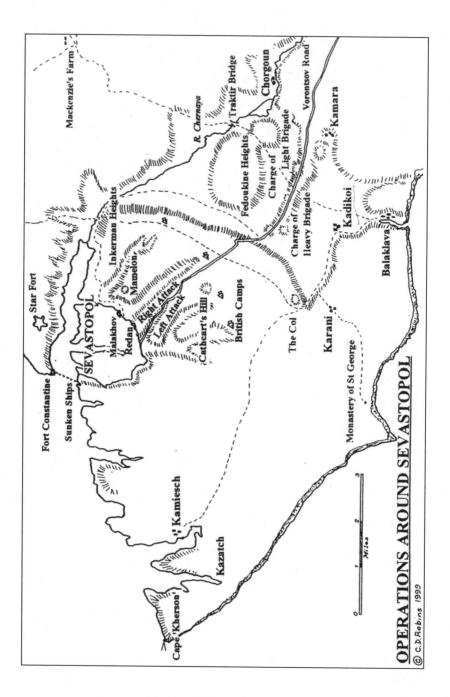

OPERATIONS AROUND SEVASTOPOL

© C.D.Robins 1999

Preface and Acknowledgements

It has been 150 years, a century and a half, since the Crimean War ended with its record of inefficient and bungled supply chains, inept planning in every part of the Government and lack of a proper command and medical staff. The Prime Minister and the Minister of War set the Army the task of capturing Sevastopol, but the Treasury denied the Army the funds it needed for the proper performance of the tasks it had to carry out.

In the time of the Crimea this was typified by the closing down of the Royal Waggon Train and by a failure to maintain a military staff after Waterloo, in the search to find economies. The chaos in supplying the Army in the Crimea resulted in the resignation of both the Prime Minister and the Secretary of State for War, but not the Chancellor of the Exchequer, who was in charge of the Commissariat and who had held up the supply of fodder for the Army. This problem of a lack of co-ordination between the tasks set the Army by the Government and the funds made available by the Treasury to carry them out continues today.

I am very grateful to Major Edward Crofton, the Regimental Adjutant of the Coldstream Guards, for allowing me to borrow one of their two original typed copies of Lieutenant-General Gerald Goodlake's Crimean letters and to entrust me with the task of editing these letters for publication. Major Robert Cazenove has helped me to locate pictures from the Regimental files. The Regimental Archivist Clerks, Corporal Bingley, Corporal Jones and Guardsman Casey have all helped me in my researches.

The Regiment also possesses a medal board with General Goodlake's medals, his Victoria Cross and his Crimean campaign medal, with clasps for the battles of the Alma, Balaklava, Inkerman and the Siege of Sevastopol, which were given by Mrs Goodlake to the Regiment.

The two identical typed copies of the letters, both dated 5 April 1899, were given to the Regiment by General Goodlake's Widow, Margaret Goodlake. The copy I used was dedicated by Margaret Goodlake, his Widow, to Edward Wilson for his faithful and loving service to General Goodlake VC.

The original copies of the letters are not in the possession of the Regiment and almost certainly do not exist. The General died in 1890, long before these letters were typed in 1899. Without his advice and in the absence of these original letters, it would have been hard to find answers to obvious mistakes. These would have not been detected by a typist, with no knowledge of the Crimean War, who was trying to decipher the text and transcribe the letters. There are frequent misspellings of names of people, places, regiments etc. 'Infantrie de Maincre' was typed instead of 'Infantrie de Marine'.

The frequency of letter writing varies very considerably over the period of the War. In certain cases this could be because of operational problems in the field, the loss of letters sent home or their loss at home. Furthermore General Goodlake did not keep the letters from his family.

In the Crimean War there was a severe shortage of writing paper; for this reason, some letters written had writing round the four edges of the paper. In some cases the paper was turned 45 degrees and lines were written at right angles to the original script. Furthermore in the earlier part of the war in the Crimea officers had to write letters in their tents on their laps or else lie on the ground and write on a piece of board. The writing was not therefore of a high standard and would be difficult to decipher, even for parents, wives or other close family members. Tables did not come available till much later in the war, when the troops lived in wooden huts.

There was also misdating of the letters, where the date and location on the letter differ from the timetable of the Guards Brigade's movements. Furthermore the matters written about in the letters took place at a different date to that of the date of the letter. In the list of the letters, there are notes on the alterations made in the dates of these letters, explaining why these changes have been made.

It has not been possible to solve all the questions that arise, especially where nicknames are used for brother officers, or to identify all the people mentioned, even after extensive research has been carried out, including research at RHQ, Coldstream Guards.

I have only been studying the Crimean War in detail since I joined the Crimean War Research Society in March 2000 and went on a Battlefield Tour of the Crimea in September of that year. My colleagues in the Society, who have studied the War extensively for many years, have helped me very much in my researches about the Crimean War, and in particular the following Members:-

Colin Robins, late Royal Artillery, the Editor of The Society's Journal, *The War Correspondent*, has acted as my mentor and guide throughout the writing of the book. He has read the proofs of the book and has suggested alterations. He has also advised me on a wide variety of subjects and in particular on the function of artillery in the war and on the munitions used in the campaign. I am greatly indebted to him for his help and advice, which I asked for and obtained on a regular basis throughout the writing of the book.

Bill Curtis, late Royal Artillery, the former Chairman of the Society, is an expert on musketry and in particular on the Brown Bess Musket, the Pattern '51 Rifle/Musket, the Pattern '53 Rifle, on other weapons and ammunition used in the War and on the drills laid down for firing rifles/muskets on the battlefield. He has given me valuable advice on the use and performance of these weapons during the Crimean campaign. Anthony Margrave has given me advice on foreign medals and on the French Army in the Crimea.

Michael Hargreave Mawson, the Society's Web Master, has given me valuable insights on the French Army and on the medals awarded in the War. Ron McGuigan has extensive knowledge of the command structure of the British Army in the Crimean War. He has helped me to define the command structure of the 1st Division and of the Guards Brigade, which formed part of this Division.

Robert Oliver, formerly a Researcher on Musketry at the Pitt-Rivers Museum at Oxford, has helped me to understand the role of Captain Augustus Lane-Fox, Grenadier Guards, who later became Lieutenant-General Pitt-Rivers, in advising and instructing the Army on the effective use of the Pattern '51 Rifle/Musket [The Minie], which replaced the Brown Bess.

John Joynson, late Coldstream Guards, has given me valuable lists of the officers of the Coldstream Guards, who served in the Crimean War. Major Brian Oldham very kindly looked through my lists of officers of the Coldstream Guards and by consulting his Great

Crimean War Index has suggested various amendments to my lists.

The late Ken Horton has advised me on maps of the Crimean War. Megan Stevens has given me valuable information on the operations of the Commissariat in the War. Keith Smith has given me valuable advice on Crimean War photographs.

Anthony James, who maintains records of officers who served in the Crimean War, has advised me on various officer records. Ed Dovey has kindly made available to me his family's research on the origins of their ancestor Private Stanlake VC, Coldstream Guards. Among other people who have helped me, my cousin, Patrick Mayhew, has kindly lent me his set of A.W. Kinglake's *History of the Invasion of the Crimea*.

Captain David Horn, the Curator of the Guards Museum at Wellington Barracks, has given me valuable advice on matters relating to the Brigade of Guards at the time of the Crimean War. He has also suggested several amendments to the Appendix on Military Terms. Mrs Bridget Webster has researched General Goodlake's family background.

I am most grateful to Dr Duncan Anderson, the Director of War Studies at the RMA, Sandhurst, for suggesting that Dr John Sweetman would be the most appropriate person to advise me on the organization of the British Army in the 1850s. Dr Sweetman, formerly the Head of the Political and Social Studies Department at the Royal Military Academy, Sandhurst, has given me valuable advice on Army organization both before and after the Crimean War. He has also helped me understand the process of reform of the Army's organization.

My brother-in-law, Bruce Lee, has given me the benefit of his knowledge and experience both as an editor and as an author of military histories.

Newstead Abbey, now owned by the Corporation of Nottingham, was formerly the home of Mrs Emilia Jane Webb, the sister of General Goodlake, [Bob in the letters]. After his death and that of his wife his pictures and other items he sent back from the Crimea were left by Mrs Goodlake to Mrs Webb. The estate finally passed to her grandson, Charles Ian Fraser. Mr Fraser sold the estate to Sir Julien Cahn, who presented it to the Nottingham Corporation. Mr Fraser gave all the Goodlake pictures and memorabilia to the Corporation and they are exhibited at the Abbey. I am very grateful to Ms Haidee Jackson, the Curator, for permission to reproduce these pictures in the book.

Simon Seely has given me much valuable advice on using my computer and Brian Cantwell has improved Kinglake's map of Captain Goodlake's operations at Little Inkerman. The other maps were drawn by Neil Hyslop.

Dr Morton, the Curator of the Royal Logistics Corps Museum, has helped me to find answers to logistical questions that arose. The Staff of the National Army Museum have helped me in my researches.

The Staff of the Bembridge Public Library has found numerous books, which I have used in my researches. Mrs Caws, who is in charge of the Newport Public Library, has helped me to research the background of people connected with the War.

I would like to thank Henry Wilson, the Publishing Director of Pen & Sword Ltd, for his help in rearranging the contents of the book, Tom Hartman for his help and my wife for her valuable assistance in checking the corrected pages.

Michael Springman
Bembridge

Introduction

General Goodlake's Family

Gerald Littlehales Goodlake was born on 14 May 1832 at Wadley House, Shellingford, Berkshire, the second son of Thomas Mills Goodlake and of Emilia-Maria Goodlake, his wife. She was the second daughter of Sir Edward Baker Bt, by Lady Elizabeth-Mary, his wife. Goodlake is a Saxon name. Thomas Godelac, Godlak or Guthlac was Lord of the Manor of Hanworth, Middlesex in 1378, and obtained from Richard II, about 1394, the Lordship of the Manor of Woxendon, now Uxonden in Middlesex. Prior to the establishment of Registers in 1536, the family resided at Letcombe Regis in Berkshire. His father served in the 5th Dragoon Guards in the Peninsular War.

From 1844 to 1849 Gerald Goodlake was educated at Eton College, where he excelled at games. On 14 June 1850 he was commissioned as a 2nd Lieutenant by Purchase into the 23rd Foot [The Royal Welch Fusiliers]. On 27 June 1851 he transferred to the Coldstream Guards, becoming an Ensign and Lieutenant by Purchase. On 14 February 1854 he sailed with the 1st Battalion Coldstream Guards to the Crimea and on 14 July 1854 he was promoted to Lieutenant and Captain without Purchase. From 17 October to 27 November 1854 he commanded the Sharpshooters of the Guards Brigade for 42 days, which included repulsing a Russian sortie on 26 October 1854, called Little Inkerman, and during the winter of 1854. For his actions in commanding the Sharpshooters on this day and on another occasion he was awarded the Victoria Cross.

Apart from Inkerman, he was present at the Battles of Alma,

Balaklava, the Siege of Sevastopol and the Battle of the Tchernaya. He was one of the few members of the British Army present at that battle, which was between the French and Sardinian Armies and the Russians. The British Army, apart from a battery of guns and some cavalry, was not involved. In October 1854 he was recommended for a Brevet Majority by HRH The Duke of Cambridge, Brigadier-General Bentinck, Colonel Upton and Colonel Lord F.Paulet. His claim was sent to London by Lord Raglan. It was refused as he had not served in the Army for six years.

During the winter of 1854/55 he served in the trenches during the Siege of Sevastopol. He claimed that he never missed a day's duty in all his time in the Crimea, but was ill on the day of the Battle of Inkerman. From 27 March 1855 to 21 June 1856 he was Deputy Assistant Quartermaster General at the 1st Division, but attached to Headquarters. He was organizing the distribution of huts until 1 September 1855, and thereafter was in charge of working parties, building roads. Apart from the Victoria Cross, he held the Crimean Medal, with four clasps, was a Knight of the Legion of Honour and held the Turkish Medal of Medjidie, 5th Class. On 6 June 1856 he left the Crimea for England.

The British Army in the 1850s and its Preparation for War

By the 1850s Britain had forgotten the lessons it had learned earlier from the successful campaigns of the Duke of Wellington in India, the Peninsular War and on the Continent. The country had been at peace since Waterloo and for the whole of this period the Duke of Wellington had been in and out of Government. In 1842 he had been appointed Commander-in-Chief for life. He had tried unsuccessfully to protect the Army from the attempts by the Treasury to reduce military expenditure after the Napoleonic Wars.

Army Organization & the General Staff

In the Peninsular War the Duke of Wellington had established an efficient and effective divisional and brigade structure, had selected and trained up a competent staff, had also set up a well-organized Military Train and an effective intelligence operation. When peace came, there was great public pressure to reduce expenditure and these organizations had been disbanded in order to save money. The lesson that armies, to be effective, need command, operational, logistical and intelligence structures had been forgotten.

Because there was no proper staff training in the British Army as there was in the German Army, the Army as a body, as distinct from individual regiments, was largely untrained. Out of more than a hundred officers on the staff, only nine had attended the staff course at the Senior Department of the Royal Military College, Sandhurst. The officers who made up the efficient general staff, built up by Wellington during the Peninsular War, had all retired or died. In the interests of economy, the Government did not feel it necessary to keep an embryonic general staff in existence in peacetime.

General Officers were able to influence the appointment of the staff officers they wanted, especially their ADCs, which in Lord Raglan's case were all his relations. However, the Secretary of State for War could appoint a senior officer as Chief of Staff, as happened when General Simpson was appointed Lord Raglan's Chief of Staff.

Without divisional organizations or manoeuvres, the Generals had no experience of handling large numbers of troops. The first Camp of Exercise took place at Chobham in 1853, at the suggestion of the Prince Consort, where 8,000 men were in camp:

> The men were splendidly clothed but they were led by officers who had no conception of military tactics. Units frequently got lost, were found by distracted staff officers advancing with smart determination and affected grimness on men of their own side, were taken off the field altogether by commanding officers who thought the 'whole damned thing' was 'a waste of time'. 'This Army', remarked an officer in the Royal Artillery, with angry exasperation, ' is a shambles.'
> A few months later, with hope and confidence and the cheers of an admiring people, it was sent to war.[1]

The Army's uniforms were completely unsuitable for a campaign in the Crimea, let alone a winter one. The officers of the Brigade of Guards wore cut-away scarlet long-tailed tunics, with large gold braid epaulettes. The men fought wearing scarlet coats. All ranks of the Foot Guards wore bearskins for the first and last time on active service. Prince Albert had designed a side-cap for the Brigade, which was worn by the sharpshooters and in the trenches. All ranks in the

Brigade of Guards wore grey greatcoats, as did many soldiers in the Russian Army.

There were no reserves available either to replace casualties or to increase the size of the Army in the Crimea, except by depleting other regiments at home. The Government had to resort to raising various foreign legions to solve this problem temporarily.

The Military Train, which Wellington had built up to be an efficient and effective organization for supplying the Army in wartime with arms, ammunition, food and materials, was finally disbanded in 1833 to save money. It was clear therefore that there was no adequate supply system in existence which would be able to provision an army in the Crimea.

No consideration had been given to the logistical problems that the Crimean Army would face: how much and what type of transport would be needed to move the troops, what systems should be set up to supply them and to keep them supplied in the field in all seasons and how they would be provided with a regular supply of munitions and suitable food and clothing, etc. The Treasury assumed, without any basis for their decision, that the Army would be able to purchase transport and find sufficient drivers for its requirements locally, which proved to be incorrect.

Army Promotion & The Purchase Of Commissions

During the seventeenth and eighteenth centuries the Crown and its Ministers wanted to prevent the appointment of officers, like those in Cromwell's New Model Army. These men had wanted to exercise political power and wished to challenge and limit the power and authority of the Commons.

Governments wished the officer corps to consist of people with a stake in the country, who were thus unlikely to act like mercenaries, revolutionaries or political firebrands. They did not want professional soldiers, but gentlemen who would regard the Army as an occupation for an amateur with private means, before he inherited his estate:

The Army had never been a profession for which an officer need prepare himself nor once commissioned to take seriously. It had consequently persisted throughout these years of peace, without a hard core of experts, without even an organization. It remained as it had been in the eighteenth century a collection of regiments, each a self-contained unit, efficient or no, depending upon the qualities of its commanding officer, adjutant and its non-commissioned officers.[2]

The exceptions to this rule were those wishing to become officers in the Artillery and Engineers, where entry to the Royal Military Academy at Woolwich was by examination.

Those wishing to join a regiment – cavalry, foot guards or infantry – had to purchase their commissions from those officers who were retiring or being promoted. It was not necessary for a candidate for a commission in the cavalry, foot guards or the infantry to attend and pass out from Sandhurst until the Purchase of Commissions was abolished by Royal Warrant on 1 November 1871.

The most senior officer of any rank in a regiment had the first choice to be promoted, regardless of merit, provided he paid the Regulation Fee. There was frequently an unofficial fee on top of this, which would be very low if the battalion or regiment was ordered for active service or for service in India, which was very unpopular. It was much higher if the unit was on home service. The reason for the lower unofficial fee was that if an officer died or was killed his commission reverted to the Crown, whereas when he retired the sum raised from selling his commission would finance his retirement. This system was very unfair to the widows of officers who were killed or who had died, as it left them without any means of support.

No fee was paid for promotions to fill vacancies caused by death on active service by the officers appointed to these posts. In the same way, appointments made because of an Augmentation, an increase in the officer establishment, were normally made without a fee being charged to those appointed.

Officers who could not pay the Regulation Fee would have more junior officers, who could afford to pay, promoted over their heads. This was both unfair and inefficient as experienced officers often had incompetent or inexperienced officers promoted over them. Finding or procuring the necessary funds was required to finance promotion up to the rank of colonel.

Promotion to the rank of major-general resulted in the colonel losing the right to sell his position to the officer taking over from him. It should be noted that all general officers of the same seniority were promoted at the same time, regardless of their merit.

Double-Rank in the Brigade of Guards

Officers in the Brigade of Guards had the advantage of holding a dual rank, their rank in their regiment and a higher rank in the Army. e.g. captain & lieutenant-colonel, lieutenant and captain, ensign and lieutenant. The double-rank privilege had been awarded to the Brigade of Guards by King James II, King William III and the Prince Regent. This had been done partly to reinforce their loyalty to the Crown and also for their bravery on the field of battle. The double-rank gave officers in the Brigade of Guards great advantages in seniority in the Army, which was reflected in the purchase price of commissions. In 1856 a lieutenant-colonelcy in the Foot Guards cost a regulation price of £9,000 plus an extra 'over regulation fee' of £4,200, making a total of £13,200, whereas a lieutenant- colonelcy in a line regiment cost a regulation fee of £4,500, plus an extra £2,500, total £7,000.[3] The double-rank was abolished in 1871 for officers commissioned after that date, but officers still serving retained their double-rank for life.

Sir Colin Campbell's position in the Crimean War provides an interesting example of the advantage of the dual rank to officers in the Brigade of Guards. Sir Colin had started the war commanding the Highland Brigade and, as he had no private wealth, he had only obtained his Lieutenant-Colonelcy by Augmentation.[4]

Captain and Lieutenant-Colonel William Codrington, who had been promoted in 1846 to a Colonel in the Army without any change in his regimental rank, started the war as a company commander in the 1 Coldstream. In June 1854 Codrington was promoted to Major-General and on 1 September 1854 became Commander of the 1st Brigade of the Light Division, in the place of Brigadier-General Airey, who became Quartermaster General. In June 1855 Codrington was promoted to Lieutenant-General as Commander of the Light Division, when Sir George Brown went home sick. When General Simpson resigned as Commander in Chief, Codrington succeeded him and not Sir Colin Campbell, who had distinguished himself in India, as well as at Alma and at Balaclava. However, Sir Colin ended his military career as a Field Marshal and was created Baron Clyde,[5] while Codrington turned down the offer of promotion to Field Marshal, as he had had experience of only one campaign.

11

Medical

The Medical Department was a staff department, which purchased for the Army medicines, bandages, etc, but it had no doctors or medical staff under its control. Each regiment had a Surgeon and two Assistant Surgeons, who established a battalion hospital. Badly wounded casualties were sent to one of the general hospitals. Although the surgeons wore uniforms, they were not officers and were treated by the Army as civilians. However, as civilians, they were subject to the Mutiny Act [The Army Act of that period.] and could be court-martialled.

No one had considered how soldiers would cook their food, as the Army provided no unit cooking facilities. No studies had been made to ensure that the soldiers' diet was suitable for the heavy tasks they had to carry out or for the hardships they had to endure.

The experience learned in past campaigns had been forgotten. No one was made responsible for the general hygiene of the Army, as Army and Navy doctors, not being officers, lacked executive power and could only recommend measures, which their superiors could and did ignore. In these times cholera epidemics, from contaminated water supplies, occurred regularly in London in summer, as the Thames was used both as a source of drinking water and as a sewer, as it was not then known that this disease was caused by drinking contaminated water. By 1894 effective main drainage systems had eliminated this disease in the main cities in England.

In the Crimea lack of knowledge of this fact caused some regiments to be careless in preventing their water supplies from becoming contaminated by their latrines. This caused cholera epidemics to break out both in Bulgaria and in the Crimea.

Ordnance

In 1847 the Duke of Wellington pointed out that the country was defenceless, as the Government had cut the purchase of armaments drastically after Waterloo. The Army had only 70 field-guns, which had last been used at Waterloo. In 1852 Lord Hardinge, the Commander-in-Chief, and Sidney Herbert, the Secretary-at-War, organized the purchase of 300 nine-pounder guns, which became the Army's moveable armament in the Crimean War.[6]

The Iron Duke had reluctantly agreed to the introduction of a new rifle, the Pattern '51 Rifle/Musket, based on the principles of the French Minie, which had been proved to be greatly superior in trials against the standard infantry musket, the Brown Bess, and the Prussian breech-loader.[7] The Duke died in 1852 and his replacement Lord Hardinge had carried on with the gradual introduction of the Minie when he had funds to do so.

The School of Musketry at Hythe, which was established in 1852, studied the tactical implications of the increased range and accuracy of the Minie. Soldiers, firing the Minie had to learn how to judge distances accurately and to set the sights correctly, in order to use effectively the increased range and accuracy of the Pattern '51, the Minie. This skill was not required when they fired the short-range Brown Bess.

Army Organization

The organization of the Army was difficult to understand, as a number of autonomous bodies, each pursuing their own objectives, shared in managing and controlling its operations and there was no overall authority. These persons were the Secretary of State for War, the Commander-in-Chief, in charge of the cavalry and infantry, and the Master General of the Ordnance, in charge of the artillery and engineers and responsible for procuring weapons, munitions and warlike stores. The Master General was also responsible for building and repairing forts and barracks. The Secretary-at-War, a different minister from the Secretary of State for War, was responsible for finance and for medical services. The Treasury managed the Commissariat, which supplied food and clothing.

All these, including the Treasury, attempted to control and manage the Army. However, this confused and illogical organization made it nearly impossible to produce a coordinated plan and to give it unity of direction. This situation, as Prince Albert said, reduced the Army to a mere 'aggregate of battalions'.[8]

During the War the record of inefficient and bungled supply chains, inept planning, the lack of a proper command system and an effective medical service showed that the Army organization was both incompetent and ineffective. These inadequacies and the horrific casualty lists made it clear to the public that reform of the Army was mandatory, if it was to survive as a fighting force. The process of reform took place during the nineteenth and twentieth centuries, ending in the reorganization of the Ministry of Defence as a tri-services ministry. This process started in 1964 and ended in 1998 with the formation of the Joint Services Command and Staff College.

Notes

1 *The Destruction of Lord Raglan, p.8,* by Christopher Hibbert, Longmans, 1961.
2 *Battles of the Crimean War,* p.19, by W. Baring Pemberton, B.T.Batsford, London, 1962.
3 *Double Rank in the Guards,* Major Colin Robins.
4 An increase in the number of officers in a battalion or regiment.
5 *Double Rank in the Guards* by Major Colin Robins.
6 *The War Office,* p. 179, Hampden Gordon, Putnam, London, 1935.
7 *The History of the Grenadier Guards, Vol.III,* pp. 153–4 and Addenda-p. XX, Gen. Sir F.W.Hamilton.
8 *The Destruction of Lord Raglan,* p.7, Christopher Hibbert.

Chapter One

The Origins and Reasons
for the Crimean War

In 1853 the Russian Empire stretched from Germany to the Pacific and its territory bordered the Black Sea, the Ottoman Empire, Persia and China. The Tsar, who ruled over this immense land, was an absolute despot whose rule was imposed by his secret police. With limited access to the sea, Russia had little foreign trade and thus was not able to develop her considerable resources. Furthermore, her road and rail links were very primitive. She lacked a warm-weather port to enable her to develop foreign trade. To further her expansionist policies, her objective was to conquer Constantinople and the Dardanelles, and thus gain entry to the Mediterranean Sea. In addition, Russia had aims to expand its empire into Turkey, Persia and India. The influence of her agents with the rulers of Afghanistan had caused the British Government considerable problems in eliminating Russian influence in this country, which threatened India's security.

In 1844 Tsar Nicholas I had made it clear to the British Government that Russia regarded the Ottoman Empire as the 'sick man of Europe' and offered Britain dominion over Egypt and Crete, provided Russia could have a free hand elsewhere. The British Government refused his offer as it had no wish for Russia to extend its borders further into Europe and Central Asia and thus to threaten the route to India.

Russia used, as the occasion for their dispute with the Ottoman Empire, the Tsar's desire to obtain protection over the Christian subjects in these territories, for which there were some historical precedents. Russia asked for this right in the spring of 1853, but the Sultan refused, as this would give Russia sovereignty over these lands.

In July 1853 Russia invaded Moldavia and Wallachia. [Modern Rumania]. The British Government then ordered Admiral Dundas's squadron of six warships to proceed to Besika Bay, at the entrance of the Dardanelles, to join the French Navy there, and if necessary to protect Constantinople from attack. The Austrian Government then attempted to use its influence to settle the differences between both parties.

The Tsar's military might had enabled Austria to put down the recent revolt by Magyar nationalists in Hungary and he was therefore sure that Austria was his ally. The Austrian Government was disturbed by the Tsar's expansionist aims in the Balkans, which could also upset its trade in Europe, as the Danube was a major trade route. They feared Russia, which controlled the German-speaking nations and had intervened in the dispute between the German Confederation and Denmark over the ownership of Schleswig Holstein. It had succeeded in obtaining the annexation of this territory by the German Confederation.

In France Louis Napoleon became President in December 1848. He was elected President for ten years in 1851 and in 1852 appointed himself Emperor Napoleon III. He was keen to demonstrate France's power on the world stage.

The Sultan was pleased that Britain and France were supporting him against Russia and put his defences in order. In October 1853 he issued an ultimatum to Russia to withdraw its troops from its territories in a fortnight. In November 1853 the Russian Fleet surprised and sank a Turkish squadron at Sinope on the Black Sea.

In January 1854 the British, French and Turkish fleets sailed into the Black Sea, as Russia needed to control this sea to be able to invade the Ottoman Empire. The British and French navies were sufficiently powerful and numerous to give the Allies undoubted command of the sea. The Russian Navy, whose warships were inferior to those of the Royal Navy, returned to Sevastopol.

In February 1854 Russia broke off diplomatic relations with Britain, but the two nations did not then declare war on one another. The Tsar was sent an ultimatum by the Allies to evacuate his armies from Rumania. He failed to do so and the British Government declared war on Russia on 5 April 1854.

[Editor's Note- *The Great Crimean War 1854–1856,* Trevor Royle, gives a full account of the development of the disagreements with Russia, which proceeded the declaration of war by the British Government.]

Chapter Two

The Letters –
Regimental Soldiering

Malta to Varna, Bulgaria
February to August 1854

GG = Grenadier Guards   CG = Coldstream Guards
SFG = Scots Fusilier Guards

Guards Brigade – Movements and Events

1854

22 February	Embarked at Southampton GG-6 Coys-*Ripon*. 2 Coys-*Manilla* CG-*Orinoco*.
28 February	Embarked at Southampton. SFG-*Simoon*
	MALTA
5 March	Landed at Malta and quartered at the Lazaretto. GG-*Ripon*. CG-*Orinoco*
12 March	Landed at Malta and quartered in the Lazaretto. GG-*Manilla* .
14 March	Landed in Malta and quartered at the Lazaretto. SFG-*Simoon*.

24 April	Embark at Malta.
	GG-*Golden Fleece.*
	CG-*Vulcan.*
	SFG-*Kangaroo.*

| 25 April | Anchor in Dardanelles. |

SCUTARI

| 29 April | The Guards Brigade landed at Scutari and encamped near Kadikoi. |
| | Lord Raglan, the Commander-in-Chief, lands at Scutari. |

13 June	Embarked at Scutari.
	GG-*Golden Fleece.*
	CG-*Andes.*
	SFG-*Simoon.*

BULGARIA

| 14 June | Landed at Varna and encamped outside the gates. |

| 5 July | Marched to Aladyn and encamped at head of Lake Devna. |

| 27 July | Marched to Gevreclek and encamped. |

| 7 August | Varna town burnt down. |

| 16 August | Marched to Hadjimmeh Village [Dschaseli] and encamped. |

| 17 August | Marched to Varna Plain and encamped. |

| 18 August | Marched to Galata Serai on the Adrianople Road and encamped. |

29 August	Marched to Varna and embarked.
	GG – *Kangaroo*
	CG- *Tonning & Emu*
	SFG. -*Simoon*

19

The Journey to Bulgaria and Invasion Plans

On10 February 1854 a Brigade Order was issued warning 3 Battalion Grenadier Guards, 1 Battalion Coldstream Guards and 1 Battalion Scots Fusilier Guards to be ready to embark at Southampton for foreign service by the 18th of the month. Each battalion was to be made up of 40 sergeants, besides the usual staff-sergeants, and 850 rank and file. The Brigade embarked on 22 February and sailed to Malta, arriving there on 5 March, to join the Army of the East. The Brigade was commanded by Colonel Bentinck, Coldstream Guards, who was appointed Brigadier-General on 21 February. The Brigade remained in Malta for seven weeks.

On 21 February Lord Raglan was appointed Field Commander of the Eastern Army.

The British Government still hoped that the naval demonstration would persuade the Tsar to sue for peace. However, as Russia did not reply to the British and French Governments' ultimatum demanding the withdrawal of Russian forces from the principalities, the two governments formally declared war on Russia on 5 April 1854. After war was declared on Russia, Lord Raglan left England for Varna on 10 April and arrived there on 29 April.

The time in Malta was well spent firing the new Minié rifle/musket on the ranges. Each battalion was issued with 200 Miniés before sailing and more were issued in Malta and in Varna, so that the Brigade was by then fully equipped with the new weapon.

From 14 April the Turkish Army in Silistria in Bulgaria had been besieged by the Russians. On 22 April the Guards Brigade left Malta bound for Scutari, so that the Army was on hand to defend Constantinople and to support the Turks if they needed help.

Silistra and Shumla were fortified towns in Bulgaria, located south-west of the Dobruja. This was the marshy area between the mountains and the coast of the Black Sea. These towns were defended by experienced Egyptian and Albanian troops, which Marshal Pashevich attacked. However, the Turks defended Silistria heroically and the Russians raised the siege on 23 June.

The Brigade arrived in Scutari on 29 April. As it was clear that Constantinople was unlikely to be captured by the Russians, on 13 June the Brigade embarked for Varna in Bulgaria, arriving there on the following day.

The British Army campsite at Varna was on wet ground and near to a stagnant lake, which caused sickness amongst the soldiers. The French occupied higher ground and suffered fewer casualties.

On 1 July the Brigade moved ten miles inland to Aladyn, on the edge of Lake Devna, which proved to be a very unhealthy place. The men suffered from typhus and dysentery and about a fifth of the men were admitted to hospital. On 27 July the Brigade marched to the village of Gevreklek, three miles away, where cholera broke out.

[Editor's Note-Cholera is an acute infectious water-borne disease, characterised by watery diarrhoea, vomiting, cramps, suppression of urine, collapse and death.]

On 16 August the Battalion moved to a seaside camp in Varna, which improved the Brigade's health.

While the Battalion was at Varna fifty-seven men died in the camp hospital, nearly all from cholera and typhus. Lieutenant-Colonels Trevelyan and Boyle MP died of disease and five other officers were invalided home.

The written orders from the Secretary of State for War, the Duke of Newcastle, instructed Lord Raglan that his first duty was to defend Constantinople. He was also informed by the Duke that the war aims of the Government were to check and repel the unjust aggression of Russia and that there was no prospect of a safe and honourable peace until Sevastopol was taken and the Russian fleet destroyed.

Lord Raglan was told by the Duke to find out as much as he could about Russian troop strengths in the Crimea and about the defences of Sevastopol. The maps available were unreliable and there was no clear idea of Russian troop strengths.

In the opinion of Lieutenant-Colonel Ross-of-Bladensburg, the Coldstream Guards historian,[1] the government suddenly decided on a change of policy to make Russia submit, as Russia had ignored both our diplomatic and our naval demonstrations. The country was losing its patience and wanted action. As the Army was not required to help the Turks, since the Russians had raised the siege of Silistria, some other task had to be found for it to perform. The government then accepted the first plausible scheme put forward, without considering the risks involved. It decided to take Sevastopol by a *coup de main*, although they were in ignorance of the strength, defences, armament and capacity of the fortress and had little idea of its layout.

The highly optimistic opinion of the government assumed that the problem could be resolved in a few months and that the Army would not have to winter in the Crimea. The government knew that both the transport system for supplies and the medical services were defective and that we had no reserves of troops to replace casualties and to reinforce the Army. It also had been informed by our diplomats that winter in the Crimea came in November, leaving only six weeks of good weather to carry out this task.

Furthermore, if this operation could not be successfully completed within the six weeks, it would be necessary to besiege this fortress. To complete this operation successfully, sufficient troops would be required to construct and defend a trench system, and also to contain the enemy's field army. This would take time and no estimate had been made of the number of troops required to carry this out. However, the decision was taken to go ahead, despite the fact that our fleet had control of the Black Sea and that the Russian fleet was blockaded in Sevastopol.

On 29 June Lord Raglan received a despatch from the Duke of Newcastle instructing him to prepare an expedition to take Sevastopol. Lord Raglan had little option than to comply, which he did against his better judgment:

> Hence the descent on Sevastopol was in the nature of an afterthought; a crude design, hastily proposed and rashly adopted, without reflection or calculation and concerted without reference to the Commanders at the seat of war, who nevertheless were forced to accept it and were held responsible for its execution.[2]

Captain Gerald Goodlake

After only four years as an officer in the Army and three years with the Coldstream Guards, the voyage to Malta must have been like a holiday, with champagne on Wednesdays and Sundays. The next journey to Scutari had been less comfortable, with sea water in his cabin. When he passed by the Plains of Troy he thought they looked like a bad grouse moor.

At Varna and in the Crimea, with the appearance of cholera and death and with the hardships of campaigning, Captain Goodlake and his brother officers would have gradually come to realize the barbarity of warfare. The death of his company commander, Colonel Trevelyan, from cholera, very early on in the campaign would have been a foretaste of worse to come.

Captain Goodlake was nearly twenty-two and a half years old when he landed in the Crimea and he was just over twenty-four years old, when he returned home at the end of the campaign. Throughout the letters he tells his parents that it is ridiculous for them to advise him what and what not to do.

On 28 April he mentions Freddy Vane, Ensign F. Vane, 7 Fusiliers, and the General, Colonel W. Codrington, both family friends. William Russell, the *Times* Correspondent in the Crimea, explains that Codrington was often spoken of as the coming man: 'The General who would arise out of the *débris* of old fogeyism, red-tapery, staffery and Horse-Guardism of the British Army'.[3]

He also writes about the Fight at Odessa. 'On 22 April 1854 a British steam-frigate, *HMS Furious,* arrived off the port of the Black Sea port of Odessa, to evacuate the British Consul and other Nationals. Despite a flag of truce, the Russian batteries opened fire. Rear-Admiral Lyons ordered fire to be returned and *Samson* and *Tiger* and two French warships, *Descartes* and *Vauban,* opened fire. They were supported by *Furious. Terrible, Retribution* and *Mogador,* and by the Royal Navy's new rocket boats, firing 24-pounder projectiles. By the end of the action twelve hours later the main magazine on the Imperial Mole had exploded, several warships had been sunk and Odessa's fortifications had been largely destroyed'.[4]

On 5 May he mentions that Scutari Camp looks just like Chobham, as in 1853, under the influence of the Prince Consort, the first Annual Camp of Exercise took place at Chobham.

On 26 June 1855 he wrote, 'No one who has not actually seen service here has the slightest idea what it is. You might read for a 1000 years about it and would not know what the reality is.' He was definitely growing up and becoming his own man.

On 25 August 1854 he writes that next Friday the Army sails for the Crimea. He says that it will be an impressive sight to see the combined fleets of England, France and Turkey, 100,000 living souls going to attack Sevastopol, just like a review of the fleet at Spithead. The fleet will cover our landing, but he says shrewdly that it will be a rougher job than the people of England expect.

The Letters

The dates of certain letters have been altered as the facts reported in them took place at a different time. The altered dates are shown in italics and the reasons for this alteration are shown below.

23

Malta – 4 March to 22 April 1854.

6 March	1854	The Club, Malta	Father and Mother

Scutari – 28 April to 13 June 1854

28 April	1854	In the harbour Constantinople on board the *Vulcan*	Father and Mother
5 May	1854	Scutari on the Quarter Guard	Father and Mother
26 May	1854	Scutari	Father and Mother
9 June	1854	Scutari, Tent	Father and Mother

Varna – 14 June to 29 August 1854

16 June	1854	Varna	Father and Mother
27 June	*1854*	The Camp about a mile from Varna	Father and Mother
27 July	1854	Camp name not known [7 miles from last camp Aladyn]	Father and Mother
8 August	1854	Gevreclek, Bulgaria	Father and Mother
19 August	1854	Varna-five miles from Galata Brun.	Father
25 August	*1854*	Varna	Father and Mother

Revision of Dates of Letters.

The dates of four letters are shown in italics. The dates and the places where these letters were written and the events mentioned in the letters did not agree with the timetable shown above. After taking into account the facts within a letter, their original dates have been amended as follows;

27 APRIL 1854, VARNA. The Army was in Varna from 14 June to 29 August 1854. In this letter it is said that the Russian troops had retreated over the Danube, which took place in June 1854. The shops at Varna are mentioned, which were all burnt down on 7 August 1854. The camp was said to be a mile from Varna, which the Brigade left on 1 July to march to Aladyn. The date has been changed to *27 June 1854.*

25 MAY 1854, VARNA. Colonel Trevelyan's death on 21 August 1854 is mentioned as just having taken place. In addition mention is made

of the imminent voyage to the Crimea, which took place on 29 August 1854. For this reason this letter is now dated *25 August 1854.*

17 JULY 1854, VARNA. The Army did not land in the Crimea until 14 September 1854. The letter was written after Colonel Yea's death on 18 June 1855 and after the sale of his possessions on 26 June 1855. The revised date taken is a year later, the *17 July 1855.* See Chapter 6.

25 AUGUST 1854, VARNA. The date of this letter has been changed to *25 August 1855*. The Army landed in the Crimea on 14 September 1854. This letter mentions the bombardment of Sevastopol and the Russian bridge across the harbour of Sevastopol from the south side to the north side. The fifth bombardment started on 16 August 1855 and the bridge was built in this month. See Chapter 6.

The Club, Malta
6 March 1854
My dear Father and Mother,

We started on Thursday morning from off Cowes, Isle of Wight and arrived at Malta at 7 o'clock on Saturday morning, averaging 10 ½ knots an hour. I had a cabin with Peter[5] and we got on capitally together. Bingham, Wildbore the Surgeon and myself the only people sick, but we got over it on the third day and were better than some of the others who were not sick at all.

We had a capital skipper. Breakfasted at 8 30, lunched at 12, dined at 4, tea at 7, grog at 9; the best of everything. Champagne on Wednesdays and Sundays. We paid 3/6d a day, government the rest. We passed Gibraltar on Tuesday morning at 5.30, had a capital view: did not stop a minute, was rather disappointed: saw land at times, the African coast nothing particular. We saw some dolphins and porpoises and some turtles floating with their heads out of the water. One day seemed just like another. We did nothing but eat, drink, sleep and smoke. The drums and fifes played after dinner from 4 till 7 and the men danced and sang in part. We had an agreeable voyage.

We disembarked on Saturday at one o'clock. Everything, luggage and all arrived safe. We were quartered on an island, three companies in the Lazaretto, four companies in Fort Manuel, one company at Fort Tigne.

The officers I am quartered with are Newton, Eliot, Dawson,

Armytage, Bingham, Dawkins, Peter and myself.[6] We have to go over to Valetta in a boat across the quarantine harbour; the whole of the Grenadiers and Fusiliers are quartered with us in the Lazaretto. We beat *Ripon* and *Manilla* hollow. *Ripon* came in Sunday morning and *Manilla* has not yet arrived: there is some report that she was seen in the Bay of Biscay with her engines stopped and her sails aback.

[Editor's Note. 3 Grenadiers were in *Ripon* and also in *Manilla*, which did not arrive until 12 March.]

Valetta is a white stone town with narrow streets on a rocky hill surrounded with every possible fortification you can conceive. The streets are paved by cutting them out of the rocks: lots of steps, stones, nice little boats, and great mules: extraordinary carriages. People stink dreadfully: women (all that I have seen.) very ugly, rather good eyes.

You can get anything you want here but very dear, much more than in England: everything has risen in price in consequence of the quantity of soldiers quartered here. There is a club we belong to, a very good one. We pay £1 subscription. Everybody talks English, which is, as you will say, a very good thing for me.

We have just got a mess-man, 4/4d a day dinner without wine, 2/6d breakfast whether we eat it or not, considered cheap here. Cooks are asking 12 to 15 guineas a month; the Grenadiers can't get one at all. They saw one who would not come under 10/- per head for dinner.

I have met several Eton fellows, one who is, (or I dare say will be), very useful, old Cooksley's son,[7] who is in the Commissariat Department.

We have an opera here: cigars 8 for 1/- very good: wine very dear. The whole battalion is to go out for Ball Practice [Range firing] tomorrow and continue every day as long as we are here, so I expect we will not have much time for ourselves. We cannot be drilled as there is no room. We can only get a 150 yards range.

Peter has done nothing but buy Maltese jewellery; he is very happy but still agrees with me that we have seen nothing half so good as England, or have been half so comfortable as when at home. We know nothing of the war, everyone here is quite ignorant. We all go about in uniform, blue coats. [Undress uniform]

I have had occasion to use my stove, as the first night we had all to sleep in barracks. I cooked some ham, and got wine, biscuits, and two old cocks which I broiled. I have a room with Peter and Bingham. The men are below as we are above. All the rooms are the same going round an immense stone building. The passage is on large arches without windows facing the two harbours below, they are all stone with nothing in them.

My bed does very well, but I am rather put to for a pillow;[8] the leather sheets are invaluable. The weather except today has been very cold.

The regiments that come after us are to be encamped on the island, so we may think ourselves lucky. We are very comfortable. It is rather amusing to see all the men smoking cigars. I have everything I could possibly want and am very well and comfortable and we have a good lot of fellows out here. Remember me to everybody and as we have been here so short a time I have no news and being rather busy, with the intention of writing soon again with best love, every good wish, and many thanks.

> Believe me,
>> Your affectionate son,
>>> Gerald Goodlake

In the Harbour Constantinople on board the *Vulcan* –April 28 1854

My dear Father and Mother

I will relate to you our voyage and the news as well as I can; if you only knew the row, bustle and confusion, you would not I hope be surprised at the brevity, or the way in which this letter will be expressed. I am quite well and hope you are also. I wrote to you a letter from Malta on the eve of our embarkation. We started on Saturday morning at 3 o'clock am, blowing hard, our skipper in doubt whether we should not have put back; we did not, and have arrived safely here. I had a cabin with five others, Peter, Armytage, Willison, Dunlop[9]. The first three days were truly wretched. All on our backs; two waves broke into our cabin, wet me through in bed, two feet of water in our cabin and remained in that state till Monday, when we began to recover, and about Tuesday got it all right and comfortable.

We had a hailstorm going through the Dardanelles, arrived at Gallipoli[10] on Wednesday 26th and saw the camps in the distance. The weather is bitterly cold, after the heat at Malta. I was much disappointed with the scenery, nothing compared to Scotland, or even to England. The usual things happened on the voyage, sails in sight and land in sight all the way, after the first two days, low mountains covered in snow. The Plains of Troy looked something like a bad grouse moor. I could not remember anything from Homer, others

27

pretended to. My opera glasses which you gave me were of great use and very good ones. I am so much obliged.

Lord Raglan had not arrived when we left Malta, it was a false alarm. We were not expected at Constantinople. I have nothing more to say about the voyage, so I will tell you about Constantinople. When we arrived at Gallipoli we got orders we were to be quartered at Scutari. We are to be embarked tomorrow and to go under canvas. I was disappointed with the place at first sight, yet I do not know what to expect more, I of course know nothing of it yet.

Three line regiments are in barracks, which causes us to grumble a little. *Freddy Vane* and the *General* are here.

The mail goes tomorrow. A fresh order has arrived, we are to disembark directly. I am ordered to my camp. I have no more time so must conclude, the mails go every eight days. I will send you a letter by the next mail.

There has been a fight with the fleet at Odessa, 3 French, 3 English steamers went for an apology for a flag of truce which the Russians fired at; they would give none so they knocked their fortifications about their ears, killed from 5 to 600. We had one man killed and 8 or 9 wounded and set some ships in harbour on fire. The three English steamers engaged were the *Terrible, Retribution* and *Fury*; they fired red-hot shot and shell. *Terrible* is 2 yards off us now, with 11 shots in her hull.

A Corporal has come after me. A thousand thanks and love to all. I will write you a long letter next mail.

Ever your affectionate son
Gerald L Goodlake

P.S. I have had a bad job to write what I have.

Scutari[11] on the Quarter Guard
May 5 1854

My dear Father and Mother,

Lord Raglan arrived on 29 April and his staff, as you will see by the papers before this reaches you, also the account of the attack on Odessa.

We are encamped in a grass field about a mile from Scutari, and are much delighted at it. The unhappy line regiments, which are billeted in barracks, are positively eaten up by the lively fleas. We are to be two hours under arms everyday, Brigade firing three times a week, so we have plenty to do. It is exactly like Cobham.

I went over by water in a caique to Stambool, Pera and Galata,[12] but was miserably disappointed; filthy dirty streets, about four yards wide, full of bestiality, and dogs, most of them mangy. Turks smoking, not caring a farthing for anything, so much so that upwards of a thousand houses were burnt down the night before last; they did not try to put the fire out, but sat down and said, 'God was great'; it was at last got under control by some engineers and soldiers. There are enormous bazaars, but I could get nothing, they sell much better things in London. They are thundering rascals, they will ask a sovereign for something and take 3/-; it is no use buying anything without a dragoman.

I had a Turkish bath which is certainly very pleasant and to be thoroughly enjoyed by everybody. There is a Divisional order to kill all the dogs round here, so of an evening, it is just light infantry skirmishing. The 23rd & the 33rd bagged 23 dogs last night; a great shame, I think, but they certainly are great thieves, coming round your tent howling all night and seeing what to devour.

There are an immense number of storks, they are so tame. I made a collection of caps in my company, bought some powder and shot and went out quail shooting and killed 17 ½ couple of quail. Yesterday I shot 12 ½ couple of quail and a hare, the top bag in camp. The quail are just coming into breed, poor creatures. There are some wild boar and deer up country; we are going to get up a party and go some day.

We see a great number of wild irregular horse coming past our camp every day to offer their services to the Sultan. They call them Bashi Bazouks; they are a thieving horrid set of rascals, but picturesque looking fellows. We are all very well and happy together.

The Brigade is separated from the other encampments by a little valley, and a brook in the bottom, an obstacle to some of the staff and a showing off point to others.

We are to be brigaded with three Highland regiments to form the Heavy Brigade. The 7 Fusiliers, 23rd, 88th, 77th, and 49th will form the Light Brigade. The Colonel[13] is furious, he says that Fusilier regiments have no business to be in the Light Division. I see a great deal of him and Freddy Vane.

I will remember you to all your friends, both Anstruthers[14] ask after you, with old Bill who is in high spirits. Astley[15] is at this moment running a man of the 33rd in and Astley has won.

Bentinck[16] informed us that we were to provide for ourselves, (the subs) with a mule or baggage horse, that we were to carry our tents, baggage and everything, and that we are allowed 1 lb of barley or

1 ½ bran a day by the Commissariat. That was all they could do for us, and the Captains of Companies are worse off still, they have to provide mules to carry the men's tents, 6 to a company. We are not allowed anybody to look after our horses, but I have managed to get our doctor, Skelton,[17] who is allowed a groom, to agree that his groom will look after my horse. Two minutes later, four others asked him the same question. That's what I call being <u>early awake.</u>

I think I have bought a horse today, about 10–12 years old, very ugly but much bigger and stronger than any of the horses out here. I picked him up in the country when I was quail shooting and gave £15 for him. They asked £30 at first; it took me a long time to beat them down; I went away several times but they came after me, and at last I concluded the bargain. I am going to call him General Brown[18] because he is such a brute; he is quiet and has not a trick in him.

All the horses and mules have arrived from Malta and were piquetted out in front of our lines; about thirty got loose, you never saw such a row in your life, kicking, biting, rearing and falling head over heels all over the place; some of the horses are much hurt. I shall piquet mine and Peter's separately. Peter is very well and I think enjoys this life very much.

A thousand thanks for your kind offers to send me anything from England, but I think I better buy the things that are used in the country; they are very clumsy but strong and durable; in addition, there is great difficulty in getting anything through the Customs House. They take off the directions and won't let you have them out unless you have a Firman (permit) from the Sultan, which is a great bore to get.

We are all going next week to see the Mosques; we go in a large party as it cost £10. Poor Bingham[19] has just come into my tent in a terrible state, because three of his horses have died on their passage out, so his governor says.

I have seen nothing since I left England either to astonish or make me open my eyes wider. I am afraid that you won't think much of this letter, but the fact is that we are so engaged with duty, cooking etc, that we hear no news or see anything hardly. I must now conclude with best love to Bob.[20] I hope she is enjoying herself and all.

With many thanks for all your kindnesses.
Believe me ever.
Your very affectionate son.
Gerald L.Goodlake.

Scutari
26 May 1854
My dear Father and Mother,

The latest news is that the Light Division start for Varna tomorrow; we follow early next week. Some French are already there. Silistria [Rumania] is closely invested and must fall if we do not come to raise the siege. The Russians have attacked it twice and have been repulsed.

I have just seen Barker, 68th Regiment, who has been up to Varna and Shumla and who gives a very good account of the place. Everybody is in capital spirits longing to have a turn at the Russians; the moment they can get any troops concentrated they will commence business.

Everyone is very well here; the men are very fat. I don't know what it will be like when they begin to march. We had an order Wednesday last to parade without stocks,[21] which is a great comfort.

We had great doings on the Queen's Birthday [Trooping the Colour.] in the Brigade, all descriptions of games; you will probably see an account in *Bells Life*. I had the misfortune to lose my little pipe and had my only suit of mufti, [plain or civilian clothes] torn to shreds off my back, for the men in a moment of inebriety, seized Astley[22] and myself and carried us round the illuminations. I hope to find my pipe and have offered a reward for it.

A poor fellow called Macnish of the 93 Highlanders was coming home last Sunday evening crossed a little gully, which owing to a terrific thunder-storm was full of water. He was washed off his feet and although an excellent swimmer was carried into the sea and was drowned; his body was not found for several days; he was the only son of a doctor in Edinburgh. Another brother officer was with him, but the branch of a tree prevented him being carried along, but he was quite stunned. Both were sober at the time.

I will now relate my adventure with General Brown, my horse. In my bargain I stipulated that he should give me a bridle and in going to fetch one he met another officer and sold my horse to him for £18, as I had not paid for him. I was savage at the time, but now I am quite delighted, as I have bought a little horse, which I think (as well as others) is about A1 in camp. I gave £25 for him which is a lot of money, but I thought I should have a good one. He is very strong and handsome. The General[23] said when he saw him "By Jove, you have got a nice one there." He is very like Earl, same colour, very

31

good action. Best love to Bob and tell her he is perhaps not quite so handsome. The Brigadier[24] has taken a great fancy to him and wants him very badly. I have been offered £30 for him at three different places, but I shall not part with him.

I have been out shooting once or twice since I wrote last; one time with Peter, who is very well and so fat. We killed 13 ½ couple of quails, 2 land quails and 1 hare. Could you please send me a dozen or two small trout flies in a letter, as there are a lot of trout and fish close by where we are going to. I wish I had bought my gun, no end of game.

Now dearest a thousand thanks for the pillow. I have not got it yet or the letter as Colonel Scarlett[25] has not arrived but no doubt I will get it all right.

Last Friday we got a *Firman,* which is a piece of paper worth £10 of our money, to see the Mosques. We were of course a large party. They are certainly immense buildings and worth seeing; you could move a Battalion of Infantry about in close column. The *Seraligo* I was much disappointed at, a sort of palace of large low rooms with very little furniture in them and one or two badly kept gardens.

About 5 miles up the Golden Horn there is a place called 'Sweet Waters' where all the Turkish women assemble on Friday afternoon, sit in groups, and sing and play music or make rather a noise and smoke. I should think that without the slightest exaggeration there are three or four thousand women, dressed in the brightest colours possible. Of course most of the male population are found there. You get a large party of fellows together and hire a large caique, which is very comfortable, and are rowed up. It is a very pleasant way of spending an afternoon.

We played a cricket match today Marylebone Club (in Asia) versus the Army. We only had one innings each, the MCA winning by 23 runs.

I am much disappointed with the Turkish tobacco, it is just like so much tasteless smoke in your mouth or at best like chopped hay.

It was a bad business losing the *Tiger* steamer in the Black Sea.[26] You will see the best account of it in the papers before this reaches you; it seems they got aground in a fog which lasted 8 days. The Russians killed one midshipman, a few sailors and the Captain Gifford had both his legs shot away. He is brother-in-law to Ben Stephenson,[27] our Brigade Major.

There seems to be a great doubt whether there will be a brevet or not, no one knows for certain; the old birds are in a great fright of being sent home. Cumming[28] is to go in three months for regulation; that is settled.

With best love to all and every good wish and my thanks for your kindnesses.

Believe me,

Ever your very affectionate son,

Gerald L. Goodlake

P.S. Best love to Bob and I hope she is enjoying herself. Stephenson Blackwood[29] is very well and attached to our Brigade. Fred Vane is in capital health and is always writing home and never gets any letters. I hope that Harry [brother] is better, best love to him. You better send my letters in future down to Horse Guards and they will forward them free. A casting line for the flies would be very acceptable. As for boiling water before one drinks it, it is all nonsense, as the water is capital anywhere.

Tent, Scutari, Asia.
9 June 1854
My dearest Father and Mother,

I received your letter of the 14th May, many, many thanks for it and for all the good wishes contained therein. I have also to thank you for the air pillow which I got yesterday from General Scarlett. I am going this afternoon to call on him and to thank him.

I should have written last mail but the 'Commissionaire' [Commissariat] stated they had a great difficulty in providing baggage animals, so Lord Raglan said two officers in each Battalion should go to buy horses. Jolliffe[30] and I went from the Coldstream, which prevented me writing sooner as we only returned yesterday. We bought three and twenty animals, averaging £14. 6s 5d each and got them all passed. The Duke of Cambridge complimented us and said that if there were any more animals wanted we would be sent. I was highly delighted to see we got better horses than the Grenadiers and the Fusiliers. [Scots Fusilier Guards.] We had great fun buying them; you can have no idea of the rascality of the Turkish nation.

On Wednesday the 31st, the Derby Day in England we had some Brigade races which was very good fun. I ran my horse, which ought to have won, but Sir James Dunlop[31] rode him so badly and lost so much at the turn. There was a great mule race which was by far the best amusement in consequence of the stubbornness and kicking propensities of the mules.

The Sultan inspected us one day. I will tell you what our Sergeant-Major[32] and the Drill Sergeant[33] thought of him. The former said he looked like an emaciated crawler, the latter like a broken down Frenchman, which is a good description of him.

I will now tell you of our reported movements or what news we have from the war. I cannot answer for the truth of all that I write, as there are such lies going about the camp every minute. We are to march to Monutain about 8 miles off on Monday, stop there till Thursday and then march to Beicos Bay above Terek,[34] when we shall either embark for Varna, or remain there for a month or six weeks as Lord Raglan says that they cannot concentrate 50,000 French and English under that time. We are very deficient in cavalry so they all say here.

The Russians tried to take Silistria by coup de main, but failed as the Turks were quite prepared, so the Russians are investing it; they will take it soon, if we do not go up and raise the siege. Everybody is anxious to do something; we have been so long doing nothing, waiting for the artillery etc.

Captain Gifford [HMS *Tiger*] poor fellow is dead, he was our Brigade Major's brother-in-law. I have also another bit of bad news, Captain Wallace in the 7th Fusiliers, one of the nicest and most gentlemanly officers in the Regiment, was thrown from his horse and killed. I think you knew him. General Adams'[35] horse kicked an Artillery officer this morning and broke his leg.

I forgot to tell you that the 7th and the 23rd have gone up to Varna about a fortnight ago. Freddy Vane and the Colonel are both well.

I have found my little pipe, a Grenadier picked it up; I think nothing of Turkish tobacco, just like dried grass.

I had a grand packing yesterday and my luggage weighs 20 stone. Peter lent me his bullock trunks[36] as my portmanteaus were too heavy. I have had to discard my waterproof bed, which is a great pity, as it weighed 28 lbs, so I have got a wooden stretcher, which is only 15 lbs, which does very well. One would think that 20 stone [280 lbs.] of baggage was a great deal, but when you take into consideration that a tent weighs over 70 lbs, pack saddle, bed, bedding, canteen, riding saddle, rope trunks, covers etc, there is not much room for luxuries.

Nothing can be better than my health I am happy to say, and I face the health of everybody though the weather is very changeable of late; the nights are very cold and yesterday it was 92 degrees in Bentinck's tent; I dined with him last night.

I must conclude now although I have told you almost nothing, but

34

what with five hours field-days, guards, piquets and the heat of the sun and being quite tired of the filthy dirty streets of Stambool and Pera, I have not much to say.

I have remembered you to all of your friends, particularly Bill[37]. I showed him part of your letter, he is still very low and very deaf, which he takes to heart a great deal; I go and sit with him very often, in fact being quartered all by ourselves, we go about from tent to tent, have letters read, talking and smoking and hearing what little news there is.

Blackwood[38] is well, although very unpopular, he is attached to us; Ramsden[39] was sent on a fatigue party for bread, Blackwood was the commissariat officer on duty and kept him waiting ¾ of an hour. Ramsden told him of it and he said he might think himself lucky he was not kept waiting four hours instead of three-quarters of an hour. He was reported, got an official wigging and then a private one. This is a great pity, as these types of little rows are not easily forgotten.

I want nothing and am tolerably happy and get on capitally with everyone. I like the 1 Battalion much better, in fact I would not want to change. We are still in doubt about the brevet, no one knows anything about it out here.

Stuart, Weasel as he is now called, Bill and Anstruther, beg particularly to be remembered to you. I am now going to have a bath with Ramsden, so with best love to all and hoping Bob is well and enjoying herself and with every good wish and thanks for all your kindnesses.

> Believe me,
> Ever your affectionate son,
> Gerald L. Goodlake

Varna
16 June 1854
My dearest Father and Mother,

Many thanks for the air pillow which is most useful. I have everything I want so pray don't send out anything as I cannot carry it and shall only be obliged to throw it away.

Now about promotion, I hope that you will do exactly as you wish and not inconvenience yourself in the least. I shall tell you what I think (supposing that I am the senior Ensign.)

In the first place no one would, nor can it be expected, to give one farthing over regulation[40] for any step at the present time. I think that if you place my name for purchase giving the regulation only, would

35

prevent Bingham, Ramsden and Willesly, who are safe to remain in the army and give their money a chance of jumping over our heads by paying the regulation themselves.

[Editor's Note- Lieutenant Lord Bingham, Lieutenant F. Ramsden, Coldstream Guards. Willesly, probably Captain Hon. W.H.Wellesley, Coldstream Guards, who landed in the Crimea on 12 July 1855; all these officers were all of about the same seniority as Goodlake. According to the purchase of commissions' regulations, provided the most senior officer was prepared to pay the Regulation Fee, he would be promoted to the next rank above before those junior to him. If he did not agree to pay, the officer next most senior to him, agreeing to pay, would be promoted above him.]

I have now been in the Army for five years and time is getting on that I should do something. For an Ensign, particularly in the Guards as on service, it is not a very agreeable thing, as what with Quarter Guards, Main Guards and fatigues. Only yesterday there were five Ensigns on duty all day, they are little better than acting corporals and have to do all the dirty work of the company, as the Captains, who are properly subalterns,[41] claim their rank, shun the dirty work of the line and do nothing.

By giving the regulation it will not prevent my getting the step for nothing, if any casualty should occur. I hear there is a chance of an augmentation,[42] which will give it me for nothing. Also, I do not think, after what the public think of Dalrymple's[43] retiring, that anyone can sell out of the regiment even at regulation at the present time, so I do not think you will have to pay anything, as there is every chance of a casualty occurring, though one ought not to speculate on that.

Now, my dear Father, I have written my views as I thought you would like to know them, at the same time I hope you will not consider them and do as you think best, which I am quite sure will suit me.

We had a very pleasant voyage from Scutari. We embarked on board *Andes* on Tuesday morning and disembarked on Wednesday at Varna, marched about a mile where we encamped in torrents of rain. It rains every day here so a French officer told me. The country looks well for sporting life; lots of wild fowl, snipe, and hares. I shall soon be after them though I have received a great loss in the shape of a gun as . . . firelock is exchanged for . . . rifle, which won't throw shot well.[44] I have 60 lbs of shot and 11 lbs of powder. A good thing too, when the Butcher said to me this morning; 'Did you ever see a man shoot a Buffalo bull'. He did this about 50 yards from the Company. It was so lean and so tough, killed at 8 o'clock in the morning, eaten at 1 o'clock the same day; any little addition to the pot is very acceptable.

I always go out shooting with my pistols and Brooks, so there is no danger with nine barrels. When I last wrote I thought that we were going to Beicos Bay,[45] but a despatch from Omar Pasha altered the state of affairs and we were sent up to Varna at a day's notice to save Silistria. There are all sorts of report here, some say the Russians have retreated, and some not. My own private opinion is that the telescope is not made through which our division will ever see a Russian soldier.

We are encamped about a mile from Varna with French and Turkish soldiers all around. Fancy we mount guard with the French, a good opportunity for acquiring the French language. I was complimented the other day on the bold manner in which I accented French words and put them in the wrong tense.

I hear we are to move thirteen miles up the country where the Light Division are encamped. Whether they are pressed I do not know, in fact anything we do is kept so dark that we can never tell until a few hours before.

I have everything that I can possibly want, for the present. I should like my old gun and a retriever dog sent out if we stay the winter, but there is a lot of time between now and then.

I wish I could show you my pony, everybody says he is very like the Earl. I have been offered £25 for him as he is the neatest in the Brigade, not a head and tail animal, but so compact and a good goer. I have not seen the cob for three weeks but the last time I saw him he could hardly contain himself. He could carry the whole of the officers' baggage, he is so strong.

Poor Bob Anstruther[46] is left behind in the hospital at Scutari; he is much better, as he strained himself going up Mount Olympus.

I will take care of myself, so pray make your minds easy.

> Believe me,
> Your ever affectionate son,
> Gerald L. Goodlake

The Camp about a mile from Varna [47]
27 June 1854.
Dearest Father and Mother

I with much pleasure received your letter and the flies enclosed for which I return a thousand thanks. I am afraid that we will not have the fish to fry, as you expect.

The Russians have retreated, worse luck, across the Danube, on account of some demonstration by Austria. We are tired of staying here doing nothing; we all expect to remain here some time, from what we hear from the French. Our own camp report says that we shall not advance to Silistria, as there is no forage nor a blade of grass between Shumla and Silistria, and very little water; if we all move on we will have to make a march of 32 miles without a drop of water. There is some talk of embarking again and going up to Trajan's Wall,[48] or Odessa, but these are only surmises. There is little or no amusement here.

When I was out the other day I saw a Zouave,[49] nearly naked, running towards me, when he saw me he hid among some bushes. I took no particular notice of him as you hardly ever meet one who is not drunk. I went on about 50 yards when I saw a poor Chasseur de Braisseur,[50] lying in the sand run through the stomach, so I got him some water, caught an arabas [bullock cart], put him in it and sent him down to the French hospital, but he was dead before he reached it. I then went to the French piquet, which caught the Zouave, who was shot the next day. Some of his compatriots came up and said that it was nothing, as he would only be shot. He said, 'Very well, I am quite ready.'

The French are always pillaging the shops in Varna, the consequence is that we suffer as we can hardly get anything. I am very well, wonderful condition. The troops are not nearly so well as at Scutari, but nothing much the matter.

I rode to the Light Division and saw Freddy Vane[51] and the General,[52] who said he had had a letter from you, both very well. The men of the Light Division are worked off their legs. Brown[53] has had such a wigging about keeping them out from 7 in the morning till 2 and 3 in the afternoon; it filled the hospital in no time. He did not allow commissionaire stores to come up such as tea, coffee, rice, porter etc. He is universally hated by both the men and officers, as he drives them out of their minds by every paltry act he can possibly think of.

You would laugh if you could see me now. I have not shaved once since I left England except my moustache, which is coming on now very well, with three weeks' growth. I am as brown as chocolate and so are all the rest of us.

My horse is universally admired, Dallas of the 56th[54], wants to buy him, he also asked after you. The English horses suffer much from the flies and from the glare of the sun, that they are obliged to go out with shades on.

Last night I heard a grand discussion going on between Jemmy Macdonald[55] and a sentry, who at every hour shouted at the top of his voice, 'All's well.' Jemmy rushed out and said, 'My good man, I know all is well; I beg you will not make that horrid noise; if anything is the matter pray go and report it, but I cannot have my slumbers disturbed'. I think a clever sketch of this anecdote would do for *Punch*.

I get on very well with everyone, and we are all very happy, but wishing to have this over and to return to England. I meet lots of Eton acquaintances out here in the different regiments. It is a fine sight to see our Division work our three battalions and three of Highlanders.

PS. I do not think it is the slightest use keeping old Chestnut. I would sell him for what he can get or give him to Gould, as I do not see the slightest chance of coming home this winter. If you should happen to fall upon a retriever, a rough hardy dog, he would be wonderfully useful here in the winter, but not till then. I think I shall ask for my gun and rifle, if we stay till then. I take great care of myself and long to come back again.

Best love, a lot of fellows will have to go home in consequence of augmentation and brevet;[56] Peter I am afraid amongst the number. Remember me to Mrs Peter.

Camp: Name not known [Gevreclek]
July 27 1854

My dear Father and Mother,

I received your welcome letters by the last mail and also the draft which has just arrived. I shall not be able to write much this mail as it goes out so early this morning. I intended to write a good long letter, but at half past 10 o'clock we were awakened and told to march at 6 o'clock next morning.

We are now encamped on a large plain about seven miles from our last camp at Allahdin,[57] a change for the better, I hope, as our men have not been as well as one could wish.

I hear good news of promotion. Bentinck has told me that the augmentation, which promotes four is to happen in the regiment, with or without purchase, he does not know; it will be a good thing either way.

I do not think that there is much chance of our fighting this year. The Russians have retreated where we cannot follow them and it is certainly too late to go to Sevastopol. Anapa is a strong place but not an important one when we have taken it. Odessa is the most likely.

We have been ordered to make fascines and gabions;[58] seven hundred men daily do it; they are paid 10d a day, so I don't think are only for practice. All the transports have arrived at Varna and the fleet is fitting up for the carrying of troops, so we are ready at a moment's notice.

The weather here is fearfully hot and will, I believe, continue a month longer, accompanied by thousands and thousands of flies, mosquitoes and wild midges. They are nearly driving me mad at the moment. Then comes the rainy season and we go into winter quarters.

If Lord Raglan has any plans, he manages to keep them very dark; his staff know nothing.

Our men march badly and will continue to do so as long as they continue to carry such tremendous weights and put on their old fatigue trousers under their white ones and wear waistcoats covered with shirt buttons, etc, with the weather as hot as it is and very little water, though what there is, is good.

George Upton[59] has taken command of our regiment. Never did I behold such a fussy, incapable old woman, the laughing stock of the Division.

My horses are very well and employed at the moment in drawing wood to make myself an arbour.

I am very well myself and attribute it entirely to drinking nothing but lemon and water, taking strong exercise and eating very little.

With every good wish and my best love to all

Believe me,

Ever your affectionate son,

Gerald L. Goodlake.

Gevreclek, Bulgaria[60]
8 August 1854

My dearest Father and Mother,

I must offer a little defence against the charges preferred against me for not writing. I do, as often as I can, but it is perfectly impossible to write every mail, as the moment one comes in, the same steamer takes the mail back; if you are on duty or not in camp when the letters arrive, you cannot possibly answer them, and you miss a mail. I will defy any one man to write by every mail, particularly as we are now up the country and post office regulations are not the same as in England.

Something awfully dangerous is on the *tapis*. Last evening we heard from very good authority that it was finally settled that we go to Sevastopol on Saturday next, the 12 August. This is no shave [rumour] and I am sure it is true. We shall reach our shooting grounds on the 16 August. I understand there are lots of birds but rather wild and strong on the wing when put to flight.

I don't see at all how we are to take it as it is so wonderfully forti-fied and the Russians, during the time we have been here, have not lost time, or opportunity in making it more impregnable. Our men are so weakened and debilitated by this hot and unwholesome country, that it will take them some time to get round, but excitement and change will do them good and the sea voyage, I hope, will entirely set them up.

I myself, thank God, am as well as if I had been in England, nothing in fact could make my health better. I attribute it entirely to the strong exercise I take, and my own idea of diet, which I think has done much.

You need not be the least afraid by my little shooting excursions. I am always well armed and the country is quite safe. I killed 13 ½ couple of quail, 3 hares, walking them up in the corn and stalking them by their call. It was the largest bag in camp; the next approaching it was 7 ½ couple with 3 guns; I cannot stay in my tent; it would kill me in a week.

We have occasional races and dog hunts, which I think are great fun. You go into the country and find a wild dog, just like a wolf. Off he goes for three or four miles, with about twenty or thirty fellows after him with spears, across the great plains, through woods, villages, etc. He is rarely caught.

God bless you my dear Father, Mother, Bob and all.

> Believe me ever,
> Your very affectionate son,
> Gerald L. Goodlake

About five miles from Varna
On the high ground on the left
of the bay as you go in.
19 August 1854
My dear Father,

I have only time to write one line as the post goes out in five minutes.

We have arrived at Varna after three days' march. The men's packs were carried for them; they are in very bad health. There is a great deal of cholera, and dysentery in the 5th Dragoon Guards, lost 32 men in three days; we and the Grenadiers have lost a great number, but the change and sea air will do them good. I myself was never better. I have not even had a headache.

We were to go home, but as they could hardly get an officer per company on parade, they would not let Peter, Ramsden, Dunlop[61] or myself go, as we were always well.

Varna is nearly all burnt down,[62] it has been burning all last week and is not out yet.

The French lost 3,000 men out of 9,000, mostly Zouaves. They went to the Dorbruja[63] without consulting Lord Raglan, found all the wells poisoned and lost 3,000 men out of 9,000, mostly Zouaves,[64] as well as 75 officers. Their return was truly awful.

We go to Sevastopol next week. I believe we go for certain. Everybody is so glad. Anything is better than remaining in this horrid country. We were going on the 12th but on account of the French not being in readiness, it is put off till the 25th. Sir R England's[65] Brigade has orders to embark tomorrow. They have nearly all the artillery on board.

I thought I would tell you about the cholera and how bad the health of the troops is, as if I did not you could blame me for not telling you the exact truth. It is always better to hear the worst, than uncertain reports. I write this to you, so you need not show it to Mother. A thousand thanks, congratulations and good wishes.

> Believe me ever,
> Your very affectionate son,
> Gerald L.Goodlake

Varna

25 August 1854

My dearest Father and Mother,

I have sad intelligence to relate. Poor old Trevelyan[66] was taken ill at 7 o'clock on Monday morning and died at 2 o'clock this afternoon of Asiatic cholera. We are very sorry for poor Trev, he was Colonel of my company and I used to mess with him. I was out on an excursion to get forage when he was taken ill; he died, just as I arrived.

Colonel Upton has asked me to take the management of his things, which are to be sold by auction on Tuesday next. We will miss him so much as he was so good natured and harmless. I am (thank God) quite well, never better. I go out shooting whenever I can and I think the strong exercise keeps me well. I go out accompanied by 6 men so that you may not be alarmed, not that there is any danger as the country is so patrolled. I killed one day 17 ½ couple of quail, 1 hare, 3 couple of doves, all my own game and top bag in camp and on another day-22 ½ couple of quail, 2 hares (bagged); we lost so many as we have no dogs.

There is not the slightest doubt about us going to Sevastopol, we go there next Friday. All last week they were practising embarking and disembarking, artillery guns and did it very well. Marshal St Arnaud [C-in-C French Army] has issued a proclamation to the French Army, that before three weeks are past, the Tricolour, Union Jack, and Turkish flag will float over the bastions of Sevastopol. Some people say this is doubtful, the Russians in particular. There are all sorts of reports about troops being conveyed from Odessa to Sevastopol, 2 divisions. I cannot believe myself, though it came from Staff at head-quarters. Everybody abuses old Dundas and he is always fighting with his Captain, Sir E. Lyons in particular.

The ships, which are told off to take us are the *Simoon* Fusiliers, *Tonning* and *Emu* Coldstream, *Kangaroo* Grenadiers: each steamer will tow 3 transports. Talk about going down to Spithead[67] to see a review of the Fleet!

The whole combined fleets of England, France and Turkey, (we won't say much about the latter) with its attendant transports, something like 100,000 living souls, going to the attack on Sevastopol. It will be a sight worth seeing and will recompense us for coming to such a vile climate as this. We have been busy ourselves in making the famous gabions.

I am sorry to tell you of your old regiment the 5th Dragoons.[68] No regiment could have landed in better order. They lost 33 men in three nights, their horses are in a dreadful state and the regiment in a state of mutiny, at least they were panic-stricken and would not do anything. Scarlett[69] was taken away as Brigadier to the Heavy Cavalry Brigade. Thompson, senior major, left at the depot at home. Le Marchant, who came in from half pay, they hate. He was taken ill so off he went; Duckworth was dying, poor fellow is just dead. Burton who is a mild man, with no service or experience, commands.[70] Scarlett took the Adjutant[71] on to his staff and they have a young fellow in his place, not fit to do the duty. The men the other day never took the horses to water but went out nutting. A more awful state for a regiment to be in cannot be conceived. They have now been marched to Varna and arrived with 91 led horses.

We have clouds of locusts flying about, which are eating everything. We're all anxious to go to Sevastopol, the fleet will cover our landing. I expect it will be a rougher job than the people of England expect.

I have been on an expedition to buy forage for our horses. We got 70 arabas[72] loads. I went with Astley[73], we slept in the villages, had a Turkish escort and were great swells and were paid every attention.

Poor Anstruther[74] has gone home, and with him have gone Blenkins of the Grenadiers, as their health would not stand the climate.

The men are much better, the last 3 to 4 days, though we have a great deal in hospital, about 116.

Pray do not be alarmed at me, I am thoroughly acclimatised and have stood the test as yet very well. I have remembered you to all your friends and they all beg to be remembered to you when I write.

I have forgotten to tell you about Tierny[75] who has certainly gone mad; he lost himself two days and two nights within a mile of the camp; he goes on in such a manner pilfering things out of official tents and using such language that they have hinted to him the necessity of "cutting his stick" which he has done. He is in general orders this evening adding cowardice to his other bad and ungentlemanlike qualities. There is not a man in the Brigade who has not thrown up his cap (hats we have none) at the news of his disappearance.

I know of no more news out here. Great excitement prevails at present. I hope the next time you hear from me I shall be entitled to a medal and feel sure that we shall have earned one.

Good bye, dearest Father and Mother.
　　　　With best love to Bob and all.
　　　　　　Ever your very affectionate son
　　　　　　Gerald

Notes

1　*The Coldstream Guards in the Crimea*, pp.52–6, Lieutenant-Colonel Ross-of-Bladensburg.
2　Ibid, p. 54
3　*The British Expedition to the Crimea*, p.425, Sir W. Russell.
4　*Crimea*, pp.149–50, Trevor Royle.
5　Peter Crawley and Lord Bingham, both Lieutenants and Captains in the Coldstream Guards. Assistant. Surgeon F.Wildbore. Lord Bingham was ADC to his Father, Lord Lucan.
6　Captains & Lieutenant-Colonels, Hon V.Dawson, W.G.Dawkins,

W.S.Newton; Lieutenants and Captains, H. Armytage, Hon G.Eliot, Coldstream Guards.

7 Deputy-Assistant-Comissariary-General A.F.Cooksley, who served in the Crimea, from the date of landing till the end of the war.

8 Lieutenant Hugh Annesley, Scots Fusilier Guards. He discovered that his bearskin made an adequate pillow when placed on a haversack full of biscuit. *Destruction of Lord Raglan*, p.42, Christopher Hibbert.

9 Peter Crawley, Henry Armytage, Sir James Dunlop Bt, all Lieutenants and Captains in the Coldstream Guards. Willison has not been identified.

10 Town on north side of the Dardanelles.

11 In Asia Minor, opposite Constantinople on the other side of the Bosporus.

12 Galata and Pera are suburbs of Constantinople.

13 Colonel Yea, commanding 7th Fusiliers, a family friend.

14 Sir Robert Anstruther, Bt, Grenadier Guards, Ensign, 1853; Lieutenant and Captain, 1855; Captain and Lieutenant-Colonel, 1861; invalided home September 1854; retired 1862; Henry Anstruther, 23rd Foot [Goodlake's former Regiment] was killed in action in the Crimea.

15 J.D.Astley, Lieutenant and Captain, Scots Fusilier Guards.

16 George Bentinck, Brigadier General, commanding the Guards Brigade

17 Battalion. Surgeon J Skelton, who served throughout the campaign, except for a period of sick leave from November 1854 to October 1855.

18 General Brown, who commanded the Light Division, was a very unpopular general, who treated the men under his command badly.

19 Captain and Lieutenant-Colonel Lord Bingham, ADC to Lord Lucan.

20 His sister Emilia Jane.

21 Stocks are leather pieces worn round the throat; see Military Terms. The Duke of Newcastle, Secretary of State for War, ordered that they be no longer worn in the Crimea.

22 See fn. 15.

23 The General is almost certainly Major-General Codrington, a former Coldstreamer.

24 See fn. 16.

25 Brigadier-General Sir James Scarlett, Commander of the Heavy Brigade at Balaklava. In 1855 he commanded the Cavalry Division.

26 On 12 May 1854, HMS *Tiger*, a 16- gun steamer, ran aground in a fog off Odessa. Capt. Gifford was killed and the crew captured.

27 Capt. F.[Ben] Stephenson, Scots Fusilier Guards, sailed as Brigade-Major of the Guards Brigade. On 28 Aug. 1854 he was promoted to

Captain and Lieutenant-Colonel and then became Company Commander of the Left Flank Company of 1 SFG.

28 Lieutenant H. W. Cumming, Coldstream Guards, was selling out and retired on 20 September 1854.

29 Stephenson Blackwood, Acting Deputy Assistant Commissary-General. In Crimea from 14 September 1854 to 5 December 1855, when he returned to England on duty.

30 Hedworth Hylton Jolliffe, Coldstream Guards. Ensign 9. 5.51; Captain 15.12.54. *Coldstream Guards in the Crimea,* p.114.

31 See fn. 9.

32 Sergeant-Major, Regimental Sergeant-Major, the most senior Battalion Warrant Officer. See Military Terms.

33 Drill-Sergeant, Senior Warrant Officer in charge of drill. See Military Terms.

34 Beicos Bay, on the Asia-Minor coast of the Bosporus.

35 Brigadier-General Henry Adams, 49th Foot, commanded 2 Brigade, 2 Division.

36 Large trunks, usually carried in bullock carts.

37 Lieutenant and Captain W. Bathurst, Grenadier Guards, whose deafness finally forced him to resign his commission.

38 See fn. 29 and Military Terms.

39 Lieutenant and Captain Henry Ramsden, Coldstream Guards. Killed at Inkerman.

40 The fee to be paid to the present holder of the position for promotion to that rank. See Military Terms

41 Subalterns. Officers in the Brigade of Guards held double rank, a rank in their Regiment and a rank one higher in the Army, so subalterns were Lieutenants and Captains, while Ensigns were Ensigns and Lieutenants. See Military Terms-Double Rank.

42 Augmentation; when the establishment of a battalion was increased, the additional officer posts were normally non-purchase posts.

43 Captain and Lieutenant-Colonel J.H.Dalrymple, Scots Fusilier Guards, wounded at the Alma and retired in 1864.

44 A firelock [shotgun] has a smooth barrel designed to project an even pattern of shot. The rifling in a rifle would distort the pattern of shot fired and project it into a far more uneven pattern than a shotgun.

45 See fn. 34.

46 See fn. 14.

47 A town on the west coast of the Black Sea, now in Bulgaria.

48 Trajan's Wall, built between Costanza on the west coast of the Black Sea in the Dobruja in Bulgaria and running west to the River Danube, about 45 miles long.

49 French colonial troops. See Military Terms

50 The French *Chasseurs à Pied* were elite infantry regiments. See Military Terms

51 Ensign 7th Fusiliers, family friend.

52 Almost certainly Major-General William Codrington, Coldstream Guards, commanding the 1st Brigade of the Light Division.

53 See fn. 18.

54 George Frederick Dallas, 46th South Devonshire Regiment; Ensign 16 May 1848. He returned from the Crimea as a Captain and a Brevet Major. See *Eyewitness in the Crimea;* his Crimean War Letters, edited by Michael Hargreave Mawson.

55 Major The Hon James W.R. Macdonald, Unattached. " He served in the Eastern Campaign of 1854, as ADC to the Duke of Cambridge, including the Battles of Alma (horse shot), Inkerman (horse shot), Siege of Sevastopol and sortie of 26th Oct." Hart's Army List, 1860, p. 68.

56 See fn. 42 and Military Terms. Brevet, a list of those being promoted.

57 Aladyn, eight miles inland from Varna.

58 Fascines, bundles of sticks, used for reinforcing trench walls. See Military Terms. Gabions, wicker baskets, filled with stones, used to build fortifications. See Military Terms.

59 George Upton, Commanding Officer, 1st Coldstream.

60 A camp site about four miles north of Aladyn, the previous camp

61 P. Crawley, F. Ramsden and Sir James Dunlop Bt, Lieutenants and Captains, Coldstream Guards.

62 On 7 August 1854 a fire destroyed a great deal of stores and most of the town. Five Greeks were caught in the act and bayoneted by the French. Colonel Lord George Paget, CO of the 4th Light Dragoons, said, "They do things better than we do in this army." *The Destruction of Lord Raglan*, p.32, fn, C.Hibbert.

63 On 22 March 1854 Marshal St Arnaud sent the French 1st Division into the Dobruja, on the west coast of the Black Sea, to attack a Russian force, which he believed had remained there.

64 See fn. 49 and Military Terms.

65 Commander of the 3rd Division.

66 Captain and Lieutenant-Colonel Trevelyan, Company Commander, 1st Coldstream.

67 Channel between the Isle of Wight and the mainland, where reviews of the fleet by the Sovereign take place.

68 His father had served in the 5th Dragoons in the Peninsular War.

69 See fn. 25.

70 When camped outside Varna, the 5th Dragoon Guards paid little

attention to their water supply and cholera spread through the Regiment. Within a week, 3 Officers and 35 Troopers died and the CO, Colonel Thomas Le Marchant, was so enfeebled that he had to be sent home. *Crimea,* p.157, Trevor Royle.

71 Adjutant 5th Dragoon Guards, Lieut. A. J. H. Elliott became ADC to Brigadier Scarlett, rode in the charge at Balaklava and left the Crimea, when Scarlett went home in April 1855. See Military Terms-Staff Uniform for more on Elliott.

72 Carts

73 See fn. 15.

74 See fn. 14; Surgeon G. Blenkins, Grenadier Guards, was sent home on medical certificate in August 1854 and returned to duty in December 1854.

75 C.G.Tierny, Coldstream Guards, Captain and Lieutenant-Colonel. Retired from the Regiment on 3 November 1854.

Chapter Three

The Development of Sharpshooting and Captain Goodlake's Victoria Cross

From 1722 to 1852, from the Seven Years War and from Waterloo up to the Crimean War, the Land Service muzzle-loading musket, called the Brown Bess, was the British infantry's principal weapon. It was given this name as it had a brown stock, instead of the previous musket's black one; 'Bess' is a derivation of the German word '*Busch*' [a barrel] meaning a generic gun rather than a specific rifle, seen again in 'Blunderbuss'.

During that period there were a number of model changes, but the infantry tactic remained the same, which was to use this weapon to provide rolling volleys, fired by formations in close order; either companies, platoons or files [file firing]. This tactic was designed to break up the enemy's formations. This was then followed up by a bayonet charge to rout the enemy and to put them to flight. The only exception was when a company was skirmishing, when the files, consisting of two soldiers, worked together in a group of skirmishers, either covering a defensive position or else working in front of an attacking force. They were, however, under the close control of officers and NCOs.

The range of this weapon was up to 200 yards, but the effective range was between 50 to 100 yards. It was not accurate for ranges over 80 yards, so for that reason it was used for firing volleys. Experienced soldiers could fire three to four rounds a minute and keep up this rate of fire for a short time without having to clean the weapon. Ten rounds in three minutes would make the barrel too hot to hold.

Some Pattern '51 Minie rifles were issued to troops fighting in the Kaffir War of 1850–53, but none of these troops fought in the Crimea. In January 1853 the first Pattern '51 Minie rifles were issued to the Brigade of Guards at the rate of twenty-five per company. Lord Hardinge, the Commander-in-Chief, directed that they were to be given to the most careful and expert marksmen. While the Guards Brigade was in Malta in March/April 1854, the Brigade exchanged more of their smooth-bore muskets for the Minie. While the Army was at Varna the Guards Brigade and the other divisions were issued with Minie rifles and handed in their muskets, except for the 4th Division, which fought the battles of Alma and Inkerman armed with smooth-bore muskets.

Ammunition returns show that no smoothbore ammunition was issued at the Battle of the Alma, as only one brigade of the 4th Division was there and was not engaged. At Inkerman, 176,670 Minie rounds were issued and only 23,150 smoothbore rounds, presumably to the 4th Division [*History of the Grenadier Guards*, Vol.III, pp. 154 and 167, Lieutenant-General Sir F.W.Hamilton].

To exploit to the full the potential of the Minie rifle/musket, a complete change in infantry tactics was required, as its increased range enabled its sights to be set from 100 to 900 yards. At short ranges, volleys could be devastating as the bullet could go through several men in a column of Russian troops, as our troops found out during the battle of the Alma and at Inkerman. Although the Minie's loading procedure was different to that of the Brown Bess, properly trained and experienced troops could fire about three to four rounds a minute.

However, the greatest advantage of the Minie was that, in the hands of a marksman, it could be used for sniping or sharpshooting at ranges of 250 to 400 yards, and even at ranges up to 800 yards, and above, at individual targets, such as enemy officers and artillerymen.

It is estimated that the accuracy of experienced shots firing at a standard target at 400 yards was 75 %, at 600 yards 60 %, and at 800 yards 25 % [W.S.Curtis, Past Chairman Crimean War Research Society].

Colonel Calthorpe, one of Lord Raglan's ADCs', reports in his letter of 13 October 1854 that Rifleman Herbert of the Rifle Brigade, on an outlying-picquet, after fixing the sights of his rifle at its extreme range, shot a Cossack officer, who fell from his saddle, the horse trotting away. Several well-qualified officers judged the distance to be downwards of 1300 yards. Rifleman Herbert himself estimated the distance to be about one thousand yards.[1]

On 16 October 1854 the First Division issued an order on sharp-shooting, stating that ten men and a non-commissioned officer from each battalion, good shots, volunteers preferred, were to be selected to act as sharpshooters, under a Captain and Lieutenant of the Brigade of Guards:

> The sharpshooters will have to approach to within 400 to 500 yards of the enemy's works, there to establish themselves in extended order (by single men) under cover of anything which may present itself to afford protection. They will endeavour to improve their cover behind any obstacle by scraping out a hollow for themselves in the ground, and they will carry with them provisions so that they will be enabled to remain, being once under cover, for many hours [even twenty-four] without relief. Whilst so established they will endeavour to pick off the enemy's artillerymen in the embrasures. The approach of the sharp-shooters to the spot they must occupy must be rapid, in a scattered order; each man acting for himself, and exercising his intelligence to the utmost of his ability.
>
> Each man will select the spot which suits him best, and be guided only in that choice by the cover he may find and the command it may give him of an effectual fire into the embrasures.[2]

Officers ordered to perform this important duty were in no way 'selected' for it, but were taken by roster. In Crimean days, as well as during the Peninsular War, it was considered that all officers were fitted to discharge the ordinary duties which their profession required of them.

Captain Goodlake's Regimental Record, held by the Coldstream Guards, states that he commanded the Sharpshooters of the Guards Brigade for forty-two days. When sharpshooting was discontinued after Inkerman,[3] owing to the shortage of men available, his parents suggested that they should establish a fund for them. Goodlake's reply emphasizes what a dangerous activity sharpshooting was. On 8 February 1855 he writes that of his thirty men, thirteen were killed, five wounded and one has been commissioned in the Rifles[4], so it only

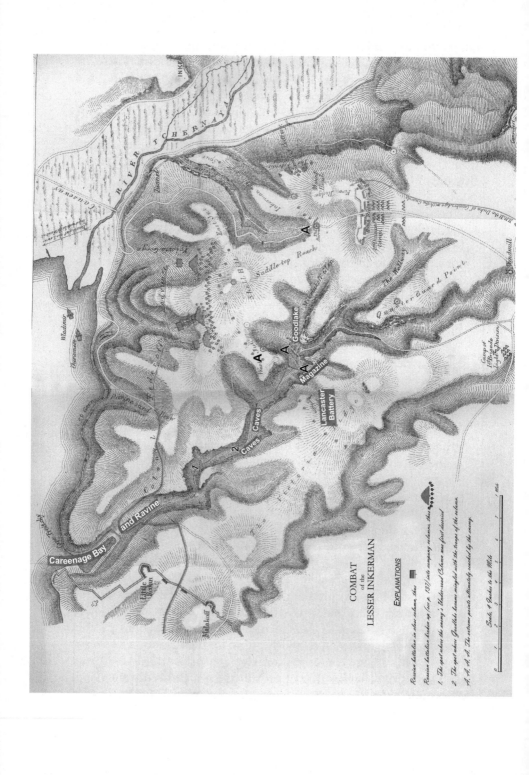

COMBAT
of the
LESSER INKERMAN

EXPLANATIONS

Russian battalion in close column, thus ▮

Russian battalions divided up (see p. 137) into company columns, thus ᵒᵒᵒᵒᵒᵒ

1. The spot where the enemy's Under-road Column was first descried.

2. The spot where Goldie's brigade bronze might with the troops of the column.

A, A, A. The extreme points attainedly reached by the enemy.

Scale, 4 Inches to the Mile

0   1   2   3   4   5   6   1 mile

leaves ten [eleven] men. 'Clothes they have in abundance. I propose the best plan would be a fund of money to be given to them on their return to England. None are married and they are composed of the most out and out blackguards of the Regiment, rob a church and use language enough to frighten a fellow into a fit.'

Kinglake explains the reason why Goodlake was the only officer with the Sharpshooters:

> Respecting the origin and constitution of this singularly and adventurous little body of volunteers under Goodlake of the Coldstream, there were two other officers who acted with Goodlake in the formation and leadership of this body namely Cameron of the Grenadiers and Baring of the Scots Fusilier Guards; but Cameron in one of these expeditions was wounded. Goodlake carried him out of the fight on his back; Baring one day was so high-handed with a man of the Rifles who he arrested in the act of retreating, so an inquiry on the subject was ordered; so that Goodlake was the only one of the three who remained free to act; and he commanded the force for a period of forty-two days, earning brilliantly his Victoria Cross. A narrative of the exploits of this force would make a volume of extraordinary interest; but I imagine there is no hope that any such will ever appear; for those who do such things are apt to be men of few words. No doubt that Goodlake, Cameron and Baring, and the men acting under them, knew well that by hanging close upon the enemy that they gained opportunities of doing really good services; but they would hardly deny, I would believe, that one motive at least, if not the main one, for engaging in these enterprises, was a love of adventure and sport.[5]

On 26 October 1854 the Russians made a reconnaissance in force on our left flank at Inkerman, this action is known as Little Inkerman. For his bravery in this action and on other occasions Captain Goodlake was awarded the Victoria Cross.

The Citation from the *London Gazette*, dated 24 February 1857, was as follows:

> Brevet Major Gerald Littlehales Goodlake-Coldstream Guards
>   For distinguished gallantry whilst in command of the sharpshooters, furnished by the Coldstream Guards on the 28th

October 1854, on the occasion of "the powerful sortie on the 2nd Division", when he held the Windmill Ravine, below the Picquet House, against a much larger force of the enemy. The party of sharpshooters then under his command killed thirty-eight (one an officer) and took three prisoners of the enemy, (of the latter, one an officer) Major Goodlake being the sole officer in command. Also, for distinguished gallantry on the occasion of the surprise of a picquet of the enemy, in November, at the bottom of Windmill Ravine, by the sharpshooters, under his sole leading and command, when the knapsacks and the rifles of the enemy's party fell into his hands.

It should be noted that the date of the action was 26 October 1854 and not the 28th. For the reasons given above, he was commanding the Sharpshooters of the Guards Brigade, not just those of the Coldstream Guards.

Goodlake then explains in his letter of 6 November 1854 the action at Little Inkerman. 'The next day (after Balaklava) on the 26th, they made a sortie from Sevastopol and attacked our left regiments, but were repulsed with great slaughter: between 7 and 800 killed and taken prisoner. I have 30 volunteer men from the Brigade, who act under me. We go out to shoot Russians and piquets. I killed 5 men, one at 300 yards through the head and one officer beating on his men at 30 yards. Most exciting. I and a Sergeant were nearly caught in a cave but we made a bolt for it and got off with a bullet through my coat and he shot in the arm.'

Kinglake describes this action as follows:

As regards the Careenage Ravine, the only troops there at first were a piquet of the Light Division (which, however, was quickly drawn in) and 60 volunteers of the Guards, commanded by Captain Goodlake.[6]

[Editor's Note: Goodlake only mentions 30 men, which is in accordance with the Divisional Order i.e. ten men from each of the three battalions. Michael Barthorp in his article on *Crimean Sharpshooters*, suggests that the 60 men may have included 30 sharpshooters from the Highland Brigade. *Journal of the Victorian Military Society*, No.69.June 1992].

The separate column had been ascending the Careenage Ravine, and at first without being visible to its nearest adversaries; for although Goodlake's sixty men of the Guards stood posted across the ravine at a spot close below the caves, there was a bend in the course of the gorge which concealed the one force from the other.

To assure himself against any ambush, Captain Goodlake (taking with him Sergeant Ashton) had gone up to examine the caves, leaving the rest of his sixty men halted across the bed of the chasm, and partly on each bank. Whilst just left for the moment without their commander, Goodlake's men were suddenly confronted by the sight of the Russian column thronging up round the corner below. The hostile force seemed like a mob, numbering about six or seven hundred men, and was pressing forward along the bed of the ravine, but also along each of its banks. Goodlake's people retreated, firing.

Kinglake notes that the Russian military authorities ignore this column, and that it is his impression that it was a battalion of Marines or seamen:

They wore dark-grey coats with black belts and caps [rather like our Chelsea pensioner], with red bands round them.[7] Goodlake himself, with Sergeant Ashton[8] at his side, was still by the caves, hemmed in by the assailants, and, debarred by the craggy and difficult ground from any possibility of effectual retreat, he thought that he and the sergeant must needs submit and be made prisoners. Sergeant Ashton, however, suggested, that if the captain and he were made prisoners, they would assuredly be put to death, in vengeance for one of their recent exploits;[9] and all notions of surrender being thereupon discarded, the alternative of course was resistance. The Russians, whilst closing in on their two adversaries, fired at them numbers of shots, which all, however, proved harmless. On the other hand, Goodlake and the sergeant fired each of them once into the nearest clump of Russians, and then, with the butt ends of their rifles, knocked away the foremost of their assailants, and ran down to the foot of the bank. There, however, they were in the midst of a mob of Russians advancing up the ravine. To their great surprise no one seized them; and it was evident that, owing to the grey cloaks

55

and plain caps they both wore, the enemy was mistaking them for his own fellow countrymen. Shielded by this allusion, and favoured too, by the ruggedness of the ground, and the obstructive thickets of brushwood, which enabled them to be constantly changing their neighbours, without attracting attention, they moved on unmolested in the midst of their foes; and, though strange, it is not the less true, that this singular march was continued along a distance of more than half a mile.

At length, with its two interlopers, the Russian throng came to a halt, and not without reason, for it was confronted by Goodlake's sixty men of the Guards, who, after their lengthened retreat, were making a stand, and had posted themselves some thirty yards off, behind a little trench, which there seamed the bed of the gorge. Goodlake, with his trusty sergeant, soon crossed the intervening space which divided the Russians from the English, and found himself once more among his own people.

When halted in front of Goodlake's men, this separate column was not far from being abreast of Federoff's[10] foremost combatants on Mount Inkerman, and may therefore have accomplished the early part of its task; but the leader, as might be imagined, sought to do more, and for his next step, to overthrow the sixty men of the Guards confronting him from behind their trench. He exerted himself with a valour and energy much admired by our people, making vehement and repeated efforts to draw forward his men; but he every time failed to get a following, for Goodlake's men, with their venturesome chief now restored to them, showed no signs of yielding; and for some time the antagonistic forces – the throng of Russians on one side, and the sixty men of the Guards on the other side – remained thus standing at bay. Desisting after a lengthy combat from their endeavours to dislodge Goodlake's men, the Russians submitted to stand debarred from any further advance; but they clung to the part of the ravine they had been able to reach, some entering the magazine grotto, where they found an abundance of food, others planting themselves in the brushwood, and behind jutting pieces of rock.[11]

In the Careenage Ravine, the enemy's discomfiture was completed by Captain Markham with some men from the 2nd Rifle battalion; but the Russians, before they succumbed, sustained a sharp combat between him in front of the magazine grotto, and seven of their number were killed, the Rifles having five men wounded. Captain Markham and Captain Goodlake between them took an officer and several men prisoner.[12]

There is further information about 'the picket job' referred to by Sergeant Ashton. The Citation for the Victoria Cross awarded to Private Stanlock DCM in the *London Gazette* of 24 February 1857 is as follows:

> No.3968 Private William Stanlock, Coldstream Guards.
>
> For having volunteered, when employed as one of the sharp-shooters in October 1854, for reconnoitring purposes, to crawl within six yards of a Russian sentry, and so enabled the officer in command to effect a surprise; Private Stanlock having been warned beforehand of the imminent risk he would run in the adventure. By preventing the sentry from giving the alarm, he enabled the others to pounce on the picket and bear their knapsacks and arms back to camp.[13]

Research by Private Stanlock's descendants reveals that he was almost certainly illiterate and that he signed his name Stanlock, Stanlake and Stanlack at different times. They have decided that Stanlake is the correct spelling, as it was the name of a farm in Devon, which they believe was the family's original home.

Kinglake states that the strength of the 2nd Division, which repulsed the attack on our left wing, was 2956 and with 30 men of the Guards totalled.2986.[14]

On 22 November Goodlake explains that he takes great care of himself. He has built a capital home and has got the materials out of Russian homes with his Sharpshooters, who will go anywhere in the world for him. He also says that Sevastopol will take a deal more trouble to take than people think. He explains that he has been nearer to it than any other Englishman, except for those who have been taken prisoner.

In his letter of 30 March 1855 he explains that the French have tried several times to take the Mamelon, which was in front of the Malakoff or Round Tower. The Mamelon was finally taken by the French on 9 June 1855. He explains that he and his Sharpshooters used to go all over it to shoot at the embrasures.

One of Captain Goodlake's brother officers, a company commander in the Coldstream, Colonel Wilson, describes the operations of Sharpshooters in the Crimea:

For some days past, volunteers from the light companies of various regiments have been engaged either in annoying the enemy's artillerymen, by firing into their embrasures, or in keeping the Russian tirailleurs, who were growing intrusive, at a more respectful distance. These duties are performed with ability in proportion to the common-sense and military knowledge pertaining to the officers employed. Two leaders of skirmishing parties Captain (now Major) Goodlake, Coldstream Guards, and a Captain of the 88th (I think) have shown marked intelligence and wariness in what to them is a novel part.

This morning a lot of our Sharpshooters got to very close quarters with a rather more numerous body of the enemy's riflemen. An eccentric combat ensured. At first everything went according to regulation; the muskets cracked sharply on both sides; but after as few minutes' 'potting,' the English, finding their pouches unaccountably empty, began to chuck stones at the "Rooshians," who wonderful to tell, slung their carbines, and replied in the same coin; so there was a bout of stone-balling between the two – a schoolboy encounter that soon ended in the 'No Bonos' scampering off amid derisive cheers from their opponents.[15]

Colonel Wilson's reference to the Captain of the 88th, the Connaught Rangers, as the leader of skirmishers, refers to Lieutenant Webb of that Regiment, who on 19 October 1854 captured several Russians. According to the regimental history[16], Webb was very short-sighted, but was an excellent officer; he always used 'a smart and plucky fellow of their Light Company' as his eyes, who always kept close to his elbow.

The history of the Rifle Brigade in the Crimea mentions another incident:

On 16th October 1854 at 3 am a party of 60 Riflemen, commanded by Captain Cartwright, were sent to the trenches as a specially selected section of 'Sharpshooters'.

Under cover of darkness, they were placed into the best

concealed positions, some only 400 yards from the Redan whose fire they were to keep down. First they silenced a mortar battery and then devoted their full attention to the Redan. Some soldiers from other regiments had been similarly employed but when the Russians opened fire they returned to their trenches in great haste. The Rifles remained in their position until nightfall, spending the whole day in no-man's land between the artillery duels of both armies. The Russians plied this open ground with shrapnel but miraculously only two Riflemen were wounded.[17]

This tactic of using static positions of Sharpshooters to keep down the fire of Russian marksmen continued, after Goodlake's mobile Sharpshooters were discontinued after Inkerman, well into the spring and the summer of 1855. These positions were around 800 to 1000 yards in advance of our lines and from any support from our infantry, and between 400 to 600 yards in front of the Russian lines.

General Todleben was responsible for organizing the effective way in which Sevastopol's defences were improved from their very unready state to becoming highly effective. He also ensured that damage from enemy action was repaired efficiently during the siege. He wrote about

the enormous losses which the enemy's riflemen inflicted on the Russian artillery. A perfect cloud of riflemen, hid in thick brushwood, opened a very accurate fire against our artillery at a distance of 800 paces. Some of our guns from time to time rained case on them, but the discharge only checked the fire of the enemy's riflemen for a minute. In another extract he states It was more the fire of rifled small arms than that of the artillery of the enemy which reached our artillerymen, of which the greater part were killed and wounded.[18]

Kinglake writes that Captain Goodlake was present at the Battle of Inkerman, that he and his sixty men heard the march of the silent battalions of General Soimonoff's army[19] and that he despatched one of his soldiers, who was unfortunately captured, to give our people warning of the approaching attack. However he fired on the approaching columns, losing six or seven men, and this warned General Codrington of the attack, who then put his troops under arms.[20]

This would appear to be incorrect as in his letter of 6 November 1854 Goodlake writes to his parents that he had been ill for a day or so (nothing at all serious) so he did not go [on 5 November], so fortunately escaped. 'I was glad when it was all over that I had not been there, though shot and shell pitched into and over our camp all day long'.

He also said his men were separate and did not go out with the battalion. So we do not know what happened to the Sharpshooters on that day. The events above may have happened with the men under the command of, possibly, the soon to be commissioned Sergeant Ashton.

Captain Goodlake's Regimental Record also says that he took part in the Battle of Tchernaya on 16 August 1855. In this battle the Russians attacked the French and Sardinian armies, which were holding the Mackenzie Heights in front of the Tchernaya Bridge and were successfully driven back with considerable losses. No British troops were engaged in this operation, so he was probably the only member of the British Army involved, in this his private Sharpshooting action. In his letter of that date he writes:

'At about half past five I was writing in my hut and heard a lot of firing. I thought it was before Sevastopol, but I heard a man observe that it was only the Russians driving in the Sardinians. So I mounted my dear old cob and positively flew to the Tchernaya, where I saw the ground covered with Russian troops trying to force the Tchernaya Bridge, which they partially did. As I came up I saw a battalion of Zouaves ordered to drive them over the bridge. I gave my cob to a Frenchman and descended in the rear of the battalion. They got to the bridge, drove them back into a thick vineyard and then I never saw before or since such fire as there was. The French extended and got from bush to bush and potted away right and left, very excitedly, and seemed to enjoy their business. There was not the shadow of fear; they fought splendidly.

'After advancing 40 yards, I got hold of a Russian needle-rifle, a capital weapon, but at first could not find any bullets to fit it.'

[Editor's Note: He must have picked a Russian M54 muzzle-loader, not a needle-rifle, converted to fire bullets through its rifled barrel. This rifle had a calibre of .720, as opposed to .700 for the French rifle, so that French rifle cartridges would fire, but not accurately. In the French rifle, the bullet was crushed by blows of the ramrod against the pillar in the breech, so that it expanded into the

60

rifling before firing [the Tamisier bullet]. The Russian Timmerhans bullet was hollow-based, so that the explosion of the powder expanded the bullet to fit the rifling .Therefore Russian cartridges would obviously be more accurate. A lot of the Russian M 54 rifles were picked up after the Tchernaya battle. W.S.Curtis, Past Chairman, Crimean War Research Society].

'The French cartridges were too small, but I put two or three together and shot away for some time. Then I alighted on a pouch full of cartridges. I got with the Zouaves, a little behind me in a ditch, and shot at about 40 yards for half an hour. I was very fortunate; I had my blue coat shot through, covered with powder and dust and mud from head to foot. I went back to the bridge after the Russians retired and a French officer ordered me to be taken up as a spy, just as I was off to get loot; so I walked off, but he allowed me to take the Zouaves with me. The general said that I had no business being there, but I might go. I said I was much obliged and that in any affair we had we would be proud to see him with our troops, his allies, and would not take him prisoner.'

On 25 August 1855 Goodlake wrote: ' We will never leave them alone from this bombardment. We are firing steadily at it; their loss must be terrible. All day long they are carrying dead and wounded to the rear. We have established a regular file-fire from right to left of our advanced works, which prevents them from mending theirs; this should have been done long ago. I am sure we would have got on much better if we had whole battalions of sharpshooters, instead of 30 or 40 or 50 men; only look at the annoyance caused to us by their rifle pits.'

The Russians learnt how effective our sharpshooting tactics were in firing at artillerymen, working their guns, and set up their own teams of marksmen, to harass our engineers and soldiers, constructing, repairing or extending trenches and batteries. Personal accounts of the war by British soldiers mention extensive use by the Russians of rifle pits and sharpshooters to prevent our engineers extending our fortifications forward.

It was necessary at times to organize raids by from 100 to 400 men to take these pits and to turn them into our positions.[21] An example of this manoeuvre was the assault on a very large Russian rifle-pit on 21 November 1854 called 'The Ovens', described by Colonel Calthorpe. He said that there might have been up to 200 Sharpshooters in this position, who were causing casualties to troops in our trenches in our left attack, as well as to the French in their advanced parallel. The attack was made by a strong company of the Rifle Brigade, which drove out the Russians and held the position against repeated counter-attacks.

[Editor's Note: Lieut Tryon, who was killed in the assault, Calthorpe says was one of the best shots in the army. Men in his company claim that he had killed over 100 Russians. During the Battle of Inkerman he spent his whole day firing at Russian artillerymen. Two men loaded for him and they said that he killed 30 Russians and wounded many others on that day. Goodlake refers to this incident in his letter of 5 May 1855. See also pages 157–9 of *Rifle Green in the Crimea*, which on page 162, mentions that the Rifles were able to approach to within eighty yards of the Redan and the Redoubt, which for four or five days did not fire a shot Goodlake refers to this operation in his letter of 6 May 1855, in which he mentions Lieutenant Bourchier, who took over from Lieutenant Tryon.]

Our soldiers then took more rifle-pits, 100 yards closer to the town [Sevastopol], turned round their defences to protect themselves from enemy fire and fired into the embrasures, at a distance of 450 yards, whenever the enemy appeared at a gun.[22]

Calthorpe reported on the 13 November 1854, that a 900 yard trench, about 300 yards in front of both of our attacks, had been dug. He said that numbers of our best marksmen would be placed in it, to reduce the fire on our trenches from the considerable numbers of Russian marksmen in rifle-pits, right the way along our front.[23] On 18 November 1854 he again mentions this battle between the Russian and British sharpshooters:

> Whereas the guns only fire in answer to the enemy's fire and vice-versa, a smart fusillade is continually going on between the sharpshooters in our musketry trenches and those in the Russian rifle-pits. He [Calthorpe] says that it is hard to know who has the best of it; our men are very sanguine, and declare that they are continually 'bowling over' the Russians.[24]

In his letter of 23 November Calthorpe says that, according to deserters, the garrison is getting very tired of the siege. Out of the 15,000 crew from the ships, which work the guns in the batteries opposed to the Allies, not more than 7,000 men now remain alive. The rest have been killed, died of disease or are in hospital, sick or wounded. In some batteries, the losses are so great that the men say they will spike their guns, rather than remain there.[25]

Michael Barthorp in his article on *Crimean Sharpshooters* says that siege warfare only required line and column manoeuvres for major assaults on the town. For the rest of the time the infantry was constructing and repairing trenches and batteries, and protecting them from enemy sorties. Furthermore, as the British batteries were about 13–1400 yards from the Russian guns, to be able to engage the Russian positions at 4–500 yards, they would be in position between 800 to 900 yards away from any infantry support, if they got into difficulties.

To operate effectively as a Sharpshooter, the order said that 'each man had to act for himself and exercise his intelligence to the utmost of his ability'. Men had not been trained in peacetime to operate in any other way than in close formation or in files for skirmishing. They had been trained to obey orders and not to use their own initiative. Furthermore the art of concealment and the ability to choose cover from fire were new skills to learn. However, the rural background of soldiers from the Brigade of Guards gave them a natural aptitude for this work. The colour of the uniform would have been a disadvantage, but because it was the winter, soldiers wore grey overcoats and Albert flat caps.[26]

This is illustrated by the remarks heard by Captain Clifford, Rifle Brigade, then a staff officer. He heard a sharpshooter say, 'This is as good as rabbit shooting' and another say, 'I would pay five shillings rather than lose this sport', thus illustrating the type of soldier, which found this work an outlet for his natural talents and emotions.[27]

However new ideas specially devised for colonial warfare, specified the need for looser and less rigid formations. By 1854, in a good well-trained battalion, it was not only the Light Company, which had the skills to skirmish.[28] Battalions could adapt to fighting in loose order as on the scrub-covered slopes of Inkerman. There, heavy Russian columns were held by extended lines of skirmishers in small groups, under junior officers or NCOs, where each man had to use his intelligence to the utmost of his ability to overcome greater numbers by using firepower rather than the bayonet.

Later on in the siege sharpshooters in static positions were used to engage enemy marksmen, harassing our trenches and batteries. However, Goodlake's operation was not only novel but well ahead of military thinking. He appeared to have a roving commission to operate where he saw opportunities. Colonel Wilson is right in his statement that Goodlake used 'marked intelligence and wariness in a novel part', i.e. irregular warfare, and that he showed 'common-sense and military knowledge'. He turned static sharpshooting, as Michael Barthrop said, 'to what in modern parlance might be called a fighting patrol.'

The Crimean War was the first of the modern wars fought with long-range rifles, which required a complete reappraisal of infantry tactics in the use of these weapons both by massed infantry and for sharpshooting [sniping]. As rifles developed and became more effective at long ranges, this trend continued during the Mutiny, the American Civil War, the Boer War and the First and Second World Wars.

Notes

1 *Letters from Headquarters,* p.101, Captain S.J.G.Calthorpe, John Murray, 1858. *Rifle Green in the Crimea,* pp. 65–6, George Caldwell and Robert Cooper, Bugle Horn, 1994.

2 *The Coldstream Guards in the Crimea,* p.120, Lieutenant-Colonel Ross-of-Bladensburg, 1897.

3 Goodlake letter. See 17 Dec.1854. 'Sharpshooting has been stopped, as we have so few duty men, so I now go out with my Battalion'.

4 Sergeant-Major Joseph Ashton, Coldstream Guards, was promoted to Lieutenant in the Rifle Brigade on 28 February 1855, backdated to 8 November 1854. *Rifle Green in the Crimea,* p.226.

5 *Invasion of the Crimea,* A.W. Kinglake, 1865, Vol. 7, p.10, fn.

6 *Invasion of the Crimea,* A.W. Kinglake, 1865, Vol.5, p.5.

7 Ibid, Vol V, p. 11.

8 See fn. 4.

9 What the Sergeant said was: 'They would kill us over that picket job'. He alluded to the fact that this little force under Captain Goodlake had lately attacked a Russian picket, taking an officer and some of the men prisoners, *Invasion of the Crimea,* Vol V, p.11, fn.

10 Colonel Federoff commanded the Russian reconnaissance in force of six battalions and four pieces of light artillery, totalling about 4300 men, plus the column of 700 men in the Careenage Ravine; i.e. 5000 men. *Invasion of the Crimea,* Vol. 5, p.5, Kinglake.

11 Kinglake notes that the magazine grotto was a cavern in which the powder for the Lancaster battery had been stored, but it was also used by the men of the neighbouring picket as a place for cooking and eating. Ibid, pp. 10–13.

12 Ibid, p.16.

13 *Britain's Roll of Glory*, pp. 42–3, Douglas H. Parry.

14 *Invasion of the Crimea*, Vol. 5, p.53.

15 *Our Veterans in Camp and before the Enemy*, pp. 222–3, a Regimental Officer, Colonel C.T.Wilson, 1859.

16 *The Crimean Campaign with The Connaught Rangers, 1854–55–56,* p.108, Lieutenant-Colonel Nathaniel Steevens, 1878.

17 *Rifle Green in the Crimea*, p.141, George Caldwell.

18 *La Defense de Sebastopol*, Gen. F.E.I. Todleben.

19 Gen.Soimonoff commanded the force of 19,000 men, which marched along Careenage Ravine to attack the British Army's left flank. Gen.Pauloff was to attack our right flank and then both forces were to come under the command of Gen.Dannenberg.

20 *Invasion of the Crimea*, Vol. 5, p. 116.

21 *Crimea –The Great Crimean War 1854–1856*, p.354, Trevor Royle, 1999.

22 *Letters from Headquarters*, pp. 186–7,Calthorpe.

23 Ibid, p. 174.

24 Ibid, p.183.

25 Ibid, p.185.

26 *The Journal of the Victorian Military Society*, Crimean Sharpshooters, Issue No.69, June 1992, Michael Barthorp.

27 *Letters and Sketches from the Crimea*, p.185, Henry Clifford VC, 1956.

28 *From Waterloo to Balaclava*, Hew Strachan, Cambridge University Press, Cambridge, 1985.

Chapter Four

The Letters –
Regimental Soldiering

The Landing, Inkerman and Winter,
September 1854 to February 1855

Guards Brigade-Movements & Events

1854   BLACK SEA
6 September   Having received orders, left Varna Bay and anchored
              in Balchik Bay.

7 September   Left Balchik Bay.

12 September   Off Eupatoria at noon.

14 September   Left Eupatoria at 1pm.

              CRIMEA
14 September   Landed [without knapsacks] at Old Fort, Kalamita
              Bay, marched three miles inland and bivouacked.

16 September   Encamped.

19 September   Marched to between Rivers Bulganak and Alma and
              bivouacked.

20 September   The Battle of the Alma; at 7.30 am the British Army
              marched to the River Alma and later fought the Battle
              of the Alma, which started at 1.20 pm and ended at
              5.45 pm.

20 September	Bivouacked about 2 miles from the Alma in the old Russian Camp.
23 September	Marched over the Steppe to the River Katcha and bivouacked.
24 September	Marched to the River Belbek and bivouacked two miles beyond.
25 September	Marshal St Arnaud resigns as C-in-C of the French Army and dies on 29 Sept. Marshal Canrobert becomes C-in-C.
25 September	Flank March, marched by Mackenzie's Farm to the Traktir Bridge over the River Tchernaya, and bivouacked on the Fediukine Heights at 9 pm.
26 September	Flank March, marched to Balaklava and bivouacked near Kadikoi.
2 October	The 1st Division marches to the Heights before Sevastopol and bivouacked near a windmill.
5 October	Tents issued.
15 October	General Liprandi arrives at Sevastopol with 25,000 Russian troops.
16 October	Divisional order issued on setting up a sharpshooting unit. consisting of 10 privates from each of the three Guards Battalions.
17–19 October	First Bombardment of Sevastopol.
24 October	Soldiers at work for 4 out of 5 nights.
25 October	The Battle of Balaklava, from 10 am to 4.30 pm.

26 October	Little Inkerman, defence of the British position on its being attacked by the Russian reconnaissance in force.
2 November	Knapsacks, left on board ship, are received by the Grenadiers and Scots Fusilier Guards.
5 November	The Battle of Inkerman, from 6.30 am to 5 pm.
6 November	Decision taken by Lord Raglan that the Army will winter in the Crimea.
7 November	The entrenchment of the Inkerman position by the Turks begins.
14–15 November	The Great Storm The eight-mile stretch of road to Balaklava becomes a morass and is impassable.
22 November	Second draft arrives of 58 NCOs & men.
17 December	Sharpshooting stopped, too few men available.
18 December	Third draft arrives of 153 men.

1855

1 January	1st Coldstream receive their knapsacks.
1 February	Guards Brigade, only some 312 men able to do duty.
2 February	Lord Rokeby arrives to take command of the Brigade.
5 February	Lord Aberdeen resigns and Lord Palmerston becomes Prime Minister.
15 February	Lime juice issued to all ranks.
23 February	Marched to Balaklava and hutted nearby. Grand Crimean Central Railway operational from Balaklava to Kadikoi.

The Invasion of the Crimea.

Without accurate maps it was necessary to reconnoitre the coastline to find a suitable landing site. Lieutenant General Sir George Brown and Marshal Canrobert made the first reconnaissance and chose the Katcha River. On 8 September 1854 Lord Raglan, together with these two officers and others, made a second reconnaissance. Lord Raglan decided on Eupatoria as a landing site for the Army.

On 29 August 1st Coldstream, consisting of 26 officers and 737 men, embarked at Varna. The Battalion was divided into two wings; the left wing and headquarters sailed in the *Simoon* and the right wing were on board the *Tonning* with the Grenadier Guards.

The Army numbered 26,000 infantry, 2000 cavalry and 60 guns. Each of the five divisions, the 1st Division, made up of the Guards Brigade and the Highland Brigade, the 2nd, 3rd, 4th and Light Divisions, were each about 5000 strong. The Cavalry Division, which consisted of the Light Brigade and the Heavy Brigade, was around 2000 strong. The French had four infantry divisions, about 7000 in all, no cavalry and 68 guns. There were also 7000 Turks attached to the French Army.

This impressive armada sailed towards the coast of the Crimea. On 14 September 1854 the troops disembarked, without any opposition from the enemy, at Old Fort, Kalamita Bay, and marched three miles inland and bivouacked.

Owing to the shortage of carts, the soldiers' packs were left on board ship, as the Medical Department advised Lord Raglan that the soldiers were too weak to carry their packs. The battalion commanding officers were not consulted over this. The officers and privates had to roll up what they needed in a blanket roll, which was carried across their shoulder and chest. For three and a half months they had no changes of clothing and all ranks were covered in lice. When the packs were recovered many items of kit had been stolen.

Lieutenant-Colonel Lord Frederick Paulet's two companies of the Coldstream Guards retained their packs.[1] In his letter of 1 January 1855 Goodlake reports that on that day the battalion had at last received its baggage.

He had to reduce the kit he took with him to the Crimea, as all officers were restricted to having one pack animal, which can carry 20 stone [280 lbs]. This load has to include a pack saddle, bed, bedding, canteen, riding saddle, rope trunks, covers, etc, so there was little room for luxuries. He discarded his waterproof bed, 28 lbs, for a wooden stretcher, 15 lbs.

In September, Marshal St Arnaud resigned as Commander-in-Chief of the French Army and died. Marshal Canrobert became Commander-in-Chief.

Alma and Inkerman

There are no letters in existence for the period of September- October 1854, so we have no knowledge of what happened to Captain Goodlake at the battle of the Alma. The casualties of his battalion at the Alma, two officers wounded, one dying of wounds and twenty-seven men wounded, did not prepare him for their losses at the Battle of Inkerman. Whereas at Little Inkerman, 27 October 1854, he played a major role, with his Sharpshooters, in repulsing the Russian assault on the Army's left flank, according to his letter of 6 November 1854 he was ill in his tent and not engaged in action at the Battle of Inkerman.

At this battle his battalion suffered the loss of eight officers killed, including the Commanding Officer, Colonel Dawson, and the Adjutant, Captain Eliot, and five officers wounded. Colonel Upton was on night duty on 4/5 November and Colonel Lord F. Paulet was ill. The next senior officer, Colonel Newton, was Field Officer of the Day. Therefore Colonel Dawson commanded and was killed at the Sandbag Battery. When Major-General Bentinck was wounded early on in the battle, Colonel Upton became the Brigade Commander. He was also wounded but remained in command of the Brigade till 15 November and was then repatriated. Out of the seventeen officers who went into battle only four came through unhurt, Captains Strong, Wilson, Crawley & Tower.[2] Three sergeants and seventy-three men of the rank and file were killed and eleven sergeants and 107 men were wounded.

The Grenadier officer casualties were three killed and six wounded and of the non-commissioned officers and rank and file there were 101 killed and 124 wounded. The Scots Fusilier officer casualties were one killed and eight wounded and the non-commissioned officers and rank and file casualties were sixty-five killed and 106 wounded.

At Inkerman, the Guards Brigade lost nearly half its strength of 1300: killed 254, wounded 367, which totals 621. The effective strength of the Brigade engaged in the battle at the end of the contest was around 679.

Every battalion had to find men for outlying piquets and for manning the trenches surrounding Sevastopol. After the battle Captain Goodlake wrote that the battalion strength, including the two companies which had been on piquet numbering 140 and who were not engaged in the battle, was eleven officers and 365 men. Overall the Guards Brigade had seven companies on trench duties, some of which were not involved in the battle.

With this great sacrifice, it is not surprising that Captain Goodlake felt very angry at the lack of recognition by Lord Raglan, when reporting to the Secretary for War of the Brigade's achievements in this battle. 'The supernatural courage displayed by the Brigade should have merited praise.'

Promotion

Goodlake's father had served in the 5th Dragoon Guards during the Peninsular War, so he feels quite at home discussing with him the complications of the Purchase System for Officers' Commissions. Promotion was one of the subjects which he mentioned frequently in his letters early on in the War. Under the rules then in force for the Purchase of Commissions the most senior officer was promoted first, provided he had paid the Regulation Fee, if not the next senior officer would be promoted over him. Therefore his name had to be placed for promotion and the Regulation Fee paid to prevent any of his brother officers jumping over his head. This payment, he says, would not prevent him from getting his promotion for nothing, if there was a casualty or if the number of officers in the battalion was increased, called an augmentation.

On 30 June 1855 he realized that he was not to be promoted, as he only had five years service in the Army and not six years, which was required for promotion to major. He was right. The recommendations of these senior officers obviously did have an effect, as he was promoted Brevet Major on 14 June 1856, having served in the Army for exactly six years.

Tactics

From 16 October to 17 December Captain Goodlake commanded a party of Sharpshooters [snipers] whose objective was to kill enemy officers and gunners. This subject is discussed in detail in Chapter 3, The Development of Sharpshooting.

Captain Goodlake had a good appreciation of the British Army's tactical position in the Crimea. On 27 November 1854 he says that Sevastopol will take more time and trouble to take than people think, as he has been nearer to it, on his sharpshooting duties, than any other Englishman, except for prisoners of war.

On 8 February 1855 he complains that Lord Raglan is very weak in his dealing with Marshal Canrobert and allows him to get the best deal for the French Army, at the expense of the British Army, whose soldiers were at work for four out of five nights.

Winter 1854

After the Great Storm of 14–15 November the roads became impassable and the supply ship *Prince* was lost, with most of the Army's winter clothing. William Russell's dispatch in *The Times* about the Crimean War, dated 25 November 1854, gave a chilling picture of the condition of the Army in the Crimea:

> It is now pouring rain – the skies are as black as ink – the wind is howling over the staggering tents – the trenches are turned into dykes – in the tents the water is sometimes a foot deep – our men have not either warm or waterproof clothing – they are out for twelve hours at a time in the trenches – they are plunged into the miseries of a winter campaign – not a soul seems to care for their comfort, or even for their lives. These are hard truths but the people of England must hear them. They must know that the most wretched beggar, who wanders about the streets of London in the rain, leads the life of a prince compared with the British soldiers who are fighting out here for their country, and who, we are complacently assured by the home authorities, are the best appointed army in Europe.

At the end of the year of 1854 William Russell wrote:

72

Why were they in tents? Where were the huts which had been sent out to them? The huts were on board ships in the harbour of Balaklava. Some of these huts were floating about the beach; others had been converted into firewood or used for stabling for officers' horses.[3]

William Russell summed up the effect of this incompetence on the fighting efficiency of the Army:

> What was the cost to the country of the men of the Brigade of Guards, who died in their tents, or in hospital of exhaustion, overwork, and deficient of proper nutriment? The Brigade [around 2900 strong originally] mustered a little over 400 men fit for duty by the middle of February 1855. It would have been cheap to have fed these men we had lost on turtle and venison, if we could have kept them alive- not only those, but the poor fellows the battle spared, but whom disease took from us out of every regiment in the expedition.[4]

About the winter of 1854–55, William Russell wrote:

> A soldier is a very dear animal. A crop of them is difficult to raise and once they have been fully grown and have become ripe soldiers, they are beyond all price.[5]

Captain Alfred Tipping, Grenadier Guards, wrote in his letter to his family after the Battle of the Alma that a French officer, noting the lack of care of our men in providing them with tents to keep out the heavy dews and the absence of any proper provision for the accommodation of the sick, remarked:

> It seems to me that your soldiers are not looked after as they should be. They merit in your hands priceless care. If you have such soldiers you should look after them as you would your eyes.[6]

Commissariat, Transport & Hospitals

In the Crimea, in the absence of an efficient and effective transport and supply operation and without a trained staff as Wellington had, even when the Army had supplies in Balaklava, it was unable to supply its front-line troops. In winter the principal shortages were clothing

73

and boots, rations, fodder for the horses, medicines and hospital supplies, tents, huts and warlike stores. Unlike the French Army, during the summer months it had failed to build all-weather roads and central stores. It could not supply its troops adequately in winter, until the railway from Balaklava to Kadikoi became operational during February and March 1855. It was later extended to the top of the Sapoune Heights, overlooking Sevastopol.

Its medical requirements, the pressing need for field hospitals and for effective ambulances for transporting battle casualties to these hospitals, were not properly considered. The ambulances, specially designed and built for the campaign, were useless and could not travel over rough ground. The aged enrolled pensioners, recruited to act as medical orderlies, were unable to operate in these extreme conditions. There were no hospital ships in existence and no trestle tables were supplied to enable stretchers to be lifted off the wet ground.

Florence Nightingale, with her nurses, had been sent out to the hospital at Scutari by Sidney Herbert, the Secretary-at-War. She and the medical staff arrived at Scutari just as the casualties from the Battle of Inkerman arrived at the hospital. They were unaware of the existence of germs. They believed that disease was caused by bad air, *miasma*, generated by decay, dirt, middens, accumulations of filth and by marshes. The sanitary measures introduced by Florence Nightingale, better cooking arrangements and diet, as well as proper nursing routines, made considerable differences to the patients' survival, especially after the Sanitary Commission had cleansed the hospital and its drains in March 1855.[7]

On 17 December 1854 Captain Goodlake writes that he is very angry about the state of the wounded. He says that the wounded are looked after disgracefully. 'There are no doctors, no nurses, no orders; all is confusion as there is no system.'

During the period from November 1854 to August 1855 he writes about the very unsatisfactory supply position in the Crimea. On 22 November he explains that, while there are plentiful stores at Balaklava, the problem is getting them up to the troops.

On 5 January he writes that on this day the battalion has only 128 men fit for duty.

The lack of a proper road from Balaklava to the camp, together with insufficient carts, made supplying the troops very difficult. However by the end of January, he says that all the men are now well off for stores and food and they are tolerably well clothed.

Some of the Army, such as the Rifle Brigade, had been on campaign, but for the others, used to living in barracks, such as the Guards Brigade, and especially the new recruits and the new drafts, there was no tradition of cooking in the field, as there was in the French Army. Many of the unwieldy and heavy camp kettles issued to troops had been thrown away by many units during the march to the Alma.

It was not till much later that consideration was given as to what diet soldiers required to combat disease and to perform their tasks effectively. The valuable lessons learnt in earlier campaigns about maintaining a high standard of camp hygiene and the prevention of disease had been forgotten.

[Editor's Note- Sir John Pringle, Physician-General to the Forces in the Low Countries in 1744, published in 1752, *Observations on Diseases of the Army*. He is the Father of modern military hygiene, attributing much army sickness to the air from marshes, rotting vegetable matter, fouling of the camping grounds by humans and animals, and from bad ventilation in hospitals, barracks and ships. He also advocated the frequent changing of camping grounds and organised messing for soldiers. All this wise advice was forgotten in the Crimean Campaign.]

On 8 February Captain Goodlake reports that the Brigade had 600 duty men and the Coldstream only 126. After the Guards Brigade moved away from the front line to Balaklava on 23 February and no longer had to carry out trench duties, he was able to report that by 28 July the Brigade's strength had increased to 1000 duty men.

His Hut

Well before the rest of the Army had huts to live in, Captain Goodlake had his own hut, built by his Sharpshooters [snipers] out of materials from Russian homes, which he wrote about on 26 November 1854. He says that, 'Another officer lives with me as well as the Battalion Quartermaster, who can get anything we want such as tools and food'.

The Letters

The date of one letter has been altered as the facts reported in it took place at a different time. The altered date is shown in italics and the reasons for this alteration shown below.

1854

20 September	Battle of the Alma	
25 October	Battle of Balaklava	
5 November	Battle of Inkerman	
6 November	South Side of Sevastopol	Father & Mother
November	War Office	Mrs Goodlake
27 November	Camp before Sevastopol	Father & Mother
17 December	Camp before Sevastopol	Father & Mother

1855

1 January	Camp before Sevastopol	Father & Mother
5 January	Camp before Sevastopol	Aunt Louisa
8 January	Camp before Sevastopol	Father & Mother
15 January	Camp before Sevastopol	Mother
25 January	Camp before Sevastopol	Father
1 February	Camp before Sevastopol	Mother
8 February	Camp before Sevastopol	Father
22 February	Camp before Sevastopol	Father

Revision of Date of Letter.

The date of one letter is shown in italics. The date and the place where this letter was written and the events mentioned in the letter did not agree with the timetable shown above. After taking into account the facts within a letter, the original date has been amended as follows;

No Date: Camp before Sevastopol. The letter mentions winter and also a draft which had just arrived on 22 November. It also mentions the more favourable treatment of the Brigade's achievements at the Battle of Inkerman by the newspapers than in Lord Raglan's despatches. The date taken is *27 November 1854*, which was when the Guards Brigade was in Camp before Sevastopol.

On the South side of Sevastopol
6 November 1854-Inkerman
My dearest Father and Mother,

On Wednesday 25 October, the Russians, being reinforced, attacked Balaklava in our rear. They tripped the poor Light Cavalry Brigade and cut them up awfully. They cut down the gunners at their guns, the Turks bolted and we lost three redoubts. As our position was not too extensive, we did not retake them. The Heavy Cavalry made a beautiful charge, but were sadly outnumbered.

The next day [26 October – Little Inkerman][8] they made a sortie from Sevastopol and attacked our left regiments, but were repulsed with great slaughter: between 7 and 800 killed and taken prisoners.

'I have 30 volunteer men from the Brigade who act under me (Sharpshooters). We go out and shoot Russians and piquets.[9] I killed 5 men, one at 300 yards through the head and one officer beating on his men at 30 yards. Most exciting. I and a Sergeant[10] were nearly caught in a cave but we made a bolt for it and got off with only a bullet through my coat and he shot in the arm'. [For this action Captain Goodlake was awarded the Victoria Cross. See Chapter 3.]

We received very little loss that day. The enemy were driven back. The Russians seemed to be very quiet from the 28th until yesterday the 5th [Battle of Inkerman] when they made a tremendous attack on the whole of our right. It rained the night before without ceasing. Our piquets were driven in and few of their rifles went off.[11]. There was a dense fog and a drizzling rain. We were ordered to march under arms and arrived just in time to repel an enormous body of Russians, which the Brigade did nobly, but they went too far, got out of control.[12]

The French Army, principally the Zouaves, advanced on the right of the British position and drove the Russians down the slope. The intervention of these fresh troops lowered the Russian morale and caused them to withdraw.

The moment the Russians fiends saw the Bearskins they sent man after man. Our men never flinched but fought as cool and were cut to pieces. We had two companies on piquet luckily, so we still manage to form a little regiment. Not a man would have returned had not the French come up and made a most splendid charge. After it was over, we found it was a fresh army [Russian] arrived from Odessa.[13] They had forwarded by carriages, arabas and every conceivable conveniences, commanded in person by Grand Duke Constantine[14].

We killed immense numbers of them, but our loss is frightful. General Bentinck was badly wounded in the early part of the fight. General Cathcart killed.[15]

My company was on piquet and my men [Sharpshooters] do not go out with the battalion. I am quite separate and as I have not been very well for the last day or two [nothing at all the matter.] I did not go, so fortunately escaped. I was glad when it was all over that I had not been there, though shot and shell pitched into and over our camp all day long. The action was from 20 minutes to 7 am till 4pm. Nothing could exceed the bravery of our men.

I will now give you the melancholy list. 17 officers went into the fight, for our Regiment, only 4 came back, not killed or wounded. We had 8 officers killed and 5 wounded. Killed Lieutenant-Colonel Dawson [Commanding Officer], Lieutenant-Colonel Cowell, Captain Mackinnon, Captain Eliot [Adjutant], Captain Ramsden, Captain Bouverie, Captain Disbrow, Captain Greville. Wounded Colonel Upton, Lieutenant-Colonel Halkett, Lieutenant-Colonel Lord C. Fitzroy, Captain Fielding and Lieutenant Amherst. There were about 80 men killed. We can only muster 365 men. 140 were out on piquet not engaged. Is it not too terrible, all one's poor friends dead?

Dunkellin has been very kindly treated, he was taken prisoner some time ago. The Scots Fusiliers have 5 wounded officers. Prentis Blair very bad, can't live. Francis Baring slightly. Shugborough, H. Drummond.[16] Men were a good deal cut up. Grenadiers, Colonel Pakenham, Sir R.Newman and Neville dead. Sturt wounded and Tipping in the leg.[17] The list, I know, is correct as it has gone out. I am writing this in a great hurry as the post is to go out directly.

We have been hammering away at Sevastopol ever since the 17th; they fire about 20 shots to our one and are far stronger than when we began. All the Artillery are crying out "let us send you chaps in with the bayonet," Every man in the army is ready to go. They will never take it without.

Poor Colonel Hood and Rowley killed in the trenches. Cameron, Davis wounded.[18]

We have an army in our rear. Sevastopol in our front and another army in our right flank and there is no doubt we shall have to winter here. Everybody knows what we have to do and all are cheerful though the poor men are worked to death. They don't get three nights a week in bed (their tents I mean). The way the wounded are looked after is disgraceful. No surgeons, no nurses, no orders, everything in confusion. No system-very bad indeed. French are far superior.

I have now not the slightest chance of coming home before winter, so please send me some winter clothing. I only have my red coat,[19] in fact just the clothes I stand up in. I have no warm clothes at Scutari. I need a good warm sheepskin cap and coat, a thick handkerchief.

The corporal has come for the mail, so I must conclude my melancholy epistle. I hope you are all well. Give my best love to all and dear Bob in particular.

> Believe me ever,
> > Your affectionate son,
> > > Gerald L.Goodlake

P.S. I ask as a particular favour that my letters are not hawked about and shown to this person and that. I know that people are anxious for news, but please tear them up when you have read them. God bless you all.

I am writing this under noise, row and all sorts of disturbances, so I dare say you won't be able to make head or tail of this letter.

The War Office
Tuesday
Dear Mrs Goodlake,

I am truly vexed to hear that you had only yesterday morning received the message which I had sent you a quarter of an hour after the Duke of Newcastle[20] had opened the bag of despatches, and more than five hours before the *Gazette* was published.

I had hoped that the delightful assurance of your son's safety would have reached you about dinner time on Sunday.

There was, as you will, 'ere this, have seen, another great battle fought on 5 November before Sevastopol. Victory again crowned the heroic daring of the Englishmen; but I fear the loss of life must have been, from all accounts, considerable.

Three generals are wounded: Adams, Bentinck and Torrens[21]

A brother and cousin serving in the Crimea now divides the interest which we feel in the progress of the war, and I hope that you will allow me to share in the advantage of the vigilant watch I keep at all hours for the arrival of intelligence. It is always of service in however trifling a degree as regards the trouble taken to render it. But the pleasure is greatly enhanced when circumstances such as these have taken off the rough edge of the obligation you bestow.

> Believe me,
> > Yours very sincerely and faithfully,
> > > E.Armstrong Vicars.

Camp before Sevastopol
27 November 1854

My dearest Father and Mother,

I have this moment received your welcome letters and a small parcel forwarded to Head Quarters. I cannot express my thanks to you for all your kindness. I will write when I can spare a moment, but we get our letters sometimes, just as the mail goes out, sometimes two mails together, sometimes three. Lord Raglan gets his mail from Chersonese[22] but ours are sent to Balaklava and if the weather is bad they may not be able to get in for several days. Such is the state of the roads that it is with utmost difficulty that we get our rations up. Only yesterday I saw some of the Light Division, bringing up their Copork[23] on their backs on a bit of stick.

It is impossible to write every mail, but I will write as often as I can. I am on outlying piquet so I have not time to write you a long letter now. I wrote one by the last mail and one two mails before. The parcel contained a wash leather waistcoat, a capital thing for which I am truly thankful. Give my love to the 'Dear Man' and tell him that his munificent present of eatables has not yet arrived, but the moment it does, I will write him a letter expressing my thanks. I will announce the arrival of all the clothing, which you have had the kindness to send out. How I am to get them up, I do not know. I think the trusty Larcombe [Soldier Servant.] will have to make several trips. It goes rather to my heart to send him, as it is up to his knees in mud.

Do not be anxious about me. I take every care of myself. I have built a capital home. I got all the materials out of Russian homes with my sharpshooters, who will go anywhere in the world for me. I am now writing in it.

If the weather was not so cold and wet and one was not constantly wet through, (which will now, thanks to you, be remedied) the cold would be nothing. We had a snow storm the other day, but it did not last long. The climate out here is much colder than in England at this time of the year. Pray don't be anxious, as I am very well off and as jolly as I can be, under the present circumstances, and am not so much of a martyr, as you think.

There is a tolerably good supply of stores at Balaklava, if only we could get them up; everything very dear, a penny for a box of Lucifer matches. One cannot think of prices.

I saw young Vivian[24] yesterday; he is a capital fellow and has shown me the greatest kindness, offering to get me anything in his power. I wish you could write to H Vivian and tell him that his son is quite well and has been so particularly kind. I cannot tell you how gratifying it is to feel how kind and how sympathetic all one's friends are.

I see very little of the Colonel; we have no time for visiting. Codrington, who at present commands the Light Division, speaks in the highest terms of him; he says he is the pluckiest and most hardworking person he ever had anything to do with. And he is no bad judge. Freddy is also flourishing. Bill, Peter and Crawley all beg to be remembered to you. Turner, the Fusiliers' Doctor, seems a very nice fellow and is liked by everyone.[25]

I see that from the last papers that the Guards are more honourably mentioned than in Lord Raglan's despatches; for all size operations, I must refer you to the papers.

There was a sortie last night, 20 or 30 of our men taken prisoner and one officer and one major mortally wounded, but the enemy were driven back. Sevastopol, in my humble opinion, will take a great deal more time and trouble to take than people think. I have been nearer than any other Englishman, except for those who have been taken prisoner. One scarcely hears the cannon, one has got so accustomed to it. We only prick up our ears at musketry.

Our draft has arrived at Balaklava and are to take two days in coming up; the men have to carry their things, their rations and their tents on their backs. What fun for them; they tell me their faces are truly laughable. They look so unhappy at all their new things lying in the mud. I must now conclude.

With best love to all, and again thanking you from the bottom of my heart, for all your sympathy, affection and kindness.

Believe me ever,

Your affectionate son,

Gerald L.Goodlake

Camp before Sevastopol
17 December 1854

Dearest Father and Mother

Many thanks for your last letter. Glad am I to hear of your all being well. May you continue so. You must know by this time all about *Simoon* and that awful storm. Nothing since has happened of any consequence.

We have had a good many reinforcements in driblets, but sickness has broken out among the newcomers to such an extent that it is positive murder to send a regiment out that has not been acclimatized. For instance, the 97th Regiment that has been attached to our Brigade for the present, because we are so weak, have up to this moment 238 men in hospital and have buried fifty-four. They have not been here three weeks. We have lost seventeen of our draft, out of fifty, besides twenty-seven in hospital, so you may suppose what danger there is in sending out drafts at this time of year. How glad we are that the 1st Battalion Grenadiers are not coming out.

I will now give you a sketch of our grievances, which are a great deal too bad, as we all know and feel out here how kind and liberal everybody is at home and how you all wish for our welfare. The following are instances, which I think ought to be known in England, as there seems to be no redress for them out here. I will commence with the hospital. We have no trestles[26] whatever. There is not a hospital in the French Army that has not got them. No dry clothes, hardly any blankets. Men come in wet to the skin, with cramps and cholera. As I have written above, not a chance have they that live on the damp ground. Few, very few, get over these choleric attacks and those that have the luck to do so are generally left with a violent fever that nothing can be done for them, or is done.

The weather has been very bad of late; the men never have a dry thread on them. It has been raining without intermission for the last fortnight.

Another application was made for a hospital marquee, which after difficulty was obtained. When it arrived it had no ropes. It has been lying on the ground for a fortnight. Requisition after requisition has been made for ropes, but to no purpose; it still remains on the ground. Sixteen poor fellows huddled on the ground in a bell tent.

Only three days ago another shameful case; a man had ophthalmia. They sent the Hospital Sergeant to Balaclava [six miles] to get some belladonna to dilate the pupil of the eye. He applied at the Medical Stores and was told that he was too late that day; he must come before 2 o'clock the next day or they would not give it to him. The hospital lost the use of its sergeant – a very important man – and the poor fellow his eyesight.

The men hate hospital to such an extent and are so badly treated that they hardly ever go there, unless ordered to or on a stretcher, when there is scarcely a chance of saving the poor fellow. Plenty more cases could I relate had I time to do so, but what I have written will show pretty plainly how things are carried out.

We are all [the Brigade] awfully disgusted at the light way in which Lord Raglan mentions the Guards on 5 November. We fought by ourselves, unsupported by any regiment, without artillery, for four hours. Three times without ammunition, against the Russians far outnumbering us in a position so central that had they retreated, the enemy would have turned their flank and been all over the camp and no one could tell what would have happened.

The real state of the case is that he is living far off, knows nothing and cares less (at least it seems so) and did not like them (the press) praising the courage the Brigade showed and the admirable manner in which they repulsed these large bodies, for showing himself up in allowing so few troops to defend a position of such importance and then not being there in time to send up reinforcements, consequently the awful slaughter the Brigade sustained.

Fortunately we had seven companies on piquet or the Drummers would have had to represent the Brigade out here. So he gets made a Field Marshal[27] and we do not get the praise, which is due. It must have been a very bloody and determined resistance, by the number of officers and men the Brigade lost, which of itself will proclaim the truth. It is natural that after the supernatural courage that was displayed by our Brigade that we expected it would have been mentioned in the despatches. But to the people, who read the account in England, it will appear that we did hardly anything, instead of bearing the brunt of it, while numbers of the Line regiments were actually running away. Our camp was full of them. There is one thing, a great consolation, which is that the whole army knows how the Brigade behaved and acknowledges the unjustness of his Lordship's despatches.

There is another part of our system, which wants altering and is a source of general dissatisfaction. The way in which the Staff are always mentioned in despatches, no matter how they behave, whether skulking in the rear or sitting behind a stone or bush (instances that can be named) they are always mentioned, while any regimental officer, sergeant or private, who undergoes ten times the hardships, by risking his life and doing his best, is scarcely or ever mentioned. When he is, it is only when he has done some foolhardy or almost impossible action from which he has escaped by the mercy of Providence, than in any other way.

I think that after all the promises Lord Raglan has made about procuring officers baggage, he might have kept them, as no one has as yet got a stick of clothing or baggage, but what he carries on his back and what one has had the luck to buy at sales or at Balaclava at exorbitant prices. I thought that our Quarter Master, who went to Scutari, would have been back by this time, but they won't give him a passage. He would have brought up some of our baggage.

I am very well, thank God, and stand the weather capitally. Sharpshooting has been stopped, as we had so few duty men, so I now go on duty with my Battalion.

Give my best love to Bob. I did not write by the last mail, as I was on piquet and did not know when the post went out and had [not] got my letter ready.

Sevastopol will be taken to a certainty, (when we do is doubtful). The Butcher's Bill [casualties.] will be awful. We, I believe, take no part in the storming. I think there is just the chance of my coming home when our reinforcements come out and when Sevastopol is taken, and also a slight one of the return of the Brigade to England after the little fortress is taken. But these are only conjectures. I remember you to all your friends whenever I meet them, and they always ask how the Governor is, etc.

I must now conclude. With best love to all, and with every good wish and thanks for all your manifold kindnesses.

> Believe me ever,
> Your affectionate son,
> Gerald L. Goodlake.

P.S. If you find an opportunity of sending me out those things which I named in my letter to Bob, I would be most grateful. How I long to see you all once more.

Camp before Sevastopol
1 January 1855
My dearest Father and Mother

A Happy New Year to you and all the family. I yesterday received a parcel containing jerseys, gloves, mittens, knife, socks, etc by Captain Briton [not identified]. I have not seen him yet to thank him. I cannot say how obliged I am and how thankful to you all. You have hit off the right things. I don't think I want anything else. It never rains but it pours, for the sleek easy-going staff promoting Raglan has at last succeeded in getting our baggage up, only fancy my delight in sleeping tonight off the ground on my stretcher.

Our draft has just arrived, which will ease our duty very much. I have been on duty thirteen days running; we only had four officers doing subaltern's duty, but in consequence of our augmentation[28] we are to begin trench work again.

I saw the Colonel two or three days ago and sent him the parcel yesterday. Both he and Fred are well, the latter very disgusted at the way things are carried on. We shall have Sevastopol in three weeks or a month at latest. We have all our guns and mortar batteries ready and are only waiting to get shot, shell and fifteen days provisions up and in we shall go, as we ought to have done months ago,

Our horses have arrived from Varna, that is to say a few of them; both of mine are lost. I bought another one yesterday but he was cut loose in the night, by the French, I think. They are such thundering rogues, they beat us into a fit soldiering. They can live where we would starve.

I have been very busy building a house, which is completed. We dine in it and have got a good fire. We are all well off now; nothing to complain of. The weather has been very cold, hard frosts and snow-storms; it suits me but I don't care for it.

What do you think I am having for dinner today? A hare I shot three days ago when I was on piquet with a Minie rifle. She was running broadside about 16 yards off; a good business.

The post is going and I have just been sent for to go on a Court Martial. So must conclude.

With a thousand thanks and every good wish for the future year.

> Believe me ever,
> Your affectionate son,
> Gerald L.Goodlake

Camp before Sevastopol
5 January 1855
My dear Aunt Louise,

Thank you so much for all your kindness and the knife, which I am sure will be very useful. I received it in parcel under the care of Captain Briton with a great many more things which I can assure you I wanted. How thankful I am that you have all been well and that Mother and Bob were staying at Ranston, an anxious time for her, poor Mother. I am afraid that we still have our work cut out before we take this place.

There is now a foot and a half of snow on the ground and the poor men are nearly frozen to death . The officers are better off, but still nothing like comfortable.

The arrangements which have made for the men are truly infamous.

We have one hundred and twenty-eight men fit for duty by this morning's state, out of over one thousand that started from England. The weather is very cold now and hard frost. Three poor officers died last night in their tents from burning charcoal and two poor men from the cold in my company. They had only one blanket and lay on the ground wet through.

We have not sufficient horses, wagons, or anything. The cavalry are turned into pack horses; they can hardly bring up the provisions.

I believe that all my parcels have arrived at Balaklava. You go on board the ship and ask for your parcel. 'Don't know'. 'Landed, where landed?' Answer: 'In some store or another.' Another answer; 'Parcels, Sir. Under the ammunition or the huts, Sir, really can't tell, Sir, somewhere or another.' There is a total want of all order or regulation. When I have the luck to get them I will write to all the kind friends and good dear people who sent them a separate letter.

I am ashamed not to have written to some of you before, but with having to grub our own wood and cook our own dinners, or get them with no tables or chairs, but lying on the ground, one has not had much time, until three days ago. I have been on duty thirteen days running, seven nights out of bed, but one draft has now arrived, so work will be easier.

My dear Aunt Louise, I have not told you much, but I thought you would like one little line to thank you for your kindness.

With my best love to dear Gran, who I am glad to hear, has been so well. Please tell good 'Mrs Waistcoat' that my having spent a few hours in the kitchen with her and Hodkiss have not been thrown away.

Remember me to her and Harris, etc. how I wish I was at dear old Ranston again; but until Sevastopol is ours, I shall never see England again, nor do I wish to.

[Letter not signed.]

Camp before Sevastopol
8 January 1855

My dearest Father and Mother,

I yesterday received your letter of 20 December. I have not received another parcel, though I believe one has arrived.

I went to Balaklava yesterday and went on board *Robert Lowe*, *Charity* and *Cosmopolitan*. *Robert Lowe* at first denied all knowledge of a parcel for me, but I saw Gregory,[29] who said there was one for me and that he would look for it and bring it up. *Cosmopolitan* said they believed they had a parcel for me but they could not get it up for at least a week, as all the boxes etc were on top of the parcels. The *Charity* parcel I have got, for which I again repeat my best thanks and which I acknowledged in my last letter. I am much obliged for all your kindness and believe I have everything I want except boots. I have only two pairs, one with half a sole and the other with the binding undone.

You, with the people at home, cannot believe the difficulty, confusion and trouble to get, find or even hear of one's things at Balaklava. You must remember there is no road up to camp, but which is up to our ears in mud and slush, no carts, and it is with the greatest difficulty that they manage to get rum and salt pork up for the troops. Some divisions have to go down and fetch it up on their backs.

I was astonished to see a statement by Sidney Herbert[30] in the House that our men had two suits of clothing and one of skins. All I can say is that there is at the moment a foot of snow on the ground and a hard frost and our men have not even two blankets to cover them. The consequence is that the hospital is full of frostbitten feet and hands. I don't mean to say that the things were not sent for them and that Sidney Herbert had not the right to expect that the men were wearing them; but one thing is certain, the men have not got them at present and are in as miserable a condition and as pitiable a state as possible.

People have sent out plum puddings and Reid[31] beer for the men, but as for getting them up here it is ridiculous.

I have made up my mind on one thing. That we shall have to exist here, if we can, till March or April, and then take this place. We shall not do so before. The weather will not permit it. Omar Pasha[32] will collect an army and attack the north side and we shall go in.

There is not a hut up yet and when one goes to bed of a night one is afraid of breaking one's red coat[33] of a morning, so stiff is it. I am very well; was never better. I run about everywhere whenever I have a moment to spare. Grub wood or anything I find; it's much the best way.

I saw the Colonel; he is so delighted with Mother's present of a chamois waistcoat, gloves etc. He came and called on me yesterday. He is very well and has seen every officer in his regiment, killed, sick or wounded. My house is the greatest blessing I could possibly have had. I always keep a good fire and, as you may imagine, have plenty of company. I do not sleep in it, as it is not quite finished at present.

You need not be in the least afraid of my hurting myself by smoking **** chip[34], as I don't smoke it unless I am hard up for tobacco. I will

87

not smoke it, as you do not like it, but you must remember that living out in the open air in piquet trenches, with no covering hardly at all, is quite different to being in England. I never drank spirits before I came out here, but now I have got to like my allowance of rum as well as any other soldier.

You have asked about me being on the staff. I would not be on anyone's staff for the world. A parcel of lazy, idle, eating, drinking, swearing fellows who don't know what soldering is and don't care, as long as they can ride about and smoke cigars, instead of looking after the poor, unfortunate and neglected men. They, to be sure, get promoted and mentioned by that sleek, easy-going, staff-promoting Field Marshal at the head of affairs. Thank God, I have done my regimental duty, without missing a day, and now know what a soldier can do and how disgracefully he can be treated.

Best love to my dearest Bob, and tell her many thanks for her letter and paper. Much obliged for sending me the pipes. I am looking forward so much for a meerschaum. My old pipe, poor dear Ramsay broke, but it is not spoilt and, one day, I hope to get it mended. I must now conclude as I am for the trenches this evening. I will let you know the moment I receive a parcel and which one it is.

With a thousand thanks and best love to all.

Believe me,

Ever your very affectionate son,

G. L. G.

Camp before Sevastopol
15 January 1855
My dearest Mother,

I have received your letter and on the same day got two more parcels one from *Cosmopolitan* and the other from *Charity*. No tongue can tell you my thankfulness for the contents. I can assure you they were much wanted and thoroughly appreciated. I am much obliged for your kindness and everyone else's. My sheepskin coat is the admiration of the camp, cap etc. I have also received my Fortnum & Mason box and a very handsome present from the 'dear man'. I have of course written to thank him but unfortunately all the brandy is all bad, turned black, tastes beastly and is poisonous, a sad pity. I am very well, never was better in my life, stronger and healthier, the cold weather suits me to a T. I only wish I had some ducks and geese to go after below the hill and that I was near you all once more.

I am very sorry Napier Sturt[35] should not only have made a donkey of himself, but also told falsehoods about me and of my smoking Cavendish tobacco.[36] I am now over twenty years of age and think I know whether a thing hurts me or not, live entirely in the open air, work hard and when I have not been able to get another tobacco, have smoked Cavendish, for how long. Why only the first three weeks we landed in the Crimea, when we only had ten minutes to smoke, certainly not more than three or four pipes a day, so make your mind quite easy on that score. I assure you I am much annoyed that Sturt should have lied so and I believe Sturt must have told the Gov. and Bob in a joking manner and that they took it seriously. I shall write him a letter and one he won't forget in a hurry. I have written enough about it and what I wrote I meant.

I am happy to say a great deal of winter clothing has arrived for the poor men who are in a sad state. The officers are doing well, can get plenty of stores but have to pay enormously for them. I have built myself the best house in the army, (allowed to be by all competent judges) window, door, fire-place, table and everything complete.

Flop [not identified.] lives with me, and so does Falconer,[37] our Quartermaster, who is one of the nicest and best fellows in the world. He can get anything, a piece of fresh meat, picks, shovels, blankets, axes, saws and in fact almost anything. I am really well off now, and very comfortable, have heaps of people to see me, or rather my house, which I again assure you is a perfect model.

Everyone here is talking of peace, I can only say I should like to hang, with my own hands, the principals on our side who propose it before this place is taken. We have a very easy duty now as we have lots of officers and very few men, trenches all night are rather bad, but one can keep the cold out well now, thanks to all your goodness.

I don't think Sevastopol will fall before April. Raglan funks, he has not pluck enough, he is afraid of the butchers bill, he takes no opportunity.

I must now conclude this letter, my dearest Mother, and again thank you for everything and all your trouble, goodness and anxiety on my account and for all your good wishes.

Believe me ever,

Your affectionate son,

Gerald L. Goodlake.

P.S. Ask Bob to send me another account book, small and flat. Please remember me to Lady Vane and Gertrude. Freddy is well and is acting adjutant. The Colonel never was better and has seen nearly every man in the Regiment sick or dead.

P.S Tell dearest Bob I drank her health in port wine on Xmas eve and I wrote her a long letter which I hope she has received. I did not forget her.

Camp before Sevastopol.
25 January 1855.
My dear Father,

I have just received your last letter and the parcel from the *Robert Lowe*, which I had almost given up for lost. I cannot say how obliged I am for all these capital things you have sent me. You could not have picked better things in the way of clothes and furs, the only thing that puzzles me is what to do with such a quantity of clothes, if we move how am I to carry them with me, I do not know.

We are now well off for everything, stores, food and the men are now tolerably well clothed and if they had fresh meat, would pick up wonderfully. *The Times* has done a great deal of good. Blythswood[38] says it has. Raggles [Raglan] has actually been seen more than once. The Staff think that the cap fits and are very sore.

I was in the trenches last night, they fired a little, two Fusiliers had their legs shot off. It was rather cold. We have no piquets now as the French have taken them over. We do trench work night and day for four days a week, but we have plenty of officers doing duty, so we are not at all hard worked. Thank God, I was never stronger or better in my life.

I can assure you I was very much annoyed that Sturt should have so far forgotten himself to have told you such an infernal lie. I can use no other term, so you must excuse me, to say I was ruining my constitution by smoking Cavendish tobacco in the way I did. You will see to what extent I smoked it in the last letter I wrote to Mother. You may make your mind quite easy on that head and put a little more trust in my good sense. When I landed in the Crimea, I had 11 pounds that I carried, as it was the most portable and the only tobacco that I could procure.

There is a great shave here about peace, I won't have it, much too disgraceful, until we have taken this place and a job it will be now. I dined with Bill a night or two ago and he asked much after you, we all read each other's letters, more or less.

My pony was stolen last night by the French, as usual I will be even with them or I will know the reason why. Rascals, talk about them, no one knows what a thief is until he has some Zouaves[39] encamped near him.

I think perhaps they may have a sky [an attempted attack] at the place in a month or so, but Raggles is afraid of the responsibility.

Markham[40] has just joined us, a capital fellow. Crawley, Dunlop and myself ought to join the 2nd Battalion, but old Strafford[41] is such a jobber. I would not go home for the world until we have this place.

You will see in Mother's letter a drawing of my hut, which was built by one man and myself with a wooden trowel and an old axe.

I must now conclude this stupid epistle, but I have nothing to say and can only repeat my thanks. With love and best wishes to you all.

Believe me ever,
Your very affectionate son,
GLG

P.S As for hutting the Army or one regiment, it is a farce. A calculation has been made that with our transport it would take five months to do it. Hard frost at present.

Camp before Sevastopol
1 February 1855

My dearest Mother,

I think I have received everything you sent me except from *Royal Albert*, *East Anglican*, *Lowe* and *Achrane*, the three letters have not arrived. There is a parcels' office at **** which is managed very well, the only thing that is.

Nothing of much importance has happened since I last wrote, except a sortie on the French trenches last night. The Muscoves came out in great force, took two batteries and killed a Chef de Battalion, five officers and fifty men. The French retook the batteries and killed a good number in return.

A Russian spy walked all through the camps and trenches and then bolted down the hill into Sevastopol, amidst a shower of bullets, but was not hit.

Poor Larcombe is very seedy, he can hardly walk he is so weak.

Give my best love to the Gov. and say that I would have written to him this mail, but I was unexpectedly wanted for the trenches at 4 o'clock p.m. in consequence of Whitehead[42] going sick at the last moment, not much the matter with him.

I am longing for the pipe, which has not as yet arrived. I am so much obliged to you.

Now my dear Mother, before I conclude this hurried epistle, I sincerely thank you and the Gov. for all your parcels and presents. I now have everything I want or could wish for. I am very well, never was better or stronger, may you all be the same, so with best love to Gov., Bob and all.

Believe me ever,

Your very affectionate son,

G. L. G.

P.S I saw Freddy Vane the other day, looking remarkably well. Love to Lady Vane, Gertrude and Harry and tell them about him. The General also is flourishing together with the Colonel, wonderful soldier in both battles, Alma and Inkerman, not touched, brute or hero. I am to the trenches till tomorrow evening. We are not hard worked, that is to say the officers, as we live out and out well, no mistake.

Camp before Sevastopol
8 February 1855

My dearest Father,

Many thanks for your amusing letter and for all the presents etc.

Nothing has been done here of any consequence since I wrote, a few shaves of being attacked and sorties nightly on the French. The weather is very curious, one day fine like the middle of spring and in two hours wind comes on with powdered snow, enough to cut one in two.

We have, as I have told you, very little to do, as we are so strong in officers and so weak in men; they are in a sad condition; they have heaps and heaps of clothing now, but too late, the mischief is done; they are shadows of what they were. At such a state have we arrived at that we cannot muster 600 bayonets for the Brigade; by this morning's state the Coldstream have only 126 duty men, the consequence is that we are, I believe, being sent to Balaklava, which is jumped at by some of the Brigade. In my opinion it will be a finishing stroke, as the place stinks aloud from dead Turks, horses, etc and the filth of the harbour, without saying anything about being sent to the rear after having done our duty at the front.

[Editor's Note, On 22 February 1855 the Guards Brigade, now with only 312 men able to do duty, was relieved of trench duties, left the Sapoune Heights and marched to Balaklava to rest and recuperate. The Brigade remained there till 16 June 1855, when the Guards Brigade and the Highland Brigade returned to the front, as the 1st Division. *The Coldstream Guards in the Crimea*, pp. 224–5 and 232, Colonel Ross-of-Bladensburg.]

There seems to be a general stir about the camp lately, all our batteries are ready, the French are making some fresh ones on the right of our position, which I hope will soon be completed and then there will be such a row as never yet was heard or witnessed.

I will tell you a story I heard around the camp yesterday. Raggers, who had been riding around a lot lately, overtook a soldier, wading up to his knees in mud, carrying a bag of biscuit up to camp. One of the ADC's touched the man with his whip and told him to get out of the way. He received no answer, so he demanded, 'Are you a soldier.' 'I was once', replied the man, 'but now I am a sojourning commissionaire [sic] mule.' His Lordship passed on and did not make a remark for some time.

You go on board the ship and ask for your parcel. 'Don't know, under the ammunition or the huts, Sir, really cannot tell'. There is a total want of all order and regulation.

I am much obliged for your intention to do something for my thirty men [Sharpshooters], but thirteen were killed, five wounded and one has got his commission in the Rifles, so it only leaves eleven men. Clothes they have in abundance. I propose the best plan would be a fund of money to be given to them on their return to England. None are married and they were composed of the most out and out black-guards [Privates] of the Regiments, rob a church and use language enough to frighten a fellow into a fit. If anything should happen to them, when they come home, I could easily assist them and do something for them, if they were deserving. Everybody is so kind about this war that I am sure an appeal to one's friends, even at a later period, would be sufficient. I do I assure you appreciate the kindness of your propositions, so I will leave the rest to your better judgment.

They have begun the railway, but the navvies are such lazy drunken fellows and get on but slowly, I cannot see the use of it now; by the time it is finished I hope the place will be ours and then we can land all our stores and embark all our guns in Sevastopol harbour; far better would it be for them to do the work in the trenches which our poor fellows are unable to do.

Our men want rest, they have regularly overworked and have had not time to cook their food, Canrobert[43] has regularly humbugged the easygoing Raggles into making the English Army to do all the work and occupy even a greater space of ground than they could manage and then when it is too late and the mischief done, give up piece by piece, piquet by piquet, as our men have died off, until the English Army is reduced to 9,800 fighting men, scarcely a Division in the present French Army. Believe it, you will not, but it is too true.

We have just heard a report that the Ministry was turned out and that Lord Derby came in; there is a great deal of excitement about it.[44]

Bill Bathurst[45] is very well and I have just heard that his cigars have arrived, an immediate visit is resolved upon. Peter Crawley is all right again and is looking very well. Sir J Fergusson[46] is much pleased at getting in for Ayrshire. The General is well, I saw him yesterday, also Freddy Vane, who I never saw look better.

My house continues to be a great attraction and is much visited. I shall be very sorry to leave it, though I would willingly give it up and stay here rather than go down to Balaklava.

I must now conclude, so with every good wish and best love to Mother, Bob and all.

> Believe me,
> Your very affectionate son,
> Gerald L. Goodlake.

Camp before Sevastopol
22 February 1855

My dearest Father,

This day last year we sailed from England, what extraordinary scenes we have witnessed. I am very thankful to say that I have had undeniably a very good time.

I am well, strong and as in as good health as possible. Tomorrow we are off to Balaklava to go into huts. I am sorry for it, not because of my hut here, but because I am sorry to leave the front now. Nothing of any consequence takes place; since I last wrote there are nightly sorties on the French, which are manfully expelled, with some fifteen killed or wounded, the average 'butchers bill.'

We had an awful day Tuesday last, N.E. wind and powdered snow, you could not keep it out, ands today it is quite fine, though a sharp frost. Liprandi[47] is to be attacked soon to find out his position and also his numbers, perhaps we will go with the reconnaissance, I hope we may.

In case there is any likelihood of a summer campaign, I wish you could send me out a small patent tent that I could carry on my back, it must not weigh more than 25 lbs, just enough to keep the dew off. It could be made of white waterproof cloth with eyelet holes and a couple or four ropes. When not used as a tent, it would be capital to lie on. It would be such a capital thing for outpost duty.

Sevastopol will require a great deal of taking yet. Jones and Niel,[48] the French Engineer, agree in thinking that the place cannot be taken until it is invested on all sides. You were quite right about Sidney Herbert and the Duke of Newcastle[49] being kicked out, you wrote it in one of your letters a long time ago; when I repeated it out here I was told it was rubbish.

I am not Adjutant; Armytage[50] is. If it had been offered me, I should have accepted it; He is my senior and is only acting. Strafford is at his jobbing tricks again. Byng will be Adjutant, after Sevastopol is taken, of the First Battalion, and Fremantle has been promised the Adjutancy of the Second.

I lost a good friend in the Duke of Cambridge;[51] if he had not gone home, he might have done something for me. I only hope he will come out again. If anyone ever spoke to him they always got a civil answer, he was believed, respected and looked up to by officers and men, and could get and did get many things for our Brigade, when they were wanted, which is not the case now.

Sickness still prevails. I have no news of any kind, we are all busy packing up for the move and I suppose will have some hard work for the next week or so. I must conclude with best love to all.

> Believe me,
> Your very affectionate son,
> Gerald L. Goodlake

Notes

1 *The Coldstream Guards in the Crimea*, Ross-of-Bladensburg, pp.66–7.
2 *Coldstream Guards in the Crimea*, pp.151 and 186.
3 *The British Expedition to the Crimea*, Sir William Russell, p.197.
4 Ibid, p.219.
5 Ibid, p.219.
6 *Letters from the East during the Campaign of 1854*, 20 September 1854, Captain Alfred Tipping, Grenadier Guards.
7 *Surgeon in the Crimea-Dr George Lawson*, pp. 9–10, Victor Bonham-Carter, Military Book Society, 1968.

8 The Russian attack on the British left wing on 26 October 1854 was designed to find out the layout and strength of our defences

9 Piquets, Picquets or Pickets – bodies of soldiers placed in front of an army to warn the main body of the approach of the enemy. See Military Terms

10 See p.62, fn. 4.

11 Misfires were caused by the firing mechanism of the rifle/musket getting wet. See Military Terms.

12 Number 8 Company, 3rd Grenadiers, under Lieutenant Colonel Lord Henry Percy, charged too far and had to be brought back to our lines, through the enemy. Lord Henry Percy was awarded the VC. *History of the Grenadier Guards* Vol III, p.232. Lieutenant-Colonel C.T.Wilson's Company, Number 8, 1st Coldstream, also charged too far and had to be led back. *Our Veterans of 1854*, pp.294–6, C.T.Wilson. Colonel E.W.F.Walker, commanding 1 SFG, charged down the slope and had to return to the Sandbag Battery. *The Scots Guards 1642–1914*, p.98, Maurice.

13 General Liprandi's Army came from Odessa.

14 Son of the Tsar.

15 Brigadier-General Bentinck, Commanding the Guards Brigade. Cathcart, Divisional Commander 4th Division.

16 Scots Fusilier Guards,killed, Lieutenant-Colonel. J. Hunter Blair; wounded, Captains G.H.Shuckburgh, H.F.Drummond, Lieut F.Baring [Adjutant].

17 Grenadier Guards, killed, Lieutenant-Colonel R. Pakenham, Captains Sir R.Newman Bt, Hon H.Neville; wounded, Captain A.Tipping, Lieutenant N. Sturt.

18 Colonel Grosvenor Hood, Commanding Officer, 3rd Grenadier Guards, killed in the trenches on 18 October 1854. Captain Rowley, Grenadier Guards, killed in the trenches by a cannon ball, 17 October 1854. W.G.Cameron, Grenadier Guards; Lieutenant and Captain, 15 July 1853. Severely wounded in the trenches when acting as a Sharpshooter. Absent on medical certificate 14 September 1854 to 13 January1855. Lieutenant F. B.Davies, Grenadier Guards. Died in December of wounds received in the trenches on 10 November 1854.

19 Full dress red coat

20 Duke of Newcastle, Secretary of State for War.

21 Brigadier-General H.Adams, Commander,2nd Bde, 2nd Div.; Brigadier-General H.Bentinck, Commander, Guards Brigade, 1st Division; Brigadier-General A.Torrens, Commander, 2nd Brigade, 4th Division.

22 From two Greek words meaning a dry island; ie a peninsula. It referred

to the peninsula south of Sevastopol. The west end of it is called Cape Chersonese.

23 Probably pre-cooked pork, which extends its life, even in warm climates.

24 Captain R.H. Vivian served with the 14th Regiment, in the trenches at the siege and fall of Sevastopol and assault on 18 June 1855. *Hart's Army List, 1860*, pp.202–3.

25 Turner has not been identified. The Surgeons of 7th Fusiliers in *Hart's Army List 1854* were John Mitchell and T.M.Smith. For the 23rd Foot, Royal Welch Fusiliers, they were Robert Smith and W.G. Watt.

26 Trestles for putting stretchers on so that they are not put on the wet ground.

27 Lord Raglan was appointed Field Marshal on 5 November 1854.

28 See p.14, fn. 4. and Military Terms.

29 George Gregory, Captain, Royal Marines. He took part in the bombardment of Odessa in April 1854 and during 1854–55 he served in the Royal Marine Brigade, which was located at Balaklava and acted as part of the local defence force, under Sir C.Campbell.

30 Secretary-at-War in Lord Aberdeen's Government.

31 Reid, a brewery company, later a part of Watney Combe & Reid.

32 Commander, Turkish Troops.

33 See fn. 19.

34 Some sort of tobacco, which is pressed into cakes and then cut into fine uniform shreds by a machine very similar to a chaff cutter.

35 Captain Napier Sturt, Grenadier Guards, wounded at Inkerman and invalided home.

36 Tobacco that has been sweetened and moulded into cakes.

37 A.Falconer, Quartermaster, 1st Coldstream.

38 A.C.Campbell of Blythswood, Renfrewshire. Lieutenant and Captain Scots Fusilier Guards, He was an MP for various seats in Renfrewshire from 1873–92. Created 1st Baron Blythswood 1892.

39 See p.45, fn. 49.

40 Lieutenant W.T.Markham,Coldstream Guards, Lieutenant, 1854. Retired 1855.

41 Sir John Byng (1772–1860) was made First Earl of Strafford in 1843. He became a field marshal in 1855 and was Colonel of the Coldstream Guards from 1850 to 1860.

42 Probably Lieutenant and Captain S.Whitshed, Coldstream Guards.

43 Commander of French Army, who replaced St Arnaud.

44 Lord Aberdeen, the Prime Minister, resigned on 5 February 1855. Lord Palmerston became Prime Minister and Lord Panmure was appointed Secretary of State for War.

45 See fn. 47.

46 Lieutenant and Captain Sir James Fergusson, Bt Grenadier Guards, retired 20 July 1855, as he had been elected the MP for Ayr in the place of Colonel Hunter Blair who was killed at Inkerman.

47 Lieutenant-General Pavel Liprandi, Commander of the Russian attack on Causeway Heights at Balaklava.

48 Major-General H. Jones, Commander, Royal Engineers and General A.Niel, Chief Engineer, French Army.

49 Lord Herbert of Lea, Secretary-at-War and the Duke of Newcastle, Secretary of State for War, both of whom resigned in 1855 because of public fury over the incompetence of Army administration in the Crimea.

50 Captain H. Armytage; Captain A. Fremantle; Captain Hon H.W. Byng, Coldstream Guards.

51 Commander, 1st Division.

Chapter Five

The Letters –
Staff Officer

Hut Building
March to June 1855

Guards Brigade – Movements and Events.

1855

March	Land Transport Corps starts operations in the Crimea.
10 March	Changed huts to the Heights west of Balaklava.
26 March	Railway line extended to British Headquarters on the Heights.
8–17 April	Second Bombardment of Sevastopol.
18–25 April	Railway line extended up the north-east valley to the Woronzoff Road to supply the 2nd and Light Divisions, with a westward branch to serve the 4th Division and the siege batteries.
30 April	The electric telegraph line completed to allow messages to be sent to and from London & the Crimea.
1 May	Fourth draft arrives, seven officers and 307 men.

3 May	First Kertch Expedition, recalled 9 May. Changed huts to the Heights east of Balaklava.
9 May	Returned to the huts on the West Heights.
19 May	Marshal Canrobert resigns and Marshal Pélissier takes over command of the French Army.
23 May	Second Kertch Expedition takes Kertch and Yenikale and successfully cuts the Russian supply lines to Sevastopol from Rostov, the River Don and the Sea of Azov.
6 June	Third Bombardment of Sevastopol.

The Railway

On 23 February the Grand Crimean Central Railway was operational from Balaklava to Kadikoi and by 26 March it had been extended to the British Headquarters on the Heights. Between 18 and 25 April the line was extended up the north-east valley to the Woronzoff Road to supply the 2nd and Light Divisions, with a westward branch to serve the 4th Division and the siege batteries. On 1 April Captain Goodlake reported that the railway could send up 112 tons a day.

The railway played a major part in the Second Bombardment from 8 –17 April. The British fired 47,000 rounds in this bombardment. On 10 March the Officer in Charge of the Siege Train reported that he was 22,987 rounds short of the requirement of 500 rounds per gun and 300 per mortar. By 10 April this had been more than made up and a far greater proportion of the larger and more damaging mortar shells were delivered.[1].

Transport & Supply

Although Lord Raglan had asked for the re-establishment of a transport corps in 1854, because of delays by the Duke of Newcastle, the Minister of War, the Land Transport Corps was not operational in the Crimea until March 1855, when it became clear that the idea, promoted by the Treasury, of using local transport was impossible, as none was available. This remedy had the disadvantage that the LTC

100

was a military body, while the Commissariat was a civilian body. Furthermore, Transport and Supply were two separate organisations, which did not promote efficiency.

Medical

The First Sanitary Commission, consisting of Dr Sutherland and other public hygiene experts, which arrived in March 1855, were given executive powers by the government to clean up Scutari Hospital. The sewers were cleaned out and running water installed. They then organized the cleaning up of Balaklava town and the harbour. Florence Nightingale told Lord Shaftesbury that the Sanitary Commission had saved the British Army.

The Kertch Expedition

The first expedition was recalled on 3 May, due to a disagreement with Marshal Canrobert. The second sailed on 23 May to cut the Russian supply lines to Sevastopol from Rostov, the River Don and the Sea of Azov, as Sevastopol was not entirely surrounded by the Allies, especially on the northern side of the harbour. The raid was completely successful as Kertch and Yenikale, which were fortified towns on the straits between the Black Sea and the Sea of Azov, were captured. A great quantity of ships and grain were taken. The capture of these towns also enabled our ships to sail into the Sea of Azov. Captain Goodlake refers to this raid in his letter of 1 June.

The Mamelon and Malakoff Towers and The Redan.

In his letter of 30 March Captain Goodlake mentions how his Sharpshooters used to operate round the Mamelon defensive tower, in front of the Malakoff. It was part of the inner ring of the Sevastopol defences and was taken by the French on 18 June 1855, when they also tried unsuccessfully to take the Malakoff Tower [The Round Tower].

It was captured by the French on 8 September 1855. The loss of this tower forced the Russians to abandon the south side of Sevastopol Harbour and they withdrew their troops over the bridge to the north side of the harbour.

The Redan was a Russian fort and part of the Russian defences, which the British failed to take on 18 June and on 8 September 1855, when the French took the Malakoff. The Redan was considered impossible to hold after the Malakoff was taken, so it was abandoned by the Russians.

Trenches

On 1 April Captain Goodlake is very worried that the British Army has too large a frontage of trenches to man. He writes that the men are worked very hard in the batteries. They work for eight hours on and eight hours off, of which two hours are spent travelling to and from the camp to the batteries. They look much beaten.

He is also worried about the effect of trench work on the mens' attitude and morale. On 14 May, he explains in his letter that the casualties arising from trench work have turned our men into funkers, as they are always looking for cover from grape and canister. They hang back in an assault and they are, like the French, very sensible. In the past they never thought they could be licked and never knew when they were.

Captain Gerald Goodlake

He writes of his great excitement on 2 March at being put in charge of the distribution of huts to the Army, and on 30 March of his appointment as Deputy Assistant Quartermaster General in charge of huts, reporting to the Quartermaster General, Major General Airey. He explains that he superintends each day from 7 am till 3 pm and then deals with the paperwork, looks after the men and rides to the various divisions to see what has been done.

On 23 April he says that he is in the saddle every day by seven or half-past seven, and attends to the loading and delivery of huts till 11 am. He then comes home to breakfast, visits his depots at the front, sees that the huts are properly sent up and delivered to the right destinations. He gets home by five or six o'clock, has his dinner, makes up his accounts and requisitions, and then writes to General Airey to report progress.

On 6 May he explains why he has joined the staff, when he was so rude about those who did. He explains this contradiction to his Mother as follows. 'When I said that I did not want to go on the Staff that only applied to becoming an ADC. I am doing a real job and have a certain amount of authority. I am on special duty and not attached to anyone'.

On 22 May he is gazetted in General Orders as a DAQMG and says that, as he is only on special duties, he will not wear staff uniform. He is still very busy on huts on horseback from 6.30 am to 6.30 pm.

He explains to his Father how hard he is working and how much more enjoyable it is than regimental soldiering, which he finds boring. He explains how he enjoys the responsibility and being his own boss. By early June he reports that the hutting work is nearly finished and he is looking out for another staff appointment.

He is disappointed that he has not been promoted to major, despite all the recommendations that he has had from his superiors. He tells his Father not to complain. He then discovers that he has not served the requisite six years. He says that he is sure his superiors, who have had their recommendation refused, will do all they can for him in the future. He was right, as he was promoted to Brevet Major on 14 June 1856, having served in the Army for exactly six years.

Life appears to be getting better, as on 1 April he writes that he has hens and turkeys and everything he wants. His hut is a palace and that there are horse races and football matches to keep the officers amused.

By 30 March 1855 he writes that the weather is delightful now, just like summer. The men are getting on well and there is not so much sickness; they have picked up well since coming down here [Balaklava]. They are now all hutted. Officers live in the lap of luxury and can buy anything they want in the eating and drinking line.

The supply situation, he writes on 1 April, has improved greatly as the railway is nearly up to the top of the hill.

On 30 March he sends a very long list of needs, including a tent, new boots, a new regimental blue coat – his original one is too small – and trousers, a forage cap, a sword and scabbard, and a saddle and double-rein bridle. He also was sent a Price's candle-power stove.

The Letters

1855

2 March	Balaklava		Father
9 March	Balaklava		Mother
9 March	Balaklava		Father
30 March	Balaklava		Father

1 April	Donkey Boy Hall	Mother
13 April	Balaklava	Father
20 April	Balaklava	Mother
23 April	Balaklava	Father
6 May	Balaklava	Father
14 May	Balaklava	Father
22 May	Balaklava	Father
1 June	Balaklava	Father
9 June	Balaklava	Father
16 June	Balaklava	Father

Balaklava
2 March 1855
My dearest Father,

We have just arrived at Balaklava from the heights above Sevastopol in great confusion. The Grenadiers moved on Thursday, the Coldstream on Saturday and the Scots Fusiliers today. The latter had their huts built for them by the former. We are all at present under canvas but will I suppose be also hutted in a week or so. It is a very hard frost with powdered snow, but two days ago we had a day like summer.

I receive all my things via Raglan's bag very punctually and I am very obliged to you, Mother and Bob, for the many many presents you have sent.

I have a good bit of news for you and I hope it will please you. If you look in the *London Gazette* you will probably see my name in it promoted to the rank of Brevet Major.

It will be a capital thing for me as I get Field Officer's allowance and do Field Officer's duty. I am happy to say I have got it from doing my duty and not for being on the staff.

Peter Crawley, I am delighted to say, is also in for gallantry at Inkerman. George Upton[2] who is now Lieutenant-Colonel of the Regiment, called me to him this morning and told me, but begged me not to say anything about it until it had appeared in the Gazette, so please don't mention it except to Mother and Bob. You may just tell Mrs Crawley, and tell her from me that Little Peter thoroughly deserves it.

I have a detachment of 100 men, placed under Woodford, AQMG,[3] to arrange and send up huts for the army. It is hard work, I am up at 7 o'clock superintending and don't get away till 3 o'clock and then have to do all the paper business, so what with looking after the men and sometimes having to ride up to different divisions and not being settled, I have my hands full, which I hope will account for the shortness of this epistle.

Many thanks for what you have done for my Sharpshooters but clothing is no use. Everybody has been so kind, there are parcels, boxes, bales, packages of all sorts full of clothing, so the men wear them till they are dirty and then throw them away.

When George Upton arrives home please call on him and thank him, as he has been very kind to me.

If there is a medal for conduct in the field I shall get one, as I am promoted for that.

Best love to Mother, Bob and all.
> Believe me,
> > Your very affectionate son,
> > G. L. G.

P.S. I hope you can make this scrawl out but my hands are so cold.

Balaklava
9 March 1855

My dearest Mother,

I will just write you one line as you appear to like a letter to yourself. How kind of the 'dear man' to send me out a Price's [candle-lit] stove. I will write to him when I have received it.

Now my dear Mother, I assure you all of us have everything we could possibly wish for; the weather since I last wrote is like summer, I was never better in my life. Freddy Vane is quite well and everybody is in good spirits, so you have nothing to be anxious about. We are much better off than you think, as we live well, feed well and sleep well and thank God and our friends and relations for it.

I congratulate and commend you for your presence of mind and courage during the last fire; there is one thing to be said, it is not the first fire you have witnessed in your house. I am so much obliged to you for your interest in my Sharpshooters, it is very kind of you. I have stated my opinion of what to do in a former letter and have told the Gov. that it is useless to send out clothing for them as they positively roll in warm clothes.

I have received so many little parcels by Raglan's bag that I cannot remember them all, or sufficiently thank you and beloved Bob for them all.

Remember me to Hodkiss [Cook?] and tell her I have told the story to everyone who has tasted her good cooking.

Remember me kindly to Mrs Crawley and tell her that her little Peter is the same he always was, to me and to everyone else, and that he is quite well, fat and as good natured as ever.

Best love to all and a thousand thanks and good wishes and for all your kindness, my beloved Mother.

I remain ever,
Your affectionate son,
G. L. G.

Balaklava
9 March 1855
My dear Father,

I yesterday received your letter of the 28th and I am happy to say all my parcels that you, Mother and Bob have sent me have turned up with the exception of the *Royal Albert* parcel. I cannot thank you sufficiently for your kindness in sending me so many and truly valuable things. I do thank you from the bottom of my heart for them all, especially the three pipes, which are so much admired; the last one sent in Peter's box is perfection and the envy of the Brigade.

We are a bit more settled now, but are going to make another move about a mile from the town; we have not been making our huts yet, but when we do they will soon be finished. I think that next week we will have the order.

Charley Fox has just arrived with my boots and some more tobacco. I am sorry to say the boots are too tight round my legs and I cannot put my trousers inside, so I have ordered them to be cut down like Wellingtons, a pity.

I must say one word about the old topic the weather. Since I last wrote we have had days just like the middle of summer, so hot you can hardly bear a coat on or stop in your tent. The roads are now in capital order and everything is going on well; sickness has decreased and everybody seems in much better spirits. We live all right and have no complaints. The men have such heaps of clothing and a little time to wash themselves.

We have a report that the Czar is dead; the staff at headquarters will bet anything you like that it is true. Lord Raglan told Sir Colin Campbell and said that he had it telegraphed from Lord J Russell from Vienna[4]; the men when they heard it gave three cheers.

The railway is progressing rapidly, as it has got about three miles already. One navvy said to another the other day, 'I say Bill, Sir Bastopol is took', so Bill says 'What be they going to do with im' ? (answer) 'Why put ''un in prison incourse.'

I went to the front yesterday to see about some huts; they seemed very busy, and said that they will open fire again within a fortnight and the assault, but I don't see it exactly.

The French had a regular good hiding the other day about a fortnight ago, I daresay you will see all about it in the papers. They attacked a Russian battery and the Zouaves went in well, but the Infantrie de Marine cut it. The Zouaves lost 17 officers and about 350 killed, wounded and taken prisoner. It seems the Russians knew all about their coming and were ready for them; the poor Zouaves were in a great way about it the next day. I have never heard so much foreign cursing and swearing in my life, but the day after down came Canrobert, addressed them, distributed 14 crosses, 30 medals, promoted two sergeants and they all became merry as 'sandboys.' I think I have given you all the news I know of what is going on at present.[5]

I look forward to our rifle match and seeing you all again and thanking you for so many things. I saw a very good dodge in a Russian rifle I took for steadying the piece; it is a little piece of iron behind the trigger guard, you put your second finger on it. I fancied it was rather a dodge, perhaps you have seen it before.

Freddy Vane is quite well and seems very happy; he is a good boy. The Colonel was not quite well when I last saw him, he had a bad cold and is much disgusted with the service. His is a hard case, no man could have behaved better, or done better, which all the authorities admit. He has seen every officer of his regiment, sick, dead or wounded, and has worked like a horse himself, but still they won't give him anything, as he is nearly the junior Colonel in the Division and they won't give him a Brigade. He declares that the moment he has served his time, which will be in a few months, he will despatch Brock, his Soldier Servant, on to Mr Steele,[Military Secretary to Lord Raglan] as he calls him, with his resignation and will retire on half pay, which he is entitled to do, after his long service.

I must again thank you for your interesting yourself so much for my Sharpshooters, but I told you my opinion in a former letter. Money will be the only thing for them on their discharge, or give them some present in the shape of a watch on their arrival in England. There are,

I assure you, bale after bale of clothes directed to the troops and they cannot use them, as they can't wear them all or carry them. This I assure you is a fact. We are <u>all</u> doing right well now and are all thoroughly grateful for the kindness and sympathy of the people of England.

I am going to write to Mother and Bob so will now conclude, with best love to all enquiring friends. I always remember you to them and they always require after you. C. Fox told me he had seen you.

Believe me ever,
Your most affectionate son,
Gerald L Goodlake.

P.S. I hope the piece of news that I mentioned in my last will please you.

Balaklava
30 March 1855
My dear Father,

You expressed a wish some time ago that you would like me to be on the staff I have just been offered a place which I have accepted. It is, I believe, a very good one, DAQMG. [Deputy Assistant Quartermaster General]. I have the entire management of hutting the army at the front under Major-General Airey [Quartermaster General]. Whether I will be kept on after the hutting is over I do not know but the opinion is that I shall, if I do the business well. I had a long talk with Airey who was very kind and civil.

He said I must have two horses as I should have a good deal of riding about. Where I am to get them or how, I do not know, as there is not the chance of getting a horse here, unless sent out from England (which is next to impossible) or buying one off some sick or wounded or dead officer.

I must also have some clothes. I shall not put on a staff uniform,[6] which I am now entitled to, as if I am only on the staff for a time, it would not be worth while to go to the expense for so short a time. But if you will be good enough, to have sent out the following things, which are positively necessary [viz]

1 Patrol tent for servants (Edgington), just big enough for two persons.
2 Pairs of Wellington boots (bow heels).
2 Pairs of Regimental trousers, 1 pair strapped inside with leather.

1 Blue coat Regimental (also large ****). I had the last from Buckmaster.

1 Forage cap and cover (Catero) Regimental.

1 Steel sword and scabbard, sling belt black.

1 Regt. belt, leather.

1 Double rein bridle.

1 Pair of spurs.

1 Saddle (I cannot get one out here, my old one is quite worn out).

1 Comb and brush.

I have only one pair of regimental trousers, which I wear everyday and the old ones, which I cannot wear. One blue coat, when I joined the guards, which is too tight and worn to a thread, and my forage cap is so shabby.

Now you see, my dear Father, I had to say yes or no, whether I could take the appointment or not. I have taken it and hope you approve of what I have done. I will tell you my reasons for accepting it. Life down here is very idle for a regimental officer. There are plenty of fatigues (cookhouse or camp cleaning duties) but what are they; one sits and smokes a cigar or pipe and talks to one's acquaintances out there and now and then speaks to a man who is not working as hard as he should; so one wastes day after day in that manner not doing much good to yourself. When we were fighting up at the front, there was some excitement, but bar an occasional turn out there is very little going on.

The duties I have to do suit me very well. I have a great deal of riding about and receive requisitions and do some writing in the evening, which is not very much but it keeps me employed all day. The pay and allowances are good. It does get one's name up at Head Quarters and it sometimes happens one may drop into a good thing by being a little known.

At all events what I have done at the present, I have done, and should you not approve of it, I can give it up, which perhaps I shall have to do at the end of the hutting. The clothes I have written for will all come in useful, for I should want them whether I was on the Staff or not.

I hope you got my letter about the Brevet Majority,[7] I am rather puzzled at it not coming out in the *[London] Gazette*. I have good grounds for saying so, as George Upton, who has always been kind to me, told me so, as did my present Colonel, Lord Paulet,

[Commanding Officer, 1st Coldstream] and last but not least Lord Rokeby. [Brigade Commander]. I hope it will not be a case of counting your chickens before they are hatched.

Now just to finish the business will you go to Cox[8] and tell them to honour my drafts, if I have overdrawn my allowances and make it right with them. I shall be put to some rather heavy expense about horses at first. I can't get one under £45 or £50 that has four legs to carry me. If you do arrange matters, I can afterwards settle up with you, when I get the pay and allowances for my appointment. My horses, with luck, would be worth more in a couple of months than at present, if I give up the appointment. I hope this is not asking too much. I have told you, as plainly as I can, how I am situated now. When I get my appointment and pay, you can deduct what you now advance from my allowance. I am not allowed anything for horses. I think I have told you all my affairs at present and I will be glad and grateful if you will manage to right all these things for me and give me your opinion.

I am much obliged for the Sharpshooters Box, which arrived safely. The men one and all begged me to thank you, Mother and Bob for all your kindness. They were very grateful for the English baccy and tea. The warm clothing was useless as they roll in it and throw it away or sell it when dirty, as I have told you before in my letters.

The weather is delightful just like summer. The men are getting on well, there is not nearly so much sickness; our men have picked up well since we came down here. They are now all hutted. I am having a Maltese hut built which with a little labour, I have made very comfortable. Poor Larcombe [Soldier Servant.] is very seedy again, he can hardly stand, as he has a touch of fever.

The officers are really living in the lap of luxury; one can buy almost anything in the eating and drinking line. The railway is nearly to the top of the hill, it will be quite there before you have read this letter. Our cavalry and our Brigade have races every fortnight. We had a football match on Tuesday, two elevens of Eton, nine Guards and Cavalry, it ended after a capital game with a goal each. So as we were only playing for fun, it was the best thing that could have happened.

I will tell you what little I know of what is going on at the front. The French cannot fight; they go in enormous masses to take some rifle pits every night. They are in front of a little hill called 'Mamelon' which is in front of the Round Tower. I used to go all over it with my sharpshooters to shoot at the embrasures. Since then the Russians have advanced 400 yards at least. The French go in with a hurroosh and are as quickly turned out again; they then draw up in line and file-fire[9] for about two hours at the enemy, who are in the pits laughing at them, so the farce ends. Sometimes medals and crosses are distributed the next day.

About a week ago the Russians made a sortie along the whole line and there was a regular good scrimmage. You will see the account of it in the papers better described than I can. Poor Browne,[10] of the Seventh Fusiliers, was shot by a man in Albanian dress, who has been leading most of the sorties this winter. He was a gallant fellow; he was struck all over and shot through and through.

They say (that is the latest shave) that we are to open up on Monday. We have a nice little present to make the Russians which is 20 13-inch shells per broadside, every ten minutes in one battery alone and their fire will always be concentrated in about 50 yards space. I don't think that they will open so soon. I give them another 3 weeks.

The Colonel is on board ship seedy, not much the matter, he was a good deal cut up by his poor brother's death, not serious, I think, cold, sore throat. Please tell Lady Vane that Freddy is on board ship at Balaklava. He is much better, in fact quite well. He has had the jaundice but is now all right. Impress on Lady Vane that she need not be the least anxious.

Peter Crawley in a great tribulation about a box value £25, which has been broken open and ransacked, the bottles smashed, the liquor drunk and nailed up again, sent through Waghorn's & Co. He has had to pay for it here as well as in London. Please make a note of that company.

I am glad everything goes well at dear old Wadley [his home].

Colonel Bruce and Hogge[11] of the Grenadiers have just arrived.

I will conclude with my best love, hoping that what I have undertaken is for the best.

> Believe me,
> > Your very affectionate son,
> > G. L. Goodlake

Donkey Boy Hall
1 April 1855
My dearest Mother,

I want you and the Gov. to make Lady Vane go to George Upton[12] and get him to persuade Lord Strafford to sanction Freddy Vane's

111

exchange to the Coldstream. Gordon, who was the other day appointed to my Regiment wants to exchange. I have spoken to Freddy about it and he will arrange it with Gordon of the 38th Regiment and then write to Lady Vane himself.[13] I will guarantee it will be the best thing for Freddy and that he will never regret it.

I am, as I wrote in my last letter, a DAQMG for the present for the hutting of the Army. The issue of huts has just been stopped and I went up to Head Quarters and I was told that I must remain idle for the present. Perhaps something will turn up. I at all events draw my pay and allowances, and was told to buy two horses. Colonel McMurdo[14] has been very civil. I see a good deal of him as I have something to do with his department in sending huts up to the front. The railway is nearly to the top of the hill; it can send up 112 tons day and night and is now a double line of rails.

I went all the way through the trenches yesterday for the first time since I came down here. I find that the Russians have a very formidable battery in the Mamelon, which is the same hill that I used to shoot at the round tower. They have advanced 400 yards on the French lines in that part of the line, since we came down here. They are fighting, night and day, in the trenches, squibbing,[15] and popping at one another, The Russians lick the French on every occasion; their men won't stand.

There were extraordinary scenes the other day at the Flag of Truce. It was just like a fair, both parties very polite offering one another tobacco and snuff. A Russian officer asked one of the 13 Light Dragoons when we were going to open fire, so he answered he did not exactly know, but it could not be today or tomorrow, as we had two Race meetings to come off.

A thousand thanks for all your parcels and presents and all your congratulations on my promotion, which I heard from Lord Rokeby was certain. Not bad, came out an Ensign, [Second Lieutenant] and a major in a year. I have indeed been fortunate.

We are all wonderfully off now: everything one would wish for in the feeding line:- twelve hens, several turkeys etc, I have got feeding at this moment under my nose. Something will be done soon which will decide whether DV, a summer campaign is at hand or we shall have the extreme happiness and pleasure of embracing our beloved relations and enjoying ourselves in dear old England. Just fancy the idle boy at Eton turned out into a working man! How you must laugh!

There is no news that I know of. I have been very busy and have hardly seen anybody.

I must now conclude, my beloved Mother, wishing you every blessing, you so well deserve, together with my best love.

> Believe me ever,
> > Your very affectionate son,
> > G.L.G

P.S. I am writing this in a great hurry, and there are a lot of fellows in my hut (palace I ought to say) so that I won't answer for this epistle being read and understood.

Balaklava
13 April 1855

My dearest Father,

By the time you have received this you will have got my last letter about the staff.

I have not much to do now, as nearly all the huts are sent up. The batteries opened fire on Monday, and have been at it ever since. We shall storm some day next week. I do not think that as yet we have done much harm to the Muscove [sic] works.

If we do not take the town next week, it will be a case of a summer campaign and hunt them out of the Crimea, stop the supplies which are perpetually getting into Sevastopol, invest both sides of the town and take our time about it. Everyone is tired of the siege, there are very few now who think there is fun in fighting and going into the trenches. It has got beyond that now.

Lord John Hay was wounded in the trenches yesterday. He is going on well.[16] They have had 84 casualties in the Naval Brigade[17] up to last night. You may have some little idea of how the fellows are worked in the batteries, when they are eight hours on and eight off, two hours of which are taken up in going and returning to camp and the trenches. The men look very much beaten. I ride to the front nearly every day to look on, but one cannot see much for smoke. The Fleet can do nothing at present.

When we assault I do not think that we shall go into the town, only take their works and knock the place down. If we do go into the town, they will shell us out in double quick time from their floating mortar batteries. There is little excitement. Fellows just stroll up to the top of the hill and smoke a pipe, and come down again with barely a remark as to how the firing is going on.

113

I have not been able to buy a horse yet, they are so scarce, Government snapping up everything and not caring what prices they give. If an officer is killed, wounded, or is obliged to go home, one of these fellows attends the sale of his horses and outbids you by a shilling.

I must now conclude, my dearest Father, this stupid letter, and with best love to Mother, Bob etc.

Believe me ever,

Your very affectionate son,

G. L. Goodlake

P.S. The Price's stove has just arrived. I have not opened it yet. I am glad my conduct has pleased you. I have been very lucky all through, thanks for everything. The General is all right again.

Balaklava
20 April 1855
My dearest Mother,

The second bombardment of Sevastopol began on Easter Monday, and lasted ten days. It has turned out to be a second failure in consequence of the timidity of our allies, the French. They are tremendous fellows to talk about assaults and going in, and then they stop. Their generals can't trust them. Canrobert [C in C-French Army] refused to go in unless every gun was silenced.

There was a sad affaire in the trenches last night. Part of the Light Division was told off to take some rifle pits, which are in front of the Redan [Russian fort]. They were taken but Colonel Egerton,[18] a very good officer, and Captain Lempriere,[19] were killed, two Engineer officers and seven others wounded as well as fifty-one of our rank & file.

Tell Lady Vane that I saw Freddy yesterday and he was quite well. I congratulated him on his promotion which he got without purchase, owing to the death of Captain Campbell.[20]

Give my love to Bob and tell her I have received her two beautiful caps, but sad to relate, if I put them down for one minute, some wretch rushes into the room and tears round the camp with one on his head. They are so admired.

You said in one of your former letters that you would like to know what I wanted for summer clothing. I want six flannel shirts, and some worsted stockings, and a thin black tie or two. I have I think a very

114

good wardrobe, with the exception of my uniform department, which I have written to the Gov. about.

Sevastopol will not be taken for a month at least. I am very busy in the hutting and wood department and am a DAQMG, a very good berth.

I must conclude now, my beloved Mother, with best love to all and thanking you again and again for all your good wishes and kindnesses, and hoping that you will enjoy yourself and don't be too anxious.

Believe me ever,

Your very affectionate son,

Gerald L. Goodlake

Balaklava

23 April 1855

My dear Father,

I have just received your letter of the 8th. I will now endeavour to answer it. I have not, I assure you, missed writing once a week to either yourself, Mother or Bob for many weeks past. You are all the best of correspondents, which I am delighted at, as it gives me greatest pleasure to receive letters from you all, but you see three people writing to one is easier done than one writing to three. I will, I assure you, be as good a correspondent as I can, but as I generally write the day before the mail goes to give the latest news, it sometimes happens that one is prevented by some unexpected event, and this mars one's good intentions. I have just received your letter, time 7 o'clock pm and I am now answering it at 2 am, so I have not had much time to consider the matter touching my Brevet Majority sufficiently, but I will give you my present views on the subject.

I can assure you as regards myself, I care little about it. When I have done my duty, gained the approval of my commanding officer, have pleased you, my parents, that is quite sufficient for me. I have been very fortunate. I have kind friends, and an opportunity, which is everything. On one point I have made up my mind, unless you *very particularly* wish it, I would sooner rot and be reduced to a private soldier, than either go to Lord Berkeley[21] or my commanding officer, or say a word about it at Headquarters. Why should I? It is not for me to say a word about it. If the Duke of Cambridge, General Bentinck, Lord Rokeby[22] and Colonel Upton recommend me and that recommendation is forwarded to Lord Raglan, and I am not thought to have served long enough by Lord Hardinge,[23] little good should I do myself, were I to make the least stir in this matter.

Some people say it is a good plan to push themselves forward and sometimes they gain their object, but as I have said before I would rather not do it. I have done so little that the less said about it the better. I consider that the Duke of Cambridge, Lord Rokeby & Colonel Upton have much to complain of. I have nothing. They have had their recommendations slighted. That is my view of the matter and so strong am I in this way of thinking, that even though I have had such a short time to think the matter over, my opinion is unalterable;

I must tell you of Colonel McMurdo's kindness. He offered to make me his ADC. I declined. I enclose his letter and my answer. I could not put one reason in my letter which was that the class of people with whom I would have to mix were not suitable to my position as I would wish. Ask Mother to write to Colonel McMurdo and his wife and thank them.

I will now tell you what my occupation is. I am in the saddle most mornings by seven or half past seven, and attend to the loading and delivering of huts, wood etc, till 11 am. I then come back to breakfast and go to my depot at the front, see that the huts are properly sent up and that they are delivered to their proper destination. I generally get home by five or six o'clock, when I have dinner, make up my accounts, requisitions etc, and then write my report to General Airey [Quartermaster General] for which duty I receive the pay and allowances of DAQMG. I have not such a great deal of spare time.

My steed is indeed seedy. I never got my ponies from Varna, they were either stolen or lost. I have at present one miserable mangy horse that was ordered to be shot by the C.O. I said I thought I could cure him. I have done so of the mange but he is very weak. I also have a mare, which I gave £6 for a good beast. However, I have a good friend in our Quarter Master Falconer, who is the best of men, and lends me his ponies. Horses are so scarce that you cannot buy them for love or money. The very first opportunity I must invest. I expect that I will have to pay, but I must do something for I am in a sad way at present.

I lunched with Lord Raglan today. He asked after all my family. He was very kind and civil.

The 10th Hussars arrived about a week ago. They and their horses are much admired. They may go well and fast on the top of the ground, but they may go under with the weight they have to carry, and in this country there are many soft and extensive valleys.

116

I hope and trust my dearest Father that you will not annoy yourself in the least about this promotion business, but consider that you have a very fortunate, and I assure you, a grateful and affectionate son.

Ever your very affectionate son,

Gerald L.Goodlake.

P.S. Poor Larcombe is very ill, he will die for certain if he is not sent home soon. I do my best to send him. I shall want a patrol tent, large size for myself and two servants to live in. I have two servants now.

Balaklava
6 May 1855

My dearest Father,

I am so obliged for the tent which has just arrived with our draft.

I expected you would say something about my going on the staff when I wrote in the winter. I certainly stated I did not want to be on the staff (by the staff I meant ADC place). What I have now got is very different. One has a certain degree of authority and can do something. I never for a moment thought or expected that I should get the place I have with my short service. How I got it I don't exactly know. Lord Rokeby, I believe, spoke to General Airey about me. How long it will last, I don't exactly know.

I am in no one's place and attached to no division, but on a special duty, so perhaps when hutting is finished I may go back to my duty. It is better than doing duty with the Battalion for what is a subaltern. A mere cipher, trotting about in the rear of his company, which may be commanded by an officer, just arrived from England, who has never seen a shot fired, and has no experience. I believe I know my duty pretty well now, and am as fit to command a company now as I ever shall be. I had a chance and took it, and am glad you approved of it. I shall not put on my staff uniform yet, or anything of that sort, until I see my way.

How about the Brevet Majority? I hope you think nothing about it. It would not do for me to move the slightest in the matter. Lord Paulet received a letter from Upton [Regimental Lieutenant-Colonel] with a kind message to Peter and myself, saying how sorry he was and that he would do all he could. You say you are pleased and our Commanding Officers say we have done our duty and that is quite sufficient for me. Let Lord Hardinge give it to whom he likes, we don't care. You may depend on it that the senior officers who have recommended us will not like to have their recommendations slighted, and

117

they will do all that can be done. I think if you reconsider this matter, you will agree with me in my view of the case, so let the business rest.

As for not volunteering, that would never do. Opportunity is everything; seldom does one have a chance. If one wants to get on, one must run a risk. 'Nothing venture nothing gain'. Look what young Bouchier got for volunteering to turn the Russians out of some rifle pits, a French Legion of Honour and promotion.[24]

I wish I could get such a chance, so does everyone else. I don't like fighting, and never wish to fight again, but we are at war and have to fight. You may as well go in a good row as stay outside and get bowled over by a stray shot, as two fellow officers were last night. It does not matter whether you are twenty yards in front of fifty yards behind, as far as danger goes.

We are all much pleased with our drafts. The Grenadiers are the best and certainly they ought to be as they have two battalions at home and ours are better than the Fusiliers.

The Kertch Expedition has just started from Balaklava with about 18,000 men. Kertch is the place, I believe, but no one knows for certain, as they started with sealed orders. We should have gone if our drafts had arrived earlier. Two Regiments of Highlanders have gone and the 71st Regiment have gone instead with a lot of French and other Regiments. It will be a nice little expedition and we much regret not going. Sir J. Brown commands.

I sent you, by Peter Crawley's brother, a diamond ring I took off the officer I shot on the 26th October [Little Inkerman], when I got a bullet through my coat and was nearly taken prisoner. I hope you will accept it and wear it for my sake. The setting is uncommon.

The siege is at a standstill at present, but I think we will see the interior of Sevastopol before you see the winner of the Derby. About the 25th of the month will be the day, as the French will be ready then, or if they are not, I shall myself begin to despair of ever taking it. They have 40,000 at Constantinople, which are coming here almost directly.

The roll of knives, forks and spoons is nearly empty, so could you send me out another. We live just as well as if we were in England, as we can get anything and everything.

I am very busy with hutting. I have not bought a horse they are awfully dear. I have attended sale upon sale. Horses, which would a month ago have fetched £15, now sell for £30 and £40 apiece. The demand is so great, as everyone is on the look out to purchase animals

1. Captain Goodlake and his Sharpshooters.   *The Chevalier Desanges.*

2. Gerald Goodlake as a young man, holding a riding whip. *Newstead Abbey.*

3. Gerald Goodlake as a young officer.   *Attributed to J. B. Harrison, Newstead Abbey.*

4. The Coldstream Guards leaving for the Crimea.

Artist unknown, RHQ Coldstream Guards.

5. Captain Goodlake defending his position below the Lancaster Battery.

Artist unknown, RHQ Coldstream Guards.

6. A Badly preserved painting of Gerald Goodlake, wearing the fur-trimmed greatcoat which he wore over his uniform when sharpshooting. He is carrying a Minie Rifle/Musket.   *James Edgell Collins, Newstead Abbey.*

7. Goodlake holding his horse outside his hut.   *Roger Fenton, 1855, Royal Collection.*

8. Colonel Walter Lacy Yea, 7th Fusiliers, and Lieutenant St Clair Hobson, with Colonel Yea's cob 'Bobby'.   *Jabez Hughes, 1883, Royal Collection.*

9. Captain Goodlake outside his hut. *Roger Fenton, Royal Collection.*

10. Captain Goodlake's Turkish pony 'Bobby', the cock from Sevastopol, the cow from the valley of Baidar and the pigeons from Colonel Zarnoski, the Commandant of Fort Constantine. Bobby was brought to England by Goodlake in July 1856. On the left is the hut occupied by Goodlake at Balaklava.

Attributed to William Luke, Newstead Abbey.

11. Captain Goodlake's pony 'The Toy' in front of the tents. This cob, the property of the late Colonel Yea, 7th Royal Fusiliers, left England with Yea and carried him through the Battles of Alma, Balaklava, Inkerman and the Siege of Sevastopol, until his death at the assault of the Redan on 18 June, 1855

Colonel Yea bequeathed the cob to Major Goodlake, who rode it to the Battle of the Tchernaya and throughout the remainder of the Campaign, until his return to England in July 1856. On 15 July 1856 'The Toy' won a cup given by Field Marshal Pelissier at the Sevastopol Races *Attributed to William Lake, Newstead Abbey*

12. Private Stanlake, VC, DCM, Coldstream Guards. *A Short History of the Regiment's Victoria Cross Holders*, Sergeant L. Pearce, Coldstream Guards.

13. Goodlake's medals: Victoria Cross, Crimea Medal with four clasps, Knight of the French Legion of Honour, Turkish Order of Medjidie 5th Class and Turkish War Medal. *RHQ Coldstream Guards.*

MR. PUNCH WELCOMES THE GUARDS.

14. *Punch,* 5 July 1856.

15. Colonel Goodlake in full dress uniform, holding his drawn sword.

James Edgell Collins, Newstead Abbey.

16. General Goodlake (seated centre) and a Group of Coldstream officers.

RHQ, Coldstream Guards

17. New uniforms of the Coldstream Guards.

| Major | | Drummer | | Drum Major | | Colour Sergeant | | Night Sent |
| | Night Sentry | | Barrack Guard | | | | Drill Sergeant | |

RHQ, Coldstream Guards

18. General Goodlake in uniform.   *History of the Victoria Cross, Philip A. Wilkins.*

Where Born _Wr Farringdon_ _Wadley_, _Berks_ Date of Birth _14 May / 18_

Ranks.	Regiments.		Dates.	FULL PAY. Whether obtained with or without Purchase; and, if by Exchange, whether with or without paying the Difference.	HALF PAY. Whether obtained by reduction, or by the Purchase of a Half Pay Commission; whether in consequence of his being from ill health incapable of Service, or under what other circumstances; and, if by Exchange, whether with or without receiving the difference.	List, and Dates of any Sieges, and Campai in which the Officer was specifying the Regimen Staff Situation he hel each occasion, and the nar Officer in the chief com
	Full Pay.	Half Pay.				
2d Lieut.	21st Fos.		14 June 1850	By purchase	Glasgow & Newcastle	Present at Alm leave Comd the Yea of Royal of Guards for the Forkie & 26 Octo
Ens & Lieut	Coldm. Gds		27 June 1851	By purchase	Embarked for Malta & went to Scutari varni	the Trenches in the w & walle of Sebastopol
Lieut & Capt	do		14th July 1854	With Purchase	Landed in Crimea 14 Sepr/54 & remained there till 6 May	Sebastopol took a Days Duty all th the Crimea Return
Bt. Major	do		14th June 1855	Brevet	employed on 2 Tin G a Batonf. Jul 1855	in Oct. 1854, for s by his R.H. Duke of Ed
Lt. Col	do		29th Novr 1857	By Purchase	29 May 53 to 8 Sep 56.	Lt Genl Bentinck col up Lt Panlet, Gd Division
Colonel	do		30 April 1869	Brevet		Clarie sent Home by h Considered not to have
Major	do		14 August 1872	Without Purchase		Service, answer of Genl

Retired on ½ pay. 7 August 1875.

If the Officer be Married,* specify					If the Officer has any legitimate Chi specify		
When.	Where.	To whom.	The Wife living at the Date of.	Minister who married the Parties, and of what Church.	Names.	Dates of Birth.	Where

* Note. A Report to be made to the War Office within Six months of the Marriage.—See *Regulations for Widows' Pensions.*

21st   Reg.t of   *Fusiliers*   with a Record of such

in case of his Death.

is first Entrance into the Army   *18 years*

...ances in which ...er has distinguished ...elf by gallant, or ...nduct, when, where, ...1 what occasion; ...er noticed in General Orders.	Wounds received in Action, specifying when, where, and on what occasion; what grant of Pay has been received; Rate of Pension; Date; and whether permanent or temporary.	Titles, Honorary Distinctions, and Medals, obtained; and if conferred for any specific Service, when, and on what occasions.	Service Abroad.		
			Period.		Station.
			From	To	
Brevet Majority 56 for Service Field.		*Crimean Medal & 4 Clasps Legion of Honor ★ Victoria Cross Order of the Medjidie 5th Class ★ For Gallant Conduct in command of the Sharpshooters during the Siege of Sevastopol. Turkish War Medal*	*Feb.y 1852 Sept. 1854*	*Sept. 1854 June 1856*	*Turkey Crimea*

rvice on	Years.		I do hereby certify, upon my honour, that, to the best of my knowledge and belief, this statement is in all respects correct and true.
	Abroad.	At Home.	
· · · · ·	*"*	*"*	
· · · · ·	*"*	*"*	———————————— Signature of the Officer.
31st Decem-} 9 · · · · }	*"*	*"*	We do hereby certify, that We are satisfied of the general correctness of this statement.
· · · · ·	$2\frac{4}{12}$	$22\frac{10}{12}$	Signature of the
· · · · ·	*Total 2 5/12 Years*		*P. Fielding Col.* Commanding Officer.
			Paymaster.

20. Goodlake (*centre*) deer-stalking in Scotland.

Newstead Abbey.

21. Goodlake in
retirement.
*Journal of the
Brigade of Guards.*

for the summer campaign. Everything is going on very well. Great improvements have been made particularly at Balaklava.

Poor Larcombe is still very ill. I am trying to send him home, poor fellow, as if he does not go soon he will die very shortly.

I must conclude, my dearest Father, with best love to Mother, Bob, and you, and wishing you every good wish, and thanking you again for all your goodness again and again.

Believe me ever,

Your very affectionate son,

Gerald L Goodlake.

Balaklava
14 May (my birthday) 1855
My dearest Father,

I yesterday received your welcome letter. I have again to thank you for all your kindness and for the execution of my commissions and for the boxes, also for the tent, tea and my other things.

The Brevet[25] has come out and I am not in it. Never mind, I am quite contented; everything has been done. You are pleased at my being recommended. I think that you will see on consideration that I am quite right in not moving myself in this matter, as things have turned out it could not have done me any good only harm. Lord Raglan knew about it, was kind enough to write himself and received an answer to this effect, that they could not give it, as I had not served long enough, but that I would not be overlooked; also I had a kind message from the Duke of Cambridge and George Upton that they had done their best and were very sorry for it. You have done all you could in this matter, and I am much obliged for the trouble you have taken.

We have had awful weather recently, rain, mud, and wind in abundance; it is now, I am happy to say, fine again.

The 10th [Hussars'] and 12th [Lancers'] horses looked much knocked up when I rode through their lines this afternoon. Cholera has, I am afraid to say, broken out again, eight cases yesterday and eleven today in the Light Division.

What a row this failure of the expedition to Kertch will make in England. There is a story about it, rather a good one. They say the reason the expedition returned without landing was because General Brown forgot his stock and said he would not fight without it. Old Yea[26] told Raggles and he told Brown who, I believe, swore fearfully.

Poor old Bill Bathurst had a medical board and is going home on account of his deafness. I am afraid he will have to sell out. Sir J.Fergusson has actually started as his constituents cannot possibly do without him, also Burton, to settle his affairs.[27]

The siege goes on much the same, frequent sorties on the part of the Russians, which are always repelled with vigour by us at least. Gortzakoff[28] has arrived with fresh troops and their camps are getting bigger every day. We are very close to one another, which accounts for the many casualties we have. I am very busy riding about all day long at my hut work etc. We have had two capital additions to our regiment, Lane and Adair;[29] in fact the draft has been very good; but we shall, I am afraid want many more;

The opinion is here, as I suppose it is at home, that Wilson[30] is in the wrong box and that Arthur Hardinge[31] has much the best of it.

I wish the Emperor of the French would come out here; we want stirring up. We are getting quite moped, much too slow, want routing, all of us. I really believe we are going to sleep. We have Eupatoria, fortunately that is where we should make our move from. We cannot move out of our present position, as we are quite surrounded. We have played the Russian game throughout; that is what makes them so bumptious about their terms for peace.

Now my dearest Father, with best love, please accept my best wishes for your kindness.

Your very affectionate son,
Gerald L Goodlake.

Balaklava
22 May 1855
My dearest Father,

I have just time to write one line. We have just received an order that the second expedition to Kertch is to start directly with 3,000 English; 7,000 French, 3 batteries; and 3000 Turks, and 1 battery; under Sir G Brown. There is a scare that the Flank Companies of the Brigade are to go, but I won't have it as I think they mean to stop at Kertch and make it a base of operations, and they would not split up our Brigade if they could help it.

I have not, as you say, been gazetted, but I have been in general orders. It ran as follows, 'Captain Goodlake, Coldstream Guards, will receive pay and allowances of DAQMG for the future', but as it is only special duty I shall not put on anything staff yet [staff uniform].

I am still very busy on huts, on horseback, at about half past six am till half past six pm. I am in capital condition never better. The weather is awfully hot, takes the skin off your face in an hour.

You asked me in your letter whether you should make the Brevet Major problem public. Write to Lord Raglan. For my part, I think it would do me the greatest possible harm and might be the cause of my leaving the army. Look at Wilson [See above] he has just about put his foot in it. With regard to writing to Lord Raglan, he knows all about it, and wrote himself to Lord Hardinge and received an answer that they could not do it as I had not got the service and they dare not break through the established rule; whether they could or not is another thing. Now, dear Father, I am grateful to you for all the trouble you have taken and for what you have done, but I am sure the best thing is to let the matter drop. I myself, as I have written before, don't care two straws about it. Lord Rokeby has written home to the Duke of Cambridge,[32] who sent me a very kind message and said he would do his best for me, which I am sure he will do.

There have been some more cases of cholera since I last wrote. Major Norton, 88th, died in eight hours. The siege you can hardly say is going on, as they never fire except at night to repel a sortie.

Freddy and the Colonel are well. Poor Larcombe is better, but he has done with campaigning; he starts for England tomorrow, and when he arrives if you would ask Byng[33] to get him leave to see his Mother and then let him go to Wadley for a fortnight, he may pull round, perhaps. The doctors here say he ought not to be kept in London but go into the country. Poor fellow, he has done well out here and has been a very good servant.

I must conclude, my dearest Father, with best love and hoping that you are all well.

> Believe me ever,
> Your very affectionate son,
> Gerald L. Goodlake.

Balaklava
1 June 1855

My dear Father,

I received yesterday with much pleasure your letter, also Mother's and Bob's. They gave me the greatest pleasure and satisfaction.

I truly and sincerely thank you for all your good wishes and kindnesses etc. and my two boxes with clothes and saddlery. Everything inside was perfection, with perhaps the exception of the sword, which is too short, fluted and not straight, but it is very light and will do. The clothes fit. I really am so much obliged; I am capitally rigged out now with the exception of shirts, which are on the road; then I shall be all right till next winter.

Affairs are going on well here, everyone in good spirits and expecting an active campaign this summer.

The second Kertch expedition[34] has been very successful; they took Kertch without the loss of one man, 50 large guns and a cannon foundry; and several sailing vessels laden with corn quietly sailed into the fleet. After the capture of Kertch they marched to Yenikale, where they are entrenching themselves as fast as they can. The Fleet sailed to Arabat[35], knocked the place about their ears, took three or four steamers and a lot of vessels laden with corn, and have opened the way into the Sea of Azov.

The Sardinians and the French have taken up positions beyond the ones the Turks abandoned at the action of Balaklava, so we can show our noses a little further and get grass for our horses.

Much obliged for your offer of sending me a horse from England, but the risk and expense is so great that it is hardly worthwhile. I now have one horse and four ponies, two very good ones. They are very difficult to get and one has to pay for them. Animals that I could have bought last year for £6, £8, £10, fetch in a moment £25, £30, £45. You cannot get a thing that has four legs and crawls for under £15. I give my beasts plenty to do. I generally ride per diem as I am out from 7 am to 6 pm nearly every day. I am in wonderful condition, never tire, and was never better in my life and I thank God for it.

Cholera has I am afraid broken out in our Brigade. The Grenadiers buried ten yesterday and eight have died today. The Sardines [Sardinian Army] have got it very badly, 28 cases yesterday General Marmora [C in C-Sardinian Army] told me himself.

Colonel Yea, I am happy to say, is quite well and highly delighted at being appointed Brigadier to five regiments during the Kertch expedition. I think he will have a Brigade this summer. He said to me yesterday, 'If I do, will you be my ADC?' I thanked him much and told him I could not because I had this present place. So he said, 'If yours is not a permanent one, I should like to have you.' So I said I would see about it. He has done right well out here and is much thought of and will decidedly be getting a turning [promotion].

Report says we open fire on Monday and the French are to take the

Mamelon, but I do not think they have pluck enough, unless they go at it in broad daylight when the eyes of the world are upon them. The Heads funk the 'butcher's bill', and as we killed so many in the last bombardment, they will just try it again. My idea is that we send an army into the interior and bully them that way for a month or two before we go in. As for taking the place, I have not the slightest doubt about it, and never had. Sevastopol will be ours, and it only depends on a single word from Raggles, and that word is 'storm.' We now have a tremendous army, 240,000 men at least, and some of them are very nasty fellows to fight against, but portions, I am sorry to say, are not worth one single rap.

I saw General Mitchell[36] the other day and he was very civil, asked after Mother and begged to be remembered.

Poor Larcombe is still very ill and is to go home by the first ship, which ought to have sailed at least a week ago. I have been at them about it and don't intend to leave them alone, I shall be much obliged to you for looking after him when he arrives in England; he has done well and worked hard.

There was a good blow up yesterday, two railway trucks full of powder. One barrel dropped off and some of the powder fell on the line. The navvies were ordered not to go on, but the lazy, drunken, insubordinate rascals did not do what they were told, so up the two trucks went into the air. I will give the railway its due, it has been an immense help in getting up shot, shell, etc, but they have been a long time about it and it is now not nearly completed.

I think you are mistaken at me having to serve two years as Captain, as the Horse Guards could not be so barefaced as to say they took as a precedent Armytage, Crawley, Boyle [all officers in 1st Coldstream]. Crawley got his promotion the same day as I did; the other two have not served two years; two cases in the same regiment.

Lord Ward[37] is here in his steam yacht, a great swell. I shall speak to him the first time I come across him.

I must conclude now, my dearest Father, thanking you again and again for all that you have done for me, with best love to Mother, Bob and all.

Believe me ever,

Your very affectionate son,

Gerald L. Goodlake.

P.S. I think another patrol tent would be of great use to put one's domestics and saddles in.

Balaklava
9 June 1855
My dearest Father,

I have only time to write you a line to thank you for your letter and for my two boxes, which arrived quite safely about ten days ago. I wrote to thank you the moment they arrived.

You will see by the electric telegraph that we have opened fire again and on Thursday night the French advanced against the Mamelon, which they took in about four and a half minutes, and two small batteries. A third and the most important one they failed in taking. They then went on to the Malakoff Tower and stood for 25 minutes within 20 paces of eight to ten guns sending grape into them. They could not get in, on account of the ditch and the banks etc., so they had to retire. The Russians followed them, turned them out of the Mamelon and hunted them into their own works. The moment they got the Russians into the open, the French let their reserves go, caught Ruski outside his works, re-took the Mamelon and again attacked the Malakoff [or Round] Tower. They, however, could not get in, so they lay outside and shot the gunners down the moment they attempted to load or fire. Darkness came on and the place appeared like a *****. We shelled the town, rockets, carcasses, blue lights.[38]

The French have lost upwards of 4000 killed and wounded. Fancy seeing such a fight as that from a hill 500 yards off. When the French took the Mamelon, three rockets went up, which was the signal for our attacking some quarries just under the Redan. Colonel Shirley, 28th, commanded the storming party and old Yea the reserve. They took the quarries after some hardish fighting, and then got into the Redan; they found little resistance at first, but were soon turned out by columns of Russians. They however held the quarries through the night, not withstanding the repeated attempts to retake them. You may conceive what a place it is; they lose about seven men an hour.

Freddy Vane is in the trenches; he was all right up to last night, I went down into the trenches to enquire.

We have lost upward of 480 men and forty-five officers killed or wounded. Nothing could be more plucky than the fighting of both parties. They fought in daylight and you could with glasses distinguish individuals, and a finer or more splendid sight was never seen. We shall storm some work or another every day now; all our batteries are up and in just about a fortnight I think we will be well inside.

Would you please send across the moment this arrives to Lady Vane and tell her that Freddy could not write as he is in the trenches, but that he is all right and got through Thursday's fight safe.

I forget to say a steamer has just arrived with capital news from the Sea of Azov. We have taken no end of provisions at Taguerof[39] [Taganrog] or some such place. They build ships there. Everything is going on, out and out well now if only we stick to them and follow them up we shall have it all our own way and then the Russians will be holloaing out for peace.

I am obliged to ride my animals' tails off all day to get through my work, so as to cut up to the trenches to see the goings on. How you would enjoy it. You can sit down and watch the whole fight without being in any danger, and you may depend on it you will never hear or see such a row again.

I must conclude now, as my servant is waiting and I am only just in time for the post. Best love to all.

Believe me, my dearest Father,

Your very affectionate son,

Gerald L. Goodlake

P.S. Sergeant Owen[40] was one of my Sharpshooters for part of the time; he was wounded at Inkerman; he is a right good man, face the devil or anything living. I am sure that he will let you know if there are any others. I don't know if they are alive or dead, the moment after they leave the regiment, The Sergeants don't even know. Best love.

Balaklava

16 June 1855

My dearest Father,

I write one line according to promise. We storm Monday or Tuesday. The Brigade go up to the front tomorrow and support the 3rd Division. You will have heard of the taking of Sevastopol before this letter reaches you. Lord help the Muscoves when we get inside not a mouse will be left alive. The men I am sure will worry them with their teeth. I never saw such a splendid sight as the taking of the Mamelon, attacking the Malakoff, and taking the quarries, The storming will be an out and out business. I think the next move will be to Odessa. The Russians will fight like rats in their holes, no mistake. I hope to have a chance of trying my new sword; it will shave now.

You cannot believe the excitement; we are, for all the world, like tigers. I believe the men would go in without arms.

I must now conclude, my dearest Father, thanking you for everything and all your good wishes. With best love to all and in great haste.

Believe me ever,

Your affectionate son,

Gerald L. Goodlake.

P.S I have served my six years on the 14th. I need not serve two years as a Captain, at least I should think not, as Armytage and Crawley did not, and many others. I think Tuesday is the day and no mistake this time.[41] Larcombe sailed a week ago in the *Saldanha*. One of my ponies is dead, £25. Rascal gave barley just before water, caused inflammation inside. Villain did not attend to orders; heard of another.

Notes

1 *The Grand Crimean Central Railway,* pp.70–71, Brian Cooke.
2 Colonel Upton was the Former Commanding Officer, 1st Coldstream, who was promoted to Regimental Lieutenant Colonel,Coldstream Guards on 1 February 1855 and thus left the Crimea and returned home.
3 Col. C.J.Woodford, Rifle Brigade, DAQMG at Army Headquarters, responsible for supplies, clothing, etc. He was wounded in the attack on the Redan.
4 Lord John Russell was acting as the British Government's Plenipotentiary at the Vienna Convention, negotiating peace terms with the Russians.
5 The Zouaves were exceedingly irritated by the Marine Infantry, who they threatened with exceedingly unpleasant quarters of an hour for their alleged retreat on the morning of the 24th. They got into their head that the Marines had not only bolted, but that they fired into those before them, who were the Zouaves. Russell heard some of them exclaim. 'Ah, if we had had a few hundred of your English, we would have done the trick, but those marines-bah'. *The British Expedition to the Crimea,* pp.227–8, W.H.Russell.
6 A blue frockcoat and a cocked hat. See Military Terms.
7 Promotion to Major by Brevet.See Military Terms.
8 Cox & Co, later Cox & Kings; every officer's pay went through this bank and thus it held accounts for all officers. This bank is now part of Lloyds TSB.
9 Rifle firing from the left or right of a company, to create a continuous volley of rifle fire to prevent the enemy from repairing their defences. See Military Terms.

10 Captain Hon.C.Browne, 7th Fusiliers, killed on 22 March 1855, during the Russian night attack on the Mortar Battery on the Woronzoff Heights.

11 Lieutenant-Colonel Hon. R.Bruce and Captain N Hogge, Grenadier Guards.

12 Colonel Upton was Lieutenant-Colonel of the Coldstream Guards and Lord Strafford was Colonel.

13 Lady Vane would have been required to find a capital sum as commissions in the Brigade of Guards were more expensive than those in line regiments, because of the double rank in the Brigade. See Double Rank in Military Terms.

14 Colonel William McMurdo, Director-General, Land Transport Corps.

15 Firing small charges of powder to dry out a weapon. See Military Terms.

16 Captain Lord John Hay RN of HMS *Queen*, serving in the Naval Brigade was wounded, but not severely, when the bombardment started on 9 April: *Despatches & Papers-The Crimea*, Vol. III, pp. 137 and 141 Captain Sayer.

17 Sailors were used to man the big guns and also to assist in carrying ladders as in the attack on the Redan. See Military Terms.

18 Commanding Officer of the 77th Regiment.

19 77th Regiment. Killed during the assault on the rifle pits on 19 April 1855.

20 Captain 20 April 1847, 7th Fusiliers, killed in action on 20 April 1855.

21 Lord Berkeley has no connection with the Regiment. He must be referring to Lord Strafford, the Colonel of the Regiment.

22 The Duke of Cambridge became Commander-in-Chief in 1856.

23 Lord Hardinge, Commander-in-Chief, British Army, took over from the Duke of Wellington when the latter died on 14 September 1852.

24 Claude Thomas Bourchier was awarded the Legion of Honour and his bravery was recorded in French General Orders. He was promoted Captain in December 1854 and to Major in July 1855. He was subsequently awarded the Victoria Cross for his leadership and bravery in this action. On 20 November 1854 three companies of the 1st Battalion of the Rifle Brigade were ordered to attack some Russians in rifle pits and caves. Lieutenant Tryon, who was in charge, was killed after the assault had been successful. Lieutenant Bourchier took charge and successfully repulsed a night attack by the Russians and consolidated the position. At this time, this medal was not awarded posthumously. *Rifle Green in the Crimea*, pp.157–9.

25 See p.45, fn. 56 and Military Terms.

26 Colonel Yea, Commanding Officer, 7th Fusiliers, who acted as Brigadier on this expedition.

27 F.H.Bathurst; see fn. 45; Sir James Fergusson Bt; see fn. 157; Captain and Lieutenant- Colonel F.A.P.Burton, Coldstream Guards, was posted home to the 2nd Battalion. on 8 April 1855.

28 Gortzakoff, Prince Michael. Second-in-Command of Russian Army.

29 Lieutenant H.J.Bagot Lane, Ensign 1855, and Lieutenant A.W.Adair, Ensign 1855, Coldstream Guards.

30 Charles Townshend Wilson, Lieutenant-Colonel, Coldstream Guards. Author of *A Regimental Officer. Our Veterans of 1854. In Camp and before the Enemy,* published in 1859 by Street. Unfortunately there is no record of the dispute between these two officers, which probably arose owing to Hardinge's staff appointments, which Wilson thought were due to his father's influence as Commander-in-Chief and not due to merit.

31 Lieutenant-Colonel Hon. Arthur Hardinge, Coldstream Guards, son of Lord Hardinge, was Assistant Quartermaster-General at Headquarters from landing to 25 June 1856 when the force was broken up, apart from a period of absence on a medical certificate from 26 December 1854 to 25 May 1855.

32 He became Commander-in-Chief on 5 July 1856.

33 See p.94, fn. 41.

34 Kertch and Yeni Kala were fortified towns on the straits between the Black Sea and the Sea of Azov. The Prince Consort suggested that an expedition to take and occupy Kertch would cut Russian lines of supply from Rostov, the Rver Don and the Sea of Azov to Sevastopol, which was not completely surrounded by the allies, especially on the north side of the harbour. The attack finally took place on 26 May 1855 and was completely successful and a great quantity of ships and grain captured. The raid also allowed our ships to sail into the Sea of Azov. P.321, *Albert Uncrowned King.* Stanley Weintraub, John Murray, London, 1997. See also p.178, fn. 22.

35 A town on the south-west coast of the Sea of Azov.

36 Lieutenant-General John Michell, Royal Artillery. He did not serve in the Crimea but in the Peninsular War. Captain John Michell was serving in the Crimea as Second Captain in W Field Battery in the Balaklava Defences, possibly his son or a relation whom he was visiting. *Into Battle*, p.35, Ron McGuigan and *Hart's Army List 1856.*

37 William Ward, born in 1813. The 11th Baron, who succeeded his father in 1835. He was visiting the Crimea in his yacht.

38 Rockets-fired from a tube, delivering, shot, shell or carcasses. See Military Terms. Carcasses, Spherical hollow shells, with several holes

and filled with incendiary material, for setting fire to buildings and shipping. See Military Terms. Blue Lights, fireworks fired by a gun. See Military Terms.

39 A port on the Don Estuary, in the Sea of Azov.

40 Unfortunately the only person with the name of Owen Owen, 4424, identified by RHQ, was killed on 1 January 1855, so it could not be him.

41 Six years' service was required before promotion to Field Rank.

Chapter Six

The Letters –
Staff Officer

The Death of Lord Raglan.
June to August 1855

Guards Brigade –Movements and Events

1855

8 June   Mamelon & Redan Quarries. The French Army takes the Mamelon and the British Army takes the Redan Quarries.

16 June   The 1st Division, the Guards and Highland Brigades, marched back to the Heights above Sevastopol.

6 June   Fourth Bombardment of Sevastopol.

18 June   Redan and Malakoff. The unsuccessful assaults by the British Army on the Redan and by the French Army on the Malakoff. The Guards Brigade forms the Reserve for the Attack on the Redan.

28 June   Field Marshal Lord Raglan dies. General Simpson takes over the position of Commander-in-Chief.

15 August   Battle of the Tchernaya. The French and Sardinian Armies defeat the Russian Army at the Battle of the Tchernaya.

16 August   Fifth Bombardment on Sevastopol.

17 August	Headquarters order issued for soldiers in the forward trenches to maintain a steady fire of musketry during the night on the Redan and on the works in its rear.
31 August	The new Pattern '53 Enfield rifle is issued to the Guards Brigade.

Captain Gerald Goodlake

On 16 June the 1st Division, with the Guards and Highland Brigades marched back to the Sapoune Heights. On 18 June 1855 the French attacked and captured the Mamelon and the British the Redan Quarries. Unfortunately the assault by our Army on the Redan and by the French on the Malakoff on 18 June signally failed, through mismanagement.

The British Army was due to storm at 8 am, after bombarding the Redan all night. After this had been agreed, Marshal Pelissier said that he wanted to storm at 3 am, without a bombardment. Captain Goodlake is highly critical that Raglan agreed, as usual, even though there was not time to issue amended orders. When the Redan was stormed, it was full of Russians, as they were about to storm our trenches and their guns had not been silenced. The signals went wrong. The supports did not come up and our men were murdered. Out of 800 men, 480 other ranks and 45 officers were either killed or wounded. The generals, he said, must make better arrangements and be more united in their plans (we want one head not four} or our magnificent armies will be sadly sacrificed. On 26 June 1855 he says that the Allies have no one with a talent for combination.

He showed great loyalty to Colonel Yea, who was killed in the attack, by buying his silver-tailed horse at his sale and ensuring it was sold to General Scarlett, who would treat the horse kindly. Colonel Yea did not want the horse to be bought by that brute General Brown.

When Lord Raglan dies, he writes on 30 June that the officers miss him, not for what he could do here, but for what he could have done for the Army at home. The men do not miss him as they feel that he did not care about them. General Simpson then took over as Commander-in-Chief.

Captain Goodlake demonstrates his grasp and understanding of tactics by pointing out that General Liprandi was in a dangerous position in the Tchernaya Valley, when he threatened our Army last winter. Not exploiting this opportunity was he felt one of our major mistakes in the war.

General Hamley[1] was present at all the major battles in the Crimean campaign and was later Commandant of the new Staff College, which was established after the War. He agreed with Captain Goodlake that General Liprandi's attack at Balaklava was a mistake, as it brought him no advantage and placed him in a perilous position:

> A great deal has been said and written by military authorities of the faultiness of our position on the plateau. It is very true that the formation of an army 'en potence' – that is, with a salient angle towards the enemy – must generally be weak and dangerous. It is clear enough that, on ordinary ground, a formation which enables the foe to throw all his force on a single point, or a single face, of your line, must be objectionable. But if the nature of the position is that the apex is unassailable, or capable of being made so, and its wings so posted that the enemy can only advance to the attack at a disadvantage more than counterbalancing the superiority of force he can bring against that face, all objection ceases; and such a position was ours.
>
> It was endangered, it is true, on 5 November, but redoubts and entrenchments subsequently made this the strongest point of our line. The left wing faced the town, and must be attacked up ravines, deep, narrow and easily defensible, or in the teeth of our siege batteries; moreover in a repulse, the pursuers might pass within the defences along with the flying enemy, and the prize might fall in our hands. The other wing could not be attacked directly, because opposite it, across the valley, rises an impassable mountain barrier. Thus an enemy's force entering the valley had Balaklava to its front, the troops on the plateau on its right flank, a mountain on the left, and the Tchernaya (River) in its rear.
>
> For these reasons, I have always considered General Liprandi's attack on 25 October on Balaklava- a mistake. His success as it was, proved of no eventual benefit to him, and during the winter he abandoned the position, which was one of great hazard.

That summer on 12 August Captain Goodlake writes that the poor fellows in the trenches beg to be shot through the legs and arms, so sick are they of burning sun all day. They are graped, shelled, canistered, round-shotted and pelted with bullets all night, 24 hours on duty and 48 hours off.

On 31 August 1855 the Guards Brigade handed in all its Minie rifles and was issued with the new Pattern '53 Enfield Rifle.

In August he writes that he has nearly finished his hutting assignment. He is uncertain about his future and may have to go back to his battalion, as the new Commander-in-Chief General Simpson, may appoint his own friends.

The Letters

The dates of certain letters have been altered as the facts reported in them took place at a different time. The altered dates are shown in italics and the reasons for this alteration are shown below.

1855

18 June	Balaklava	Father
22 June	Balaklava	Father
26 June	Balaklava	Father
30 June	Balaklava	Father
3 July	Balaklava	Mother
17 July	Balaklava	Father
28 July	Balaklava	Mother
12 August	Balaklava	Father
15 August	Battle of Tchernaya	
16 August	Balaklava	Father
25 August	Balaklava	Father

Revision of Dates of Letters.

The dates of two letters are shown in italics. The dates and the places where these letters were written and the events mentioned in the letters do not agree with the timetable shown above. After taking into account the facts within each letter, their original dates have been amended as follows;

17 JULY, VARNA. The Army did not land in the Crimea till 14 September 1854. The letter was written after Colonel Yea's death on

133

18 June 1855 and after the sale of his possessions on 26 June 1855. The revised date taken is a year later, _17 July 1855._

25 AUGUST, VARNA. The date of this letter has been changed to _25 August 1855_. The Army landed in the Crimea on 14 September 1854. This letter mentions the bombardment of Sevastopol and the Russian bridge across the harbour of Sevastopol from the south to the north side. The fifth bombardment started on the 16 August 1855 and the bridge was built in that month.

Balaklava
18 June 1855
My dearest Father,

It is with real sorrow that I commence this letter, having to tell you of the death of our poor dear friend Colonel Yea [Commanding Officer, 7th Fusiliers]. A more disastrous day could not have happened to us. We made a general assault and owing to the greatest mismanagement signally failed. The poor dear Colonel was shot at the head of 'the forlorn hope'[2], close to the Redan. The last time he was seen he was crawling wounded with his cap on the point of his sword, calling to his men to come on; he was then seen to fall over on his back. The Russians have possession of his gallant body. Poor fellow, his death has caused the greatest sensation. 'Poor dear old Yea' is in everybody's mouth. I cannot tell you how I feel his death; he was always so kind to me. His regiment is fearfully cut up. Our men fought as well as men could do, but they were fairly slaughtered.

I will now try and give you an account of this sad day's work. You may suppose that in the excitement and confusion of the day, it is difficult to give a true and correct account but I will do my best. The Batteries being ready and Lord Raglan and Pélissier having at last agreed to an assault, they fixed 18 June as the day. The French were to attack the Malakoff Tower and force their way into the town, and also take the batteries on the extreme left. The English were to attack the Redan Garden Batteries. Storming parties were told off, scaling ladders etc, and they were to bombard all Sunday evening. Pellissier sent word to Raglan, after every plan was explained to those concerned, that instead of storming at eight o'clock on Monday morning they must storm at three am instead. Lord Raglan gave way as usual, and issued fresh orders, which could not be promulgated on account of the short space of time. The Light Division was ordered to furnish a portion of the storming party and the poor Colonel was to lead the 'forlorn hope' with Lieutenant-Colonel of the 23rd, who is badly wounded.

[Editor's Note: The Redan was a strongpoint south-west of the Malakoff, attacked unsuccessfully by the British Army on 18 June and 8 September 1855. The Redan was evacuated by the Russians, when the French Army took the Malakoff on 8 September 1855. Lieutenant-Colonel Daniel Lysons, Commanding Officer 23rd Foot [RWF], was, in fact, only slightly wounded. Lieutenant-Colonel Thomas Shadforth, Commanding the 57th Foot, which were the storming party, was killed.]

Everything went wrong. We attacked with 800 men instead of at least 8,000. The Russian works were crammed with men and were just preparing to make a sortie on us. The Redan guns, which were supposed to be silenced, all opened up and the poor storming party were murdered. The signals went wrong, supports never came up and the Russians being in such enormous force positively cheered on our men with cries of 'Come on, English!' The French were repulsed three times and lay the blame on us, as they say we made such an ineffective attack on the Redan, and therefore did not draw off the fire sufficiently from them, and that the Malakoff is a perfect citadel and if they had taken it, they could not have held it on account of the shipping [guns on Russian naval boats].

Of course we, on the other hand, lay all the blame on Pélissier for having altered the plan at the last moment. One thing is certain, that a more disastrous, ill-planned and managed affair could not be. Some people will talk of our having lost our prestige; it is not the case, our soldiers could not have done more or behaved better, there is not one man that would have not gone singly and be butchered, as the poor fellows were who attacked today. What could 800 men not supported do against a tremendous work with ditch, abattis,[3] parapet, etc, guns not silenced, but double-shotted with grape, canisters[4] and bullets and the enemy in such numbers, actually preparing an attack on our trenches.

After this sad failure, Lord Raglan ordered the attack to cease and the troops marched back to their camps. The Brigade came up from Balaklava on Saturday and acted as reserve but was not the least engaged. They are now in the trenches. Just before I started for Balaklava (where I continue to live), I sent to Freddy Vane to see if he was all right, which I am happy to say he was, because he was in the quarries just under the Redan the whole time. What an awful night and day he must have had. Please send to Lady Vane and let her know, with my love, in case Freddy should not have written.

Now, my dear Father, this is as near to the truth of this sad day's work as I can at present make out. What a different letter this is to the one I expected to have written this mail. My opinion is that we should have attacked as Lord Raglan had previously arranged at eight o'clock in the morning, after a good bombardment, but never with 800 men, 8,000 is under the mark. Then again, when the mischief was done, leaving off in the middle, Lord Raglan, if he had been a man, would have sent in the whole British Army. The loss would have been terrible, but we should have gained our object without doubt and it would have cost fewer lives in the end. It was such a disappointment to the troops when the attack was ordered to cease. That we shall take the place there cannot be the shadow of a doubt, as I have said before, but if the generals cannot make better arrangements and cannot be more united in their plans and opinions (we want one Head not four Heads) our magnificent armies will be sadly sacrificed.

The poor dear Colonel left two letters, one for Lord Vivian[5]and the other for his sister, Miss Yea; if you would write to Lord Vivian and tell him that if there is anything in the world that he wishes done for poor Yea, how truly happy I will be to do it. I can write now on no other subject as I can hardly think of anything but the poor fellows so many that I knew. General Sir John Campbell[6] was killed and an immense number of officers.

My box arrived quite safely with the shirts, tobacco etc. I am so much obliged to you all, I will write in future every mail, until something is settled.

We are too deep in to think of returning, on we must go, so why not go really ahead ? It is awful to see how many valuable lives are frittered away.

God bless you my dearest Father, Mother and all of you. I hope I may never have to write such a sad letter again, with best love to all.

Believe me ever,

Your very affectionate son,

G. L. Goodlake

Balaklava
22 June 1855
My dearest Father,

I have just time to write you one line, and then I go to the poor dear Colonel's sale. I am truly glad to tell you that his gallant body was recovered at the Flag of Truce, three days afterwards; he was buried immediately, nearly the whole Division attending.

You cannot conceive the sensation his death has caused throughout the entire army, regretted sincerely by both men and officers. Even those in his own regiment who used to abuse him, admit his great loss; he was considered one of the best officers in the army and kept his regiment in the best order. He has left me the cob – so kind of him. I think of bidding for the silver-tailed horse. Old General Brown wants to buy him, at least he did a short time ago, but the dear Colonel said that he hoped if anything happened to him, old Brown would not get his horse. He hated Brown. Poor Brock [soldier servant] is so cut up; he has gone to Pearson of the 7th Fusiliers[7] who will make him a capital master.

The Colonel, I am sure, from what I have heard lately, fancied he would be killed. He was always counting the time when he should have served 30 years, when he intended to retire instantly, unless they made him General. This failure has caused great dissatisfaction throughout the army. Our Generals, I am happy to say, know whose fault it was, as it has had this effect on them. General Estcourt,[8] very ill indeed, not expected to live. General Brown is very ill, gone on board ship. General Pennyfather has gone home ill. General Eyre ditto, not home. General Codrington[9] ditto, on board ship. Raglan has not uttered a word since 18 June.

Will you give my love to Lady Vane and tell her Freddy is all right and quite well, he was not touched but had a narrow shave. He was at one time told off for the 'forlorn hope'[10], not one officer out of ninety-seven who led that day came back alive, or not wounded. This I think speaks enough for them.

I will write a long letter next mail and tell you all the Camp opinions and shaves. This failure has been a grand thing for the croakers. I must now conclude my dearest Father.

With best love to all,
      Believe me ever,
         Your very affectionate son,
           G. L. Goodlake

Balaklava
26 June 1855
My dearest Father,

Thank you for your last letter. I must write next time to Mother and Bob.

On Friday was the poor Colonel's sale. I bought the silver-tailed horse. I will tell you the circumstances. Old General Brown wanted to buy him some time ago and the Colonel made this observation: 'I wouldn't sell him to that old brute. I don't want to sell the horse, and if anything happens to me I hope he will never get the horse.' I told Scarlett [nephew of General S] of the horse and recommended him as he is such a perfect charger, and especially as his Uncle told him to look out a horse for him. He bid £100, Pearson, Brown's ADC bid [for old B.] £105. I did not wish old Brown to get the horse so I bid £110 and he was knocked down to me. It was a tremendous price to give but he is a very good sound horse. If General Scarlett[11] likes him, I told young Scarlett[12] he might have him, as I recommended him and as he was too high a price for me.

If he does not, I will sell two of my ponies for £25 each, which I can get, and make that go towards paying for him, and as you have made it all right at Cox's,[13] I will make it all right with you before long with my extra pay. Please don't mention about old Brown as it might come to his ears and he may do me a bad turn, especially as he is a man in authority at present. The horse is looking wonderfully well.

The poor dear Colonel left me the cob, which has a slight cold. You cannot think what a sensation there is still in the army about his death. He was considered one of our best officers. People are rather downcast at present and it is a grand time for croakers; but we shall have the place yet though the Muscoves are up to every move. What do you think they have done now! They have put four feet of earth on their ships and made them fire and shell proof and lined them inside also.

Our Generals are in a bad way. Poor Estcourt died yesterday of cholera and fever. Brown has gone on board ship having fainted several times from weakness. Penneyfather has resigned and gone home. Codrington very seedy on board ship, Eyre is wounded and Raglan has never uttered a word since the 18 June.

In fact those in authority who were concerned in that piece of butchery are ashamed and very cut up about it. I myself, must own that I think we are in rather a fix. In the first place we have not got a man that anyone can name who has any talent for combination, either in the French army or in our own. Next, the position of the place is naturally so strong and I do not think it is possible to turn it in any way and we cannot get out-we are actually shut in.

On the Balaklava side they have a line of hills or cliffs so that they are so well fortified both by nature and also by art. Then we cannot attack the North side without fighting a tremendous battle at the [River] Belbec.[14] The Russians have made it a most formidable position and also there is no water nearer than the Belbec, which is six miles from the North side and it would take an enormous army, as it would be obliged to protect its rear. Attacked in front and on its left flank and there is no good landing place in front, I am sure they will not attempt it. Therefore there is only one line left that I can see, which is to go safely on quietly, and then we must assault again and do the thing properly, not send 800 men and never back them up. The greatest difficulty is the ships and rafts with guns on them, they are the very devil. We cannot touch them at present and they are the greatest thorn in our sides.

We had a most tremendous thunderstorm at Balaklava yesterday, it washed away huts, four or five men were drowned, tore the rails of the railway up, and did no end of mischief.

I must conclude my dearest Father, thanking you for the box etc, and with best love to Mother, Bob and all.

Believe me ever,

Your very affectionate son,

G. L. Goodlake.

P.S. Larcombe will have arrived by the time this reaches you. I am so much obliged for your promise to look after him.

Balaklava
30 June 1855
My dearest Father,

I have just received your letter of the 14th, but long before you receive this letter, you will have heard of the death of poor Raglan. He is a great loss to the army, not perhaps so much as a Commander of the Forces out here, but as a man with a good head and would have done much for the army, if he had got home. He is much lamented by the officers; one and all agreed about his being a kind, good-hearted gentleman that ever lived. I think that from what I have overheard among the men that they were glad he is out of the way. They fancied that because he was not often seen that he did not care about them enough.

What a break up of Headquarters! Estcourt's sale took place today; things went dear. All Raglan's staff go home directly with the exception of Hale [not identified] who will have to stay some time just to show his successor how things are carried on etc.

I really was very stupid about the time I have been in the Army, I fancied I had served for six years on the 14th of this month instead of five years. I shall if I live, please God, till next year, it will be close to my Lieutenant-Colonelcy. I can see my way quite clear by that time. If we stay another winter in the Crimea, the army will have scarcely an officer. I know at least fifty who have taken their oath that they will not stop for another winter in the Crimea; if they are not allowed to sell they mean to resign.

There is quite a lull in the Camp today. What with the failure of the 18th and the generals dying and going home sick, we are not making much progress in the siege. At present they are erecting a battery or two to try and touch up the shipping, but I am afraid they will have to invent a larger range machine than any we have out here to do it. The French declare they will not go in unless the ships are smashed. If we could manage them we should assault directly, at least that is my idea. I think we are sure to remain another winter in this country. What can't be cured must be endured.

The Russians sent back poor old Yea's sword and also Sir John Campbell's, very civil of them. I myself did not intend to go on the Colonel's staff, I only gave an evasive answer. He seemed to wish it so that I could not say no, exactly. He was always so kind to me; I feel his loss so much.

I have given up all hope of being home by next winter and as everything is so dear now it is not worthwhile keeping animals to eat their heads off. As for sending my red coat home, I have only one here and cannot spare it.

My hutting business is nearly over; about another three weeks will finish it. Whether I go back to my regiment I have not the slightest idea. Poor Raglan dying may have something to do with it. You see there will be an entirely new lot[15] and they will have to put in their friends. It is rather a pity as I got on well with the old ones and they knew me and were always very kind. Simpson[16] is the Commander at present. I daresay people at home have as many and as different opinions as we have out here, as to who is the right man to put in this responsible situation. <u>No one who has not actually seen service has the slightest idea what it is. You might all read for 1000 years about it and would not know what the reality is.</u>

Now I will just relate a fact that occurred last week. Lord Panmure[17] wrote to General Simpson to ask him if he would show somebody (a swell I believe; I don't know, but that does not matter) round the French and English trenches and go with him. What on earth could Lord Panmure be thinking about. The French have upwards of 40 miles of trenches. Fancy a man in his position making such a request. Everybody who comes out here owns that everything he sees is quite different to what he had heard and expected.

Writing about trenches, what a lot of funkers they are making in our army; we have lost so many men and so many are wounded constantly that they are always looking out for cover. They are quite right to do so, but what an effect it has on them. When they are wanted to storm they hang back a bit. Look at the officers' 'butcher's bill' that will show they were well forward. There never will be any mistake about them.

I am sure that if our army was to take the field and had to storm a position like the Alma there would not be an officer left. The men are getting like the French soldiers, very sensible; they see their danger and the effect that grape and canister has upon them. There is not the idea, which there used to be, that they never could be licked and did not know when they were licked. I beg leave to say I am not croaking. I only remark what has struck me during the last few months. I am one of the few who thought that we were fighting against out and out good men; we are better and that is all.

You have mentioned in your letter that you don't want me to bathe and that is quite sufficient for me. I have one little favour to ask and that is that my letters are not shown about. A gentleman dined with me last night and he made this remark: 'Oh, Gerry I saw several of your letters last summer.' 'Indeed,' said I, 'Who showed them to you?' 'Oh, your people. Several people saw them and I have often heard others talking about some of your accounts.' Now I made this point a particular strong one before I ever came out and I had my promises about it and have written about it often. I only wish my letters shown to Mother and Bob, unless private is put on them and that means that the letter is only to be read by the person it is directed to. Now my dear Father, I hope you won't mind doing this, but everyone has his weaknesses and one of my very many ones is this. I have written very plainly and I hope you won't mind what I have said.

You ought to have had £5 on the Ascot stakes. How unlucky about the Chester Cup. Oulston should win the Leger in a canter, if he meant to.

I must now conclude as it is past 12 o'clock pm and I must be up at 6 o'clock.

My box of shirts came to hand. Everything inside is good and useful. I repeat my thanks. Best love to all and . . .

Believe me, my dearest Father,

Your very affectionate son

G. L. Goodlake

P.S. I give you all great praise for your corresponding powers.

Balaklava.
3 July 1855
My dearest Mother,

I just send you one line. I received yours and Bob's letters this morning.

What a shocking affair the 18 June. The poor dear Colonel, how he is missed out here and how sorry all his friends will be in England.

There is nothing going on, the siege is quite at a standstill, no one has the same opinion of whom our new Commander-in-Chief will be. I think we will assault in three weeks or so. The French are to make a battery in 5 hours, with 14,000 men, which if they succeed and destroy the shipping, Sevastopol will be ours.

Cholera is on the decrease I am happy to say and things are looking pretty well. I think it will be the case of another winter. I am still very busy with my hutting; I shall finish in about another month. Whether I go back to my regiment or not, it is impossible to say. The break-up at Headquarters is a great blow to me as they all knew me and were very kind and civil.

Also love to Lady Vane and tell her that Freddy is quite well, though worked very hard and is in good spirits.

I must beg dear mother that my letters are not shown. I met a man, who told me he had seen several of them last summer. Remember the promises I received. No one is to read my letters, but the Gov., You and Bob and if the word 'Private' is put on any of these, no one but the person it is directed to is to read it. On the fulfilment of this will depend my correspondence. I have no news and very little time, so must conclude.

With best love to you all.

Believe me ever,

Your most devoted son,

G. L. Goodlake.

P.S. Poor Raglan's funeral takes place today. The road from Head-quarters to Kamiesch[18]will be lined with Troops and the Brigade of Guards will furnish the Guard of Honour.

The shirts are perfection. I would not send any more tobacco for the Sharpshooters, as it will diminish the fund. A pipe apiece they would value so much more. They are now supplied with everything they want, but of course you can do as you like.

Balaklava
17 July 1855

My dearest Father,

We are all at them hammer and tongs, it began last night at 10 p.m. I think the whole place depends on our moving the ships, if we do, it's all over but the shooting, as far as the south side goes. If we cannot smash the ships, it is a case of investing or making an incursion into the country another winter.

The night before last the Muscoves made a tremendous sortie on the Mamelon, but were repulsed with loss. We have nearly come to the end of the fleets, another week will finish them. Everybody seems to say that I am right.

I sold the poor dear cob horse, Silvertail, to General Scarlett for £110; he was much too high a priced horse for me; he has got a good kind master who will take good care of him. The cob is very well, but his legs swell so if he is not worked every day; he is very fat.

The Colonel's kit was sold under the superintendence of Captain Dixon of the 7th, who kept everything he thought that his friends might like and just sold the things that were perishable. I got one or two things for Mother and Bob. Brock[19] has gone back to England with Pearson[20] of the 7th, Brown's ADC; he has taken him as a servant. No one can get his discharge now unless he has served his time, so I am afraid there is no use thinking about him till the war is over. You will most likely see him in London.

I cannot help laughing at the extraordinary number of letters I

143

receive from all quarters saying 'whatever you do don't bathe.' I have not bathed as you don't wish it, but at the same time, what do the doctors say about anyone who is sick and has had fever or diarrhoea: 'If only he can get to the Monastery[21] or sanatorium, where he can bathe, it will do him so much good'.

Everyone bathes, mind I am not going to bathe, as you don't want me to. It is all very well to sit at home in England and say don't do this or that, you cannot, nine times out of ten, help doing it. Do you remember telling me whatever I did, not to sleep out at night. Why, what do 8000 men and officers do every night but sleep out. Our nature has quite changed out here; what we could not do when we left England, we can do now with impunity. As I said in a former letter, with all due respect to our good people at home, they are not competent to give much advice to people out here; one must be guided by one's own common sense and circumstances. I hope you will excuse the freeness of my opinion, but ask anyone who has been out here and returned home.

I would be most obliged if you could send me out '*Bell's*'[22] regularly. Peter takes it but he lives at the Monastery now, and it is so difficult to get hold of the paper, when one wants it.

I suppose Larcombe [Soldier Servant] will have arrived by this time. I am obliged to you for your kindness to him poor fellow. I have little doubt that if he lands safely he will get over it, as his sea voyage will have done him a great deal of good.

I have no more news and nothing more to say.

I am very well and hope you are also. I must now conclude with the best love to Mother and Bob and with every good wish and thanks for everything.

Believe me ever.

Your very affectionate son.

G. L. G.

P.S They are not firing so heavily now, an officer has just come down from the front and says they only opened for a few shots. Freddy Vane is quite well. I have just heard that he is thinking of taking the paymaster-ship of the 23rd. I have never heard of such a thing, I am off to lecture him on his folly; tell Lady Vane and Harry not to allow it for a moment; if I can't turn him, he could not make a greater mistake.

Balaklava

28 July 1855

My dearest Mother,

It is your turn to have a letter. I have just received yours of the 14th.

All the poor dear Colonel's things were sent home by the Paymaster of the 7th, Captain Dixon. I was so glad he was made CB;[23] only what a shame he did not get it before, after Inkerman.

[Editor's Note: Prior to the establishment of the Victoria Cross, there was no medal to record gallantry in the field by junior officers. The Medal for Distinguished Service in the Field, which later became the Distinguished Service Medal, was awarded, together with a gratuity, to warrant officers, non-commissioned officers and private soldiers. Campaign medals were awarded to all ranks.]

I have sold the horse to General Scarlett and begged him to take care of him and never let him be ill-treated. He knew the Colonel and said he would never part with him, and he should never be abused.

There is a good deal of grumbling about the CB. Paulet Somerset's[24] case is much talked about. There is one thing. They can and will never please everybody.

I think I may say I have safely landed another appointment as the Huts are finished, as I have the superintendence of timberwork etc, much the same sort of work.

I think we will have a go about the 7 or 8 of August. I don't think we [Guards Brigade] shall be engaged, as we shall be sure to be in reserve. If they cannot take the place without our Brigade, I don't think we will be much good, as we have not 1000 duty men in the whole Brigade.

I would be much obliged if you would order *Bell's Life*[25] to be sent to me, as now I am separate from the Brigade; papers are so useful out here as after you have read them, you can give them to the men in hospital; also two or three little pocket account books.

If you think of sending William [manservant] away, tell him I will give him a trial. He would suit me and I am sure that I could manage him. He would be very useful to send on errands, valet me and wait at dinner. I have five horses, the Cob and four ponies, and they have plenty to do. He could have his passage out here for nothing and he is also rationed for nothing.

I think another winter is a certainty. What a bore; if we succeed in a week or fortnight in taking the South side, still there is plenty more to be done. I am afraid it is the case. One thing we will be well prepared and in comfortable quarters.

I must conclude, my dearest Mother, hoping that you are all well and with best love to Gov., Bob, Tom [Brother], Gran. and all.

Believe me ever,

Your affectionate son,

G. L. Goodlake.

P.S. Please tell Bob to send my clothes by Hayter and Howell, [shipping agents] sending them by individuals bores them a great deal, you hardly ever get them, they lose them and say I am sorry but someone walked off with that parcel of yours. No one has a conscience out here. I fancy taking things; theft is considered no crime to the French.

Balaklava
12 August 1855

My dearest Father,

I yesterday received your letter. I think you will be quite mistaken with regards to the taking of Sevastopol [south side] the next time we try. I cannot possibly conceive how we are to fail. It's true we failed the time before, but that was when we did not try. Everything is going on well; we should have been ready by the 12th, but the Russian have been firing so heavily on our working parties and we have been giving it back, and two ships with 13 and 10 inch shells did not arrive, so we will have to wait about three weeks longer.

What a lot of people, I know, are going to be married. Wilson in the 7th Fusiliers, a great friend of the poor Colonel's, has just married a Mother's beloved girl with £50,000, and his brother, wounded at Alma, has married a girl with £120,000.

We had a great shave [rumour] out by the last mail that the Scots Fusiliers and the Coldstream were to have three Battalions each. I hope they won't do it for a year and then that would make me Colonel.

I was offered by General Windham[26] his first ADC place. He came up and said he did not know either me or my family; but if I liked I might go on his staff. I thanked him much, but as I have landed my present place, I of course declined.

We are sure to winter here. I have quite made up my mind. We shall be very comfortable, though very dreary. We have advanced a good way into the country, beyond ****[27]; it is the most lovely scenery, such pretty villas and country houses. The French, of course, have sentries over each and have ransacked everything; they have a lot of champagne (very dry).

I was looking at the position of Liprandi's army,[28] which threatened us in the winter. You never saw such a trap as they were in, if we had known the country. I am sure that our not having chained up entirely Liprandi's army was one of the greatest military blunders we have committed, since we engaged in this war.

I think we will take the south side without the slightest doubt. Our ships will then look in and dislodge them from the north side; they will then evacuate, as there will be nothing for them to stay for. We shall then winter and make ourselves comfortable and have a perfect army by next spring, then quietly hunt the Muscoves systematically out of the Crimea, throw up lines to Perekop,[29] leave 40,000 French and Turks there, ask sharp terms of Russia and then say to Austria, 'You have helped Russia as much as you can without fighting the Allies and now the time for false modesty on our part being past. Here is an army of about 270,000 who have got very little out of Russia and we are just ready to have a shy at you and Russia'. She won't accept the challenge at any price and she will just have to tell Russia that peace it must be. So about next year I expect the war to be over, not much before.

One thing is certain, that if they don't give leave in the winter, more than half the officers will resign. The poor fellows in the trenches positively beg to be shot through the legs and arms, so sick are they of the trenches, burning sun all day, graped, shelled, canistered, round shotted and pelted with bullets[30] all night, 24 hours on, 48 hours off.

I am very comfortable in my house at Balaklava. I have a good stable and kitchen and am very well off. I would be obliged that if when you send anything out to me, you send it by Hayter and Howell. I assure you it is the only way, trusting to individuals is the worst way in the world. Many a time when your parcel arrived in the Crimea, the man you gave it to forgot all about it. It is put into his regimental store at Balaklava and that is the end of your parcel. My trousers are in tatters, I should have had them a month ago but Colonel Lewis and Lord Stuart[31] have not arrived. I should have had them a good month ago.

I think that Bob and Mother like Ryde very much, as the Vanes and so many of their friends are there.

I must conclude this very stupid letter, but there is nothing going on now, but I am scampering about all day. I am glad to go to bed early at night. Best love to Mother, Bob and Tom.

Believe me ever,
Your very affectionate son,
G. L. Goodlake

Balaklava
16 August 1855
My dearest Father.

I have just come in after having witnessed a model action between the French and Sardinians on one side and the Russians on the other. I will now describe what I saw as well as I can. At about half past five I was writing in my hut and heard a lot of firing. I thought it was before Sevastopol, but I heard a man observe that it was only the Russians driving in the Sardinians. So I mounted the dear old cob and positively flew to the Tchernaya[32] where I saw the ground covered with Russian troops trying to force the Tchernaya Bridge, which they partially did. The Sardinians when I came up were retreating as they had advanced up the hill, against Russian guns firing grape. They could not stand against it and retired. They fought well I believe.

As I came up I saw a battalion of Zouaves ordered to drive them over the Bridge. I gave my cob to a Frenchman at the top of the hill and descended in the rear of the Battalion. They got to the bridge, drove them back into a thick vineyard and then I never saw before or since such fire as there was. The Russians, from their hill, were pounding every sort of missile over the people's heads and the French doing the same. The French extended and got from bush to bush and potted away right and left very excitedly, but nevertheless had their wits about them, and seemed to enjoy their business. There was not the shadow of fear; they fought splendidly.

After advancing 40 yards, I got hold of a Russian needle rifle, a capital weapon, but at first I could not find any bullets to fit, the French cartridges were too small, but I put two or three down together and shot away for some time, when I alighted on a pouch full of the proper cartridges and an officer's sword.[33]

I got with the Zouaves, a little behind me in a ditch, and shot at about 40 yards for half an hour. I was very fortunate; I had my blue coat shot through, covered with powder and dust and mud from head to foot. I went back to the bridge after the Russians retired and a French officer ordered me to be taken up as a spy, just as I was going to get loot; so I was walked off, but he allowed me to take the Zouaves with me. The general said I had no business there, but I might go. I said I was much obliged and that in any affair we had we would be proud to see him with our troops, his allies, and would not take him prisoner.

I will tell you that I put the killed and wounded at:-

Russian Force altogether	60,000
Russian Force actually engaged	15,000
French Force up to 10 o'clock (They had large reserves after that)	35,000
French Force engaged	12,000
Sardinians engaged	15,000
Russian loss	2,000 (killed and wounded)
Russians	500 (killed)
French Loss	600 (killed and wounded)
Sardinian Loss	200 (killed and wounded)

This is the estimate I made and gave this morning. I am now writing at about 1 o'clock today. This may be all wrong.

The reasons the Russians lost so many men and had so many prisoners taken was that there was no cover close to the Tchernaya and then an open plain. When the Russians got safe into cover, the French whenever they tried to get out pounded them awfully, so a great number laid down their arms. I never enjoyed a day more. One thing struck me, which was how little one cared and how insignificant were the six and nine pounders to what we had been having day after day. The 13 inch shells[34] were so different-one quite despised them (the others). I never saw men behave better than the French did in my life and I never saw a heavier fire.

The Russians are advancing on the Tchernaya, the army is ordered under arms at 4 am tomorrow. I don't think it will come to anything, only a feint while the Russians bolt clean out of the Crimea. How can they stop it, both flanks and their rear are threatened? If only we had pluck, the Russians could not exist.

I am glad Sir R. Airey[35] is going home. He is, bar no man, the person who should command this army. He has the eye of an eagle; he will get over any difficulty and he is besides a thorough man of the world, a perfect gentleman. He has been very, very kind to me. See if what I have said doesn't turn out true. We shall have him at the top of the tree, thankless office that it is, put there by the *Times* and kicked out by the *Times*. What a position for the Commander-in-Chief of England's Army.

Glad am I to hear such good accounts of you, Sir, and the dear Mum. I am going to write her a line, but I have little time for writing letters.

I am so much obliged for my trousers, which arrived by old Lewis[36] quite safely; they are just the things. I must conclude as I have not been on my rounds or done an atom of business today. So with my best love to Mother and Bob.

Believe me,

Ever your very affectionate son,

G. L. Goodlake

P.S. The papers will give an account of this action. I expect the French think a great deal of it.

Balaklava
25 August 1855

My dearest Father,

I have not had a letter from you for the last three mails, and I think that one batch of letters must have been lost.

We are still hammers and tongs at this place, but you will see notwithstanding the opinion of people at home, that we shall not take this place until it is properly invested.

I think you will hear one morning that the place is ours and that the spade and pick are not to be denied. The Ruski have made a bridge across the harbour; they made it in two nights, that is to say they put it together and made it available for transport. I think it is a sign of weakness, as they must have thought of it before and as I don't think they funked much, before the present time. They are gradually getting hemmed in and they see they cannot stand much longer.

[Editor's Note – Sevastopol Harbour is split in two by the sea and has north and south sides. The south side was finally taken by the Allies on 9 September 1855, after the French took the Malakoff Tower on 8 September, which commanded the south side. The Russians then evacuated all their troops to the north side by a bridge across the harbour.]

The firing and shelling is positively terrible in the trenches at night. The French have over 150 casualties in 24 hours and many more if there is a sortie.

People in England think that we should invest the town and cut off the supplies. We do not have <u>half</u> enough men to do it; how could we supply ourselves with water from the north side. We should have to

150

keep up a communication from the Belbec,[37] six miles away. How many wagons do you think are employed daily by the Russians in transporting water to the North Side – 23,000 wagons. Tom Steele[38] told me yesterday.

We will never leave them alone from this bombardment. We are firing steadily at it; their loss must be terrible. All day long they are carrying dead and wounded to the rear. We have established a regular file-fire[39] from right to left of our advanced works, which prevents them mending theirs; this ought to have been done long ago.

I am sure we should have got on much better if we had whole battalions of Sharpshooters, instead of 30 or 40 or 50 men; only look at the annoyance caused to us by their rifle pits.

What extraordinary accounts the papers have of what is to be done with the newly purchased Rhone boats. Some say to go in with a rush at the Harbour. What nonsense; the Russians batteries would sink the whole lot in an hour. I expect the Emperor of the French, who is the only man that looks ahead, has brought these up so that in the event of our failing to take the place before winter; he will order an ex-pedition of some 20,000 men to the Sea of Azov,[40] disembark near Perekop,[41] break up the road and bridges and land again at Eupatoria,[42] break up the road there, just before winter comes, so that the Muscowes will have great difficulty in getting supplies.

I hear that the Emperor of the French has promised that not a man who wintered here last year shall winter this. He is sending vast reserves up here and taking the old Crimean soldiers (there are not so many) to winter comfortably at Constantinople. I dare say the fellows who have been out here the whole time will have three or four months leave. Am sorry no chance for me, nor would I go till this place is taken, much as I would like it.

Wednesday 28th
I could not finish my letter yesterday. Nor did it matter as the post does not start till this evening and I had a noisy lot of fellows in my tent. There is a report that we are to move 11 miles up country on Friday, which I think is very likely, as the ground wants changing.

Poor Peter's horse died today of inflammation and Bouverie's[43] I do not expect will live out the day. It is partly their own fault, they will gallop them so and bring them in hot, give them their fill of cold water; so they must stand the consequences. I have bought upwards of about 20 horses for fellows out here and I am happy to say they have all

151

turned out well. I could have turned £20 easily, if I had liked, the price averaging from 30/- to £6, for ponies without shoes, but very hardy good little animals, which live on nothing. I hear our new Ensign [2nd Lieutenant.] is to come from the ranks. I will certainly bring home my horse for her [Bob] in the winter and one for Tom [Brother.]

I will write whenever I have a moment, but I have so little to say and hardly know anything about the war except from the papers, which may appear strange.

I must now conclude, so hoping you are all well, and with best love and thanks for the flies, etc.

Believe me ever,

Your very affectionate son,

Gerald L. Goodlake

Notes

1 *The Story of the Campaigns of Sebastopol*, pp.334–5, Lieutenant-Colonel. E. Bruce Hamley, 1855, William Blackwood. Reprinted 2003 by The Naval & Military Press, Uckfield.

2 The advance guard of a hazardous attack. See Military Terms.

3 Abattis, a rampart of trees laid side by side with the branches towards the enemy. See Military Terms.

4 Double shotted with grape: Loading a gun with two projectiles. See Military Terms.

5 Charles, Lord Vivian. Born 24 December 1808, he succeeded his father in 1842, who had been a Lieutenant-General and Master-General of the Ordnance. Lord Vivian retired as a Major in 1842 and was Lord Lieutenant of Cornwall. Lord Vivian was probably acting as Colonel Yea's Executor.

6 Commanded 2nd Brigade 4th Division. Temporarily in command 4th Division after Inkerman.

7 Brevet Major R.L.O.Pearson, 7th Fusiliers. 'He served in the Eastern campaign from April 1854 to July 1855 as ADC to Sir George Brown, including the battles of Alma, Inkerman, Siege of Sevastopol, attack of the 18 June and expedition to Kertch.' *Hart's Army List – 1860*, p.162. He left the Crimea with Sir G.Brown in July 1855, when the General was invalided home. From 2 December to February 1855 he was ADC to Admiral Lord Lyons. He exchanged into the Grenadier Guards in 1855.

8 Adjutant-General.

9 Pennefather commanded a Brigade in the 2nd Division. He commanded the Division very successfully at Inkerman as Sir de Lacy Evans was sick. Major-General Sir William Codrington became Divisional Commander

Light Division after Sir George Brown was wounded at Inkerman . He later became C-in-C in the Crimea. Major-General William Eyre became Divisional Commander 3rd Division in August 1855 and Corps Commander in December 1855.

10 See fn. 2 and Military Terms

11 Brigadier-General Scarlett, commanding the Heavy Cavalry Brigade at Balaklava.

12 Captain and Lieutenant-Colonel Hon W.F.Scarlett, Scots Fusilier Guards, Extra ADC to his Uncle, Brigadier-General Scarlett.

13 See p.123, fn. 8 and Military Terms.

14 The Belbec flows into the Black Sea just north of Sevastopol.

15 The new Commander-in-Chief will choose his staff and will probably appoint his friends.

16 Lieutenant-General Sir James Simpson. Initially Chief of Staff and, after Lord Raglan's death, Army Commander until he was replaced by General Codrington in October 1855.

17 Secretary of State for War in Lord Palmerston's Government, 1855–58.

18 The bay west of Balaklava which the French used as a port to supply their Army.

19 Lieutenant-Colonel Yea's Soldier Servant.

20 See fn. 7.

21 St George's Monastery is situated on a cliff overlooking the Black Sea, west of Balaklava and west of the village of Kadikoi.

22 Pierce Egan (1772–1849) began publishing in 1824 in London, a weekly paper, which developed into a well-known sporting journal *Bell's Life*. In 1859 *Bell's Life* was incorporated into *The Sporting Life*.

23 Companion of the Order of the Bath. Normally only awarded to senior officers.

24 Paulet Somerset, ADC to his uncle Lord Raglan. Captain and then Lieutenant-Colonel, Coldstream Guards. In Goodlake's eyes this would have been an unmerited award to a non-fighting soldier.

25 See fn. 22.

26 Commissioned Coldstream Guards. Chief of Staff to General Codrington when he became Commander-in-Chief. .

27 Either the Valley of Baidar, west of Balaklava or the Valley of the Belbec, just north of Sevastopol.

28 Lieutenant-General Liprandi responsible for the Russian Army in the Tchernaya Valley.

29 Town on the isthmus which joins the Crimea to the mainland.

30 Canisters etc, grape-shot, cannon balls and bullets from rifles and muskets. See Military Terms.

31 Colonel C. Lewis, Grenadier Guards. He landed in the Crimea on 13 August 1855 and remained there till the end of the war. He acted as Battalion Commander of the 3rd Grenadiers for two months in August 1855, until Colonel Foley took over on 8 October 1855. Baron Stuart De Decies was raised to the peerage of the United Kingdom in May 1839. Born 8 June 1803. Lord Lieutenant of County Waterford and Colonel of the Waterford Militia.

32 River between the right of the British position at Inkerman and the Mackenzie Heights.

33 Chapter 3, The Development of Sharpshooting, pp. 58–9.

34 13 inch shells were fired from mortars. See Military Terms

35 Quartermaster-General.

36 See fn. 31.

37 See fn. 14.

38 Colonel Tom Steele, Coldstrean Guards, Military Secretary to Lord Raglan, later General Sir Thomas Steele. He rode with the Coldstream Guards in their attack on the Russians at the Alma.

39 See p.123, fn. 9 and Military Terms.

40 An inland sea to the east of the Crimea, with an entry to the Black Sea through the Straits of Kertch.

41 See fn. 29.

42 A town on the west coast of the Crimea, north-west of the Allied landing place at Kalamita Bay.

43 Possibly Peter Crawley. Although he mentions Captain Bouverie's horse, the animal must have belonged to someone else as he had been killed at Inkerman; all three were in 1st Coldstream.

Chapter Seven

The Letters –
Staff Officer

*Capture of Sevastopol and Road Building
September 1855 to January 1856*

Guards Brigade-Movements & Events

1855

5 September   Sixth and Last Bombardment on Sevastopol.

6 September   Malakoff and the Redan. The French Army captures the Malakoff. The British Army is unsuccessful in taking the Redan.

8–9 September The Fall of Sevastopol. The Russians evacuate the south side of Sevastopol, which the British and French Armies then occupy.

20 September   A parade is held for those who landed in the Crimea before 1 October 1854 to receive medals and clasps.

4 October   5th Draft arrives of 8 officers and 207 men

11 November   General Simpson resigns and Lieutenant-General Sir William Codrington is appointed Commander-in-Chief of the Army in the Crimea.

19 December   Goodlake reports that the Balaklava to Sevastopol road, which he and his workforce repaired, is now properly made up and can handle traffic.

28 December   Badges of the Battles of the Alma and Inkerman and of the Siege and Capture of Sevastopol are to be enscribed on the new Colours of the three Battalions of the Brigade of Guards that served in the Crimea.

Captain Gerald Goodlake

On 4 September 1855 he correctly guesses that the Russians will make a bolt out of the south side the moment we take the Malakoff. They did this by building a bridge of boats across the harbour and then evacuating their Army to the north side of the harbour.

After his criticism of the British Army's failure to take the Redan on 18 June, it is surprising that he makes no reference to the British Army's second failure to take the Redan on 8 September. This is almost certainly because the French captured the Malakoff on 8 September and the Russians evacuated the Redan that night, which the Allies then occupied.

In his letter of 1 September he mentions the successful naval action in the Baltic against the Russian forts there. On 9 August 1855 the British Baltic Fleet, commanded by Rear-Admiral Sir Richard Dundas, bombarded and destroyed the forts at Sveaborg, a fortified island off Helsinki in the Gulf of Finland, occupied by the Russians. He also mentions Vice-Admiral Sir Charles Napier, who was dismissed from being Baltic Fleet Commander in December 1854 for failing to operate effectively in the Baltic. He was replaced by Rear-Admiral Sir Richard Dundas.

On 1 September he is given another important job, as the Balaklava road was placed under his charge. He has 500 workers, and has to tell them off and set them to work. He says that this will be a very difficult job as the greater part of the road is clay-bottomed. With the enormous amount of traffic the stones sink down and the clay works up. He says that he will catch it if the road is impassable in winter

The completion of this road, before the onset of winter, would have had a very high priority. Thus, by 4 September he writes that he is in charge of 900 men who he puts to work. He says that they are the laziest brutes.

After the British Army's capture of the south side of Sevastopol on 9 September he writes, on 18 September, that this task has been extended to superintending the formation of a large road from

Balaklava to Sevastopol. He now had some 4000 men to set to work. He has little time available to write letters.

By 19 December he writes that he has more time now that the road is finished and hutting is nearly done. He says that, after being busy for so long, idleness comes over him. 'I sometimes sit for hours doing nothing but thinking'. On 10 January 1856 he is able to report that the road stands well and that one can canter along it from end to end.

William Doyne, a qualified engineer and the Superintendent of the Army Works Corps, was in charge of both railway maintenance and road building in the Crimea, and especially the construction of a new all-weather road from Balaklava to British Headquarters on the Heights. This had to be finished before the onset of the winter weather. The road building operation in the Crimea is described as follows:

> Doyne had an enormous force of troops at his disposal, released by the end of the fighting before Sevastopol. By the 6 October he had 6000 men, and two weeks later he was managing 8600 troops, 1000 Croat labourers as well as 1000 of his own men. They had laid the staggering quantity of 60,000 tons of road metal, when the six and a half miles of road between Balaklava and the British Headquarters was opened on the 10 November, seven week after construction started in earnest.[1]

It is also mentioned that Captain Henry Clifford VC, Rifle Brigade, was superintending 2000 troops in the construction of the road. Captain Goodlake was performing a similar function with his 4000 men. Both of them would have been carrying out William Doyne's instructions for constructing the new road.

On 11 November, General Simpson resigned as Commander-in-Chief and was replaced by Lieutenant-General Sir William Codrington.

He also mentions the arrival of Alexis Soyer, the Chef of the Reform Club, in the Crimea. He came out at his own expense but with the Government's approval, with his patent-efficient portable stove, to show how rations could be cooked. He was inventive and forward-looking. Battalions did not have centralized cooking and soldiers were given their rations to cook. Unfortunately there was no tradition of field cooking in the British Army as there was in the French Army.[2]

By 1 January 1856 Goodlake could boast that the British Army was now in a most luxurious state. The French Army was in a bad state and not much better off than we were last winter. The transports of the three armies were lamentable. The English Army was the best fed, the French Army was miserably fed.

The Letters

The date of one letter has been altered as the facts reported in it took place at a different time. The altered dates are shown in italics and the reasons for this alteration are shown below.

1855

1 September	Balaklava	Father
4 September	Balaklava	Mother
8 September	Balaklava	Father
18 September	Balaklava	Mother
17 November	Balaklava	Mother
19 December	Balaklava	Mother

1856

10 January	Balaklava	Father
15 January	Balaklava	Mother

Revision of Date of Letter.

The date of one letter is shown in italics. The date and the place where this letter was written and the events mentioned therein do not agree with the timetable shown above. After taking into account the facts within the letter, the original date has been amended as follows;

17 NOVEMBER 1854. The date of this letter has been changed from 1854 to *17 November 1855*. The letter mentions the return home of Lieutenant-General Airey to take up the position of Quartermaster-General of the Army at Horse Guards. He left the Crimea on 11 November 1855.

Balaklava
1 September 1855
My dearest Father,
I am so much obliged for your kindness to Larcombe. As for getting his medal when it arrives here I will do so, but I very much doubt the arrival of any of them.

Sveaborg is good news. Charley Napier must shut up; he is nobody now. Our Generals and Admirals have lost all their dash. I want to see the fleet go in and when the action is over, there ought not to be a mast standing; it would be the cheapest and quickest way of settling this business. The Fleet don't half fight.

The French think a great deal of the action on the Tchernaya. I had no idea the Russians lost so many, about 6000, the French put it at, but that is a throw over the mark.[3]

Your prophecy is wrong about the time of assault, like a good many of mine. There is a great deal too much apathy in our camp. The system of hut work would be very advantageous. I would make Heads of Departments responsible to have so much work done by such a time, instead of which, they go dragging on, now and then put on a spurt, but that is rare.

There was a tremendous explosion in the Mamelon three nights ago, which killed about eighty and wounded 200 etc, knocked the bottles off the shelves at Balaclava (six miles).

I think that the anniversary of the Alma will be the day. The French lose 100 a night, and two nights last week they lost eighty-nine and eighty-seven in the night attack alone. Farquharson[4] in the SF Guards was shot through the right hand, Colonel Walker[5] severe contusion on the head from a piece of shell last night. Harry Drummond[6] is going on well.

Much obliged for getting me warm clothing. Winter here is inevitable. I think that peace is certain this winter after Sevastopol is taken.

I have a great deal to do now, as the road is placed under my charge. I have 500 creatures; 200 Army Work Corps, and I have to tell them off and set them to work. It will be a very difficult job, and I am afraid of the result, the greater part of the road being clay-bottomed and so the stones sink down and the clay works up with the enormous amount of traffic. I intend to do my very best, as I shall catch it if the road is impassable in winter.

I must now conclude, my dearest Father. With my very best thanks for everything.

Believe me ever,
Your very affectionate son,
Gerald L.Goodlake

Balaklava
4 September 1855
My dearest Mother,

Last mail, I promised to write you a long letter. What to tell you I don't know, as one day here is just like any other. I am very much obliged for *Bell's Life* which I got all right.

The assault will not take place for some time, as the French are going to correct all their saps,[7] which will take three weeks at least. They are working, in a measured way, doing everything by miles; they will not hurry themselves in the least and must be reinforced. The great drawback in this is the immense loss of life in the time taken. I believe the Russians will make a bolt out of the south side, the moment we take the Malakoff.[8]

I will now give you a list of my winter things and will be much obliged if you will get them together. I waterproof (very long with hood), 1 pair of ditto trousers, 12 pairs of worsted socks, 6 flannel shirts (the flannel to be well shrunk), 1 shooting jacket, thick and warm, 1 trousers and waistcoat with arms, 6 pairs of dogskin gloves, 12 collars and a black scarf, 1 shooting cap, 1 pair of leggings, some sealing wax and a sponge. Baccy is very short. If you and the Gov.will get these things together for me and start them about October 1, I shall be much obliged. I will write to Bob about my uniform etc.

I don't think that you could have got all my letters, as there have been many subjects that I asked questions on and I have not had any answer. I did not get a letter for two mails. However I do get a great number and look forward to post day with the greatest pleasure.

Soyer[9] is out here, he has a small camp and his patent stove; he makes very good dishes out of the rations, but he can't do it in the short time the men have to do theirs in. I think the stoves are capital things when the camp is stationary, but would not do in the field. They are nothing more than a large cauldron with a fire underneath and a chimney up the opposite side; on the same principle as John Genter's copper for the dogs at old Wallery's, but a little more portable. The health of the army is good and better than it has ever been.

I have charge of over 900 men. I put them to work and that is about all; they are the laziest brutes, real <u>Brutes</u>, Mother, and some of them good enough to knock one down,

I saw Freddy Vane the other day and he looked the picture of health and impudence. I must now conclude, my dearest Mother, this stupid letter.

Believe me ever dearest Mother,
Your ever affectionate son,
G. L. Goodlake

Balaklava
8 September 1855

My dearest Father,

We go in at 12 today. I think that this time it will be all right; it depends entirely on the French being able to take the Malakoff. There has been a slight noise going on for the last 48 hours. We have burnt two ships and blown up a magazine or two. The 2nd Division storms, the Light Division supports, the 1st and 4th Divisions are in reserve; there are no half measures in this. The thing up to this period has been well managed, no one except the stable [headquarters] knew about it till 5 o'clock yesterday. The Sardinian 1st Division has come up to storm. I must conclude, as I am anxious to see the fall of the little tower, which has caused us so much trouble.

Poor Buckley[10] of the Scots Fusilier Guards was shot through the heart yesterday; you will remember him well, Sir Radnor's grandson, a better natured or pluckier soldier never lived. He will be a great loss to his regiment and to the Brigade.

God bless you my dearest Father and mother and all.

Ever,
Your affectionate son,
G. L. Goodlake

Balaklava
18 September 1855

My dearest Mother,

I have received your two letters and I am glad you are all well. I have not written to you for some time as I have hardly a moment to do anything, as I am superintending the formation of a large road from Balaklava to Sevastopol, having some 4,000 men to set to work.

How glad you must be at the fall of Sevastopol. There is hardly any news; there is talk of a move up the country on Wednesday, but I do not think they will go. Camp is so dull now; we have nothing to look forward to, except blowing up the docks and buildings etc. and making ourselves comfortable for the winter.

I will send the pony back at the first opportunity. I have spotted a

161

good strong horse at about £35, to do my duty with this winter. I have given Dunkellin's horse[11] away, as he was always on his head or his knees and could not stand my work. The fact is that I have hammered him to pieces. I did not like to sell him, so as I gave nothing for him and got some work out of him, I gave him away.

My staff things have not arrived yet. I want for nothing that I know of, besides what I have written for. Baccy I am very short of, and Price's candles[12] for the stove I am running short of. I live uncommonly well, one can get anything here one wants, though one has to pay for it.

I have amassed a roll of Russian leather, but I don't want it opened or touched until I come home: two boxes went by the Alma steamer.

Colonel McMurdo has recovered and expects Mrs McMurdo out here shortly.

There is the greatest possible grumbling at the French being allowed to pillage and that the English army has taken away what pillage the authorities can find; so one has to be careful now when one pillages, as the general orders are so strong on the subject. It is a great pity; it makes our army so dissatisfied.

I must now finish, my dearest Mother, with best love to all and every good wish and a longing to see you all again. I could never have moved an inch homeward until this place has fallen, but there is talk of leave this winter for three months and I hardly know what to say about it now. God bless you all, my beloved Mother.

Believe me ever,
Your very affectionate son
Gerald L. Goodlake

Balaklava
17 November 1855
My dearest Mother,

Many thanks for the beautiful pipe you sent me which arrived safely. You cannot think how it is admirably coveted by my friends. I have no doubt that it will colour well.

I have just got a load off my mind. My pony, Bobby, is on board The *Queen of the South* and starts this morning for England. I got Gordon of the Fusiliers to let him go as his horse. He has accompanied General Simpson home. Young Gordon,[13] behaved very badly; having promised to apply for a passage for him, he wrote to me and said that he had done so, and that it was all right. He did not do so; he never applied at all; he sneaked out of the Crimea, having told me a falsehood. But I went to Headquarters myself and told them that Gordon had two horses going home instead of one, got the warrant signed and put the pony on board ship. I give you my word that I am more than happy that the pony is on board, as the Gov.[14] and Bob seemed so anxious for him, than if I had received £500.

The Brevet [promotion list] is out but I have not seen it. Some fellows are badly treated. I must own that I think I am rather so. Pray don't make any application for it if you wish to oblige me. For myself I do not care, but I feel my family would have liked to have seen me be a major. But Mother, you may be quite happy, for one thing that I don't mind saying that you have a son who has never missed a day's duty, since he started from England, and my conduct has been approved by every officer I have been under, and all my friends have been disgusted about the way I have been treated. Mind you, don't ask again for the Brevet Majority.

General Airey starts tomorrow for England as Quartermaster-General there. He has been a good kind friend to me. I hope the Gov, when he goes to town, will thank him for all his kindness. Let me beg of you not to say a word about it again to anybody. I would sooner be reduced to a private soldier than any of my friends should ask for it.

Poor Colonel McMurdo[15] has been ill with brain fever; his wife is with him. I call often to enquire, but I have not seen him yet.

Give my love to all. Thank Tom's intended for her kind useful gift. Give the bridegroom my very best love and every good wish. What would I give to be present at his wedding. I must conclude, my beloved Mother.

> Ever your very affectionate son,
> Gerald. L. Goodlake

Balaklava
19 December 1855
My dearest Mother,

I blame myself for not having written to you for so long a time, but I know you will forgive me. I have had much more time lately, that is in the last week, as the road is finished and the hutting nearly done, but after being busy for so many months idleness came over me dreadfully. I can sit for hours at a time merely thinking not speaking; home, I can assure you, is generally uppermost in my thoughts.

I sent by Peter Crawley[16] a silver bracelet with an old Arabic inscription on it. It was taken from the wrist of an Arab chief who was found among the wounded when Sevastopol fell.

The cold today is intense, a fine frost; we have had some snow today. I am going with a cavalry and infantry escort to hunt arabas[17] among the hills and shall be away some days towards Baidar.[18]

The Land Transport Corps[19] was found to be in a terrible state by Colonel Wetherall[20] that there is hardly any transport allowed for the army.

I have in my hut a good fire, and the inkbottle standing on the hob when I dip my pen in it, before I can exhaust the ink, it is frozen. The *Sardinia* is in and I have got the tea, for which a thousand thanks, I long for my other things.

The new Quartermaster-General[21] is very kind and civil to me. Lady E. Pusey is his sister, is she not ?

Everyone here is conjecturing in his own mind what we shall do next year, some think Asia, others Kaffa.[22] I do not believe that anything is settled; there is ever a peace party. I do not belong to the latter. How I do wish that they could pitch into Austria.

I am learning surveying from one of the engineers of the Army Works Corps. I want a prismatic compass and a small box of instruments sent out as soon as possible; if I can manage this I will be much more fit for my place; I have application but not talent. I think I shall be able to manage it.

I hope by this time my pony, Bobby, will have arrived safely.

Life in camp is dull for the regimental officers. There are some Divisional amateur theatricals coming off soon. I am going, I believe, on New Years night, to one in the Light Division. I visited Sevastopol on Saturday, an interesting sight. They are working hard in the docks, preparing them for their destruction. I brought away several sticks and pieces of granite to make paperknives of. It is quite astonishing the stupendous amount of labour the Russians must have got through in the defences and public works of Sevastopol. They shelled us a good deal from the north side; about nine shells fell into the docks while I was there, killed two men and wounded three of the 18th. They have killed very few considering, since the town was taken.

With best love to the Gov. Bob, and relatives etc; wishing you and them all, a Happy Christmas.

Believe me ever,
Your very affectionate son,
G. L. Goodlake
P.S. I received your letter of the 24th and Bob's.

Balaklava
10 January 1856
My dearest Father,

I did not write to anyone last mail as I was making up the Fleeting books[23] etc. The Army, with the exception of the L.T.C. [Land Transport Corps], is hutted.

I must now thank you sincerely for my boxes, which I have received safely. Everything has arrived and is to my entire satisfaction. I am as well clothed and as well hutted here in my comforts and luxury as any man in the Army, and as even the most fastidious could wish to be.

One pipe with a bone mouthpiece, sent by Mackenzie for you, is certainly and without exception the best pipe I ever saw in my life. I look at it and I need not say others do too. Cook's things are very good; everything with the exception of the tightness of my shooting jacket; I freely forgive him. White's boots perfection, with the exception of the leather long boots being too tight across the knee joint. I have had them altered. Stilton cheeses very good etc. No one can be happier or better off than I am, except being at home. I am truly grateful and thankful. I am glad you like Bobby. I wish he had been a little larger.

You need not be afraid of my being caught by Cossacks in the least. I have only been out shooting twice. I asked for a day's leave and went into the country near Baidar with Astley, with some natives to beat. I was very fortunate, having killed two roe deer right and left, at eighty-five paces, running as hard as they could, with Blane's[24] small Wilkinson rifle.[25]

I was sorry that Nate and Blundell did not get a shot at deer. Blundell killed a hare.[26] We only saw one woodcock and one other hare. We had capital accommodation in a Tartar House,[27] and enjoyed ourselves much.

I have sent home some embroidered jackets and scarves presented to me by the Pasha. I had an unfortunate accident. My interpreter, whom I took with me to carry Sir James Dunlop's gun, which he kindly lent me, had a fall owing to the slippery nature of the ground and broke it short at the stock. I have sent it home and should be much obliged if you would have it restocked for me and send it to the Guards Club, for Sir James Dunlop.[28] The rammer is broken and will require mending. Poor little man, I hear he has lost £250 a year, as his agent has bolted.

I see by your last letter that you are directing my letters to Balaklava. Please continue to direct to Headquarters as usual, as I belong there although I live at Balaklava.

The road stands well; one can canter from end to end without a single rut.

Now a word about the war. You will know what we are going to do sooner than we shall out here. My own idea is that about 20 March, Colin Campbell[29] will start either for Asia (it depends so much on Omar Pasha) or will act either from Kaffa[30] or Kertch and work this Crimean Army. I believe Kars[31] fell in consequences of the jealousies of Omar Pasha, not caring to relieve it in time. He thinks he was slighted and had not the weight he thought he ought to have when here last summer. I am not one of his greatest admirers, I cannot forget that when he was at Euphrates for many months last summer during the siege, with 4,500 Turks, cavalry etc., he never cut off one single convoy; after him I blame the authorities at home for not sending sooner to relieve the place

You cannot blame our Commanders-in-Chief, at least the English ones, now-a-days for not doing anything or undertaking expeditions, as they have become little better than chief clerks to the Secretary-at-War. That electric telegraph,[32] what good has it done us what harm ??? Panmure[33] sends out insulting rubbishing idiotic messages, which are ludicrous and ridiculous. I don't believe that Codrington could send 500 men anywhere without being obliged to telegraph home to know if he might do so.

The [Peace] Commissioners are to be ready on 9 March. You will see, I think, that what I predicted in October last year will come off. I mean that the Russians will maintain their position on the Mackenzie Heights[34] and north side, and it will take us all we know to make them evacuate the Crimea.

The British Army is in the most luxurious state and yet there are grumblers. D----- them, lazy idle beggars, who think that a fatigue or a guard is a bore.

The French army is in a very bad state. I don't think that they are much better off than last winter. Their army has been drained of 20,000 of their best soldiers, owing to the sagacity of the Emperor Napoleon. He, having drafted all the best men in the French Army into the Guards, which he now has around him and can depend on them for a good stock of business.

The transports of the three armies are lamentable. The English Army is the best fed, as it is, the French are miserably fed. I do not expect to move from here for months and months myself. Sir Colin will go somewhere with four Divisions and cavalry. We cannot move the whole army. I do not think that the French have 8,000 more fighting men than we have; they are great humbugs, you can never get to the truth, and a good job too, I mean for the French Army.

You need not be alarmed about the cold and weather and my being frostbitten. I never remember so mild a winter as this and it is like last year in England, with the exception of now and then one day or so when the cold is intense.

People like writing home and lying about the hardships and rubbish, nothing of the sort. I can assure you that, if half the people knew how happy and comfortable we are, they would be enraged beyond measure.

My horses are all well. I see few others in such condition. Bandages, soft socks and brushes have all arrived. I am much obliged.

I will call on Nightingale[35] and see him. I have not met him before. The Highlanders are rather out of my line of business, but I can idle now, as no one has much to do. I still get up at seven. I do not think that I could lie in bed of a morning now. I wake generally at half-past five.

Nothing could be more civil than our new Quartermaster-General. I expect to be attached to him next spring to undertake and see special orders carried out. I have an idea that way, as I often have rides with him inspecting places all round the country. I am going with him next week to pilot him round the French outposts.

I am going to write to Bob this mail about a lot of little things, loot etc. Anything in the world that you wish to have, I will just take it at once; a lot is intended for you, but I think it would be better to wait and see everything together and then take your choice.

I must now conclude, my dearest Father, hoping that you will enjoy yourself in London and get a good moor in Scotland next year and with love and sincere gratitude for all your kindness to me.

> Believe me,
> Your very affectionate son,
> G. L. Goodlake.

Balaklava
15 January 1856

My dearest Mother,

I am afraid you must be angry with me for not having written to you for such a long time. I must first begin by thanking you a thousand times for all you have sent me, especially the leather regimental breeches, which are much admired and greatly appreciated. Everything has come in good order, with the exception of the candles, which I told you about in a former letter.

You will, I know, be happy to hear that I have everything I can wish for, clothes, plenty to eat, drink, smoke, horses, servants, and in the greatest luxury, and I have to thank you, Mother, for the greatest part of it, which I do most sincerely.

There is nothing whatever going on now. Paper chases take place twice a week now. I have never been out, as I don't care about trifling with my horseflesh, which is particularly good, I am pleased to say at present. There is also a theatre at the 4th Division where very good acting goes on. I have been once, but it is a long way from Balaclava and I have to be at work by half-past seven. I am going tomorrow to Baidar, about some more arabas, as we find them very useful now. The Army Works Corps has shut up, so there is a report that the Russians mean an attack, but I do not think it is likely. The French officers have been confined to camp for several days past.

The weather here is very changeable, from frost and snow we had a rapid thaw, then a deluge of rain with quite a muggy heat; today it has changed in an hour to a very sharp frost with a cold N.E. wind; it is just one of these sort of days that frost bite people if they are not prepared, but on the whole with the exception of these sort of particularly intense cold days, I do not think the weather here is so cold as it is in England.

I have sent home a Tartan embroidered cloth, which I intend for you, my dearest Mother. I must now conclude as I am going to write to my dearest Bob. With best love to Gov. etc, and thanking you again and again for all you have sent me out.

Believe me ever,

Your very affectionate son,

G. L. Goodlake

Notes

1 *The Grand Crimean Central Railway.* p.123, Brian Cooke.
2 *The Destruction of Lord Raglan*, pp.264–5, C.Hibbert.
3 See pp. 142–4. Goodlake originally estimated the Russian killed and wounded to have been 2000.
4 Captain and Lieutenant-Colonel James Farquharson, Scots Fusilier Guards.
5 Colonel Edward Forrestier Walker, Commanding Officer, 1st Scots

Fusilier Guards; evacuated to England after being wounded in November 1854. He returned to the Crimea on 29 October 1855.

6 Captain Hugh Drummond, Adjutant, 1st Scots Fusilier Guards, was killed in action in August 1855. Lieutenant and Captain Hon R. Drummond, Coldstream Guards, died of disease on 2 October 1854.

7 A narrow trench dug for protection against enemy fire. See Military Terms

8 The defensive tower. See p.98.

9 See fn. 2.

10 Captain and Lieutenant D.F. Buckley, Scots Fusilier Guards, was killed in action in an advanced sap in front of the Redan on 7 September 1855. Sergeant James Craig and Drummer Smith then went to search for him, but found he was dead. They brought in his body under murderous fire and for this act of gallantry each received the Victoria Cross. *The Scots Guards 1642–1914*, Vol II, p.111, Major-General Sir F. Maurice.

11 In his letter of 23 April 1855, Goodlake explains that the Colonel had ordered that Lord Dunkellin's mangy horse should be shot. He managed to persuade the Colonel to allow him to attempt to cure it, which he must have done, but not completely.

12 See Military Terms, Price's candles.

13 Captain R.H.Gordon served with the 38th Regiment throughout the Eastern Campaign, including the battles of Alma and Inkerman and the siege of Sevastopol. He commanded the party of the 38th which was engaged in repulsing the sortie on 20 December, for which he was honourably mentioned by Lord Raglan and promoted into the Coldstream Guards. He then sold this commission and exchanged into the 42nd Regiment. *Hart's Army List 1860*, pp. 255–6.

14 He refers to his father.

15 Director-General Land Transport Corps, later Commandant Military Train.

16 Brevet Major, Coldstream Guards. Promoted for gallantry at Inkerman.

17 Carts

18 A town on the Woronzoff Road, west of Balaklava.

19 Responsible for transporting and supplying the Army with food and materials. See Military Terms.

20 Colonel Sir Edward Wetherall, DAQMG Turkish Contingent at Kertch, until the fall of Sevastopol and thereafter Director-General of the Land Transport Corps.

21 Major-General the Hon Percy Herbert, AQMG, 2nd Division in the

Crimea. From November 1955 he replaced General Airey as Quartermaster-General.

22 Port on the Gulf of Kaffa on the Black Sea which is on the Kaffa/Kertch peninsula about 100 miles east of Sevastopol.

23 Despite making enquiries about this term from the Museum of the Royal Logistics Corps, it has been impossible to find out the meaning of this word. This must therefore be a misspelling It is far more likely to be Hutting Books, giving details of the distribution of huts to each regiment, battalion or military unit.

24 Lieutenant and Captain S.J.Blane, Scots Fusilier Guards; Assistant Engineer in charge of Croatian labourers.

25 From 1804 James Wilkinson took over his father-in-law's gunsmith business. His son Henry expanded the business to include sword-making. Up to the Great War, they remained noted gunmakers, while also being swordsmiths. See Military Terms.

26 Nate and Blundell have not been identified.

27 A house of timber construction, with shutters, surrounded by an open veranda with a tiled roof; the veranda posts might have been ornately carved with Islamic designs. Inside there would be carpets on the walls and not on the floors. The furniture would be mainly divans, low tables and no chairs.

28 See p.43, fn. 9.

29 Major-General Sir Colin Campbell, commanding Highland Brigade 1st Division; then Commander, Highland Division and finally Corps Commander.

30 See fn. 22..

31 A town in Asia Minor, defended by the Turkish Army, which was later taken by the Russians.

32 In April 1855 a telegraph line was laid from the Monastery of St. George near Balaklava to Cape Kalagria 30 miles north of Varna and then to Vienna, from where messages were routed to London.

33 See p.147, fn. 17.

34 The hills above the Tchernaya River, named after a Scot who served as an Admiral in the Russian Navy.

35 Arthur C. Nightingale, Lieutenant, 93rd Foot, Sutherland Highlanders.

Chapter Eight

The Letters

Peace and the Army's Return Home.
January to May 1856

Guards Brigade-Movements & Events

1856

16 January   Russia accepts the Austrian Government's suggested terms for peace.

1 March   6th and last draft arrives of 8 officers and 263 men.

30 March   Peace of Paris signed, ending the War.

2 April   An Armistice is declared. Peace terms are communicated to the several armies engaged in the war.

17 April   Review of British and French Armies by the Russian General Staff.

3 June   3rd Grenadiers embark at Kamiesch Bay in HMS *St Jeanne d' Arc*.

4 June   1st Coldstream embark at Kamiesch Bay in HMS *Agamemnon*.

6 June   Lord Rokeby, Commander of the 1st Division, left the Crimea accompanied by Captain Goodlake.

11 June   1st Scots Fusilier Guards embarks at Kasatch in the *Princess Royal*.

28 June	1st Coldstream disembark at Spithead and travel by train to Aldershot Camp.
1 July	3rd Grenadiers disembark at Portsmouth and travel by train to Aldershot Camp.
4 July	1st Scots Fusilier Guards disembark at Portsmouth and travel by train to Aldershot Camp.

Foreign Service: 2 years and 126 days. [856 days].[1]

Malta	48 days.
Scutari	45 days.
Bulgaria	75 days.
Crimea	627 days
At Sea	61 days.

8 July	Windsor Castle Parade. The Guards Brigade parades before HM Queen Victoria. A representative body of officers & men hear Her Majesty's address.
9 July	Hyde Park Parade-The Guards Brigade make its public entry into London to join the other four Guards Battalions to march past Her Majesty and to give the Royal Salute.

1857

26 June	Victoria Cross Investiture in Hyde Park for officers and men awarded the Victoria Cross. Her Majesty Queen Victoria awards this medal to all the recipients, including Major Goodlake.

Peace

On 16 January the Russians accepted the Austrian Government's Peace Proposals and on 30 March 1856 the Treaty of Paris was signed ending the War. From 2 April 1856 there was an Armistice in the Crimea.

In the final outcome, however, the war had achieved its objectives:

In any case in 1856, Russia had been decisively beaten and its military power revealed as a sham. In the short run, the threat to

India had been neutralised and in the longer term the Royal Navy still controlled the Mediterranean. In that these limited objectives had been met, for Britain at least, the outcome of the Crimean War was more satisfactory than anyone in the country could have dared to hope at its outset.[2]

Despite the disorganized state of our Army, it was clear that we only won because of the amazing bravery of our soldiers, fighting against superior odds, and because we had made fewer mistakes in the campaign than the Russians. The Press and the British Public held the government responsible for the unnecessary deaths of brave men from disease and from the ineffective organization of the Army's logistical, medical and hospital services.

Charities had appealed successfully for funds to supply the Army with food and clothing to make up for the failure of the Commissariat and the Treasury to provide these necessaries. The Prime Minister, Lord Aberdeen, and the Secretary of State for War, the Duke of Newcastle, had been driven from office in 1855. Florence Nightingale, the much-revered heroine of Scutari, throughout her long life, reminded the public of the debt that the country owed to the soldiers of the Crimean War.

Casualties[3]

The cost in casualties was, however, high as the table in the Appendix for the 1st Battalion Coldstream Guards shows, which lists the figures for effective strength and casualties. Of the 2060 NCOs and rank and file who served in the Crimean War 81 (3.9 %) were killed in action, 54 (2.6 %) died of wounds and 564 (27.6 %) from disease, totalling 699 (33.9 %). If the total figure of 111 of those invalided and discharged is added to those who died, total losses reach 810 (39.3%).

The staggering figure of 2785 NCOs and privates, that is 35.2 % of the total force, were admitted to hospital. The same figure for the officers was 17 (18.7 %).

Out of the 92 officers, who served in the war, 9 died in action, 1 from wounds and 3 from disease, making a total of 13 (14.1 %). The total loss in officers, including the 7 invalided, was 20 (22.0%). The figure of officers who died in action or from wounds, including the 8 officers who died at Inkerman, was 10 (10.9%) as against 135 (6.5%) for the NCOs and privates.

The wounded were 243 NCOs and privates (11.8 %) and 7 officers.

The Regimental System

The one strength the British possessed was the regimental system, whereby each regiment had a pride in its name and a determination that their behaviour on the field of battle would at the least equal their successes and honours won in the Peninsular and Waterloo campaigns and would thus add to their glory. Gradually throughout the campaign, the various regiments adapted to the conditions and by the end of the war the conditions in the camps, the feeding, clothing, hygiene and medical services were all superior to those in the French Army. By the second winter Florence Nightingale was very impressed by the standards of hygiene in the camps of the Guards and the Highlanders.

Despite the chaotic state of the Army at the beginning of the war, the regimental system did not let the country down. Let Lieutenant-Colonel Ross-of- Bladensburg's words provide the epitaph for the brave men who served throughout the horrors of this campaign:

> The successes gained were not due to the skill of the Government, which directed the struggle, On the contrary, our statesmanship had little or no claim upon our regard on this occasion. For, the military achievements, under disastrous conditions, were justly a cause of pride to our country, and were worthy of the best traditions of a glorious past. These achievements were solely brought about by that indomitable bravery, discipline and power of endurance that have ever characterized our soldiers, as well as by the admirable system, which made British regimental officers and men second to none that existed, at that time, in any other European army. To the rank and file, and to those who led them in the field, is all the merit to be ascribed, and not to any other body of Englishmen.[4]

Captain Gerald Goodlake

On 10 and 15 January 1856 he writes proudly, 'My horses are all well. I see few others in that condition. There are paper-chases twice a week now, but I don't go out as I don't care about trifling with my horse-flesh, which is particularly good.'

On 16 April he backs his cob 'The Toy' to win in a steeplechase. He says that Turkish and Arab ponies are no good and English horses such as 'The Toy', his cob, would lick their heads off. Everyone roars with laughter and when 'The Toy' appeared the crowd of both British and Russian officers roar, 'Where is his cart, where is his wagon?' To their mortification and astonishment Toy won. The prize was a cup, made out of a Russian grenade, and £35.

On 15 January 1856 he writes that he has everything he could wish for, clothes, plenty to eat, drink, smoke, horses, servants and that he is in the greatest luxury. He says that he has to thank his mother for the greatest part of it.

On 15 February 1856 he proudly tells his parents that the present Quartermaster General from Headquarters [Brevet Colonel Percy Herbert] complimented him on the hutting and said that he could, if he wished, go and live in idleness in Balaklava for a month. He does not wish to do this, but instead is learning surveying, under Mr Wakefield, who made the public roads in Australia.[5]

In his last letter from the Crimea in May 1856 he says he is now competent to survey any wood, county or river sufficiently for military purposes and that he has surveyed his own establishment.[6]

In this letter he also says that he is wonderfully well but that he thinks his family will say that he looks rather old. His beard is not a good one, as it comes out very much now. He says that he will not trim it off until they have had one sight of it.

He refers, too, to an incident involving HMS *Stromboli*, a paddle gunboat, of shallow draught, with six guns. On 3 June 1855, after the capture of Kertch, it bombarded Russian coastal traffic in the Sea of Azov and thus cut off Russian supplies coming from that area and from the mainland. Taganrog, situated to the north east of the Sea of Azov, near the estuary of the River Don, was a major supply base where stores were stacked on the beach, but the port could only be approached through shoals.

Commander Cowper Coles, who commanded *Stromboli*, had a raft constructed which could pass over the shoals, carrying a 42-cwt gun. Lieutenant Horton, of *Ardent*, equipped his pinnace with a 32-pounder to bombard the Russians. There was also a division of light boats, carrying rockets and one gun. The British and French forces destroyed all the stores, vessels and Government buildings at Taganrog without loss of any of their men or vessels.[7]

On 4 June 1856 the 1st Battalion Coldstream Guards embarked at Kamiesh Bay and sailed for England in HMS *Agamemnon*, arriving at Spithead on the 28 June. It then travelled by train to Aldershot Camp.

On 8 July the Guards Brigade paraded at Windsor before HM the Queen. On the following day, the Guards Brigade made its public entry into London to join the other four Guards battalions to march past Her Majesty and to give the Royal Salute.

On 26 June 1857 Major Goodlake received his Victoria Cross from HM The Queen at the First Victoria Cross Parade in Hyde Park.

Personality

It is interesting to see him gaining confidence during the campaign, enjoying taking his own decisions and gradually becoming a seasoned campaigner. He certainly had very strong and affectionate relations with his family. He was careful to tell his father that in certain matters relating to promotion, he must do what he thinks is best, no doubt because his father was paying the Regulation Fee. He said however that if his father did complain to Regimental Headquarters about his failure to be promoted, he would be so ashamed that he might leave the Army.

He was very caring towards his mother, who he was sure organized all his food and clothes parcels and he sent her various presents, including a diamond ring and some satin towels.

His style of living was very Spartan; he ate little, only drank lemon and water and took strong exercise, which included shooting quail and hares so as to vary their very monotonous diet.

He was very astute and well organized. When he found out that he would not be allowed a groom in the Crimea, before anyone else, he asked the battalion doctor if he could share his groom. He was certainly very enterprising in building a hut for himself, before anyone else in the Army was hutted, and also in arranging for the Quartermaster, with his ability to supply most needs, to live with him. In his words, this was being 'early awake'.

His skills as a negotiator were well developed, as he enjoyed buying and selling horses. He was quite knowledgeable about looking after them and curing them from disease and was perhaps a bit of a horse-coper.

He was very brave, tough and resolute and enjoyed dangerous situations such as sharpshooting. He was very quick to canter down to the Tchernaya Valley to take part in the battle between the French and the Russians, and enjoyed shooting at the Russians at close range, and having his blue coat cut by bullets He was very self-assured in telling the French general, who said that he ought not to have been there, that he would always be welcome at any fight the British Army had with the Russians. Furthermore they would not arrest him if he took part.

He was resolute and was quite prepared to remain in the Crimea till Sevastopol was taken, and he was furious with those who wanted peace without honour.

His attitude over staff appointments is illuminating. He was only interested in jobs which give him authority and was not interested in ADC jobs, where one was doing what one was told. He justified his taking the DAQMG position as it gave him authority, allowed him to make decisions, to formulate plans and to implement them. He was happy to set himself objectives and to be judged on achieving them. He liked being given authority and was a risk taker,

He was a leader with good people-handling and management skills, who led by example. He was well able to manage large groups of people, military, civil and foreign, set them objectives, monitor their work and persuade them to achieve these objectives. His work in successfully organizing the hutting of the Army and the building of roads, which needed a work force of up to 4000 men, was impressive, as he had no previous experience of this type of work. Even though he would have certainly had good technical advisors from the Engineers and no doubt good non-commissioned officers, there was the requirement to set to work teams of navvies, to manage them and to ensure that they met the targets set, both for the amount of work completed and for the quality of that work.

The experiences of all the soldiers who had gone to war for the first time were well summed up by Colonel Hamley:[8]

So ended, too, our first campaign. Hitherto I, and doubtless most others my contemporaries, had viewed in a kind of epic light the men of Wellington's campaigns, beside whose rich and stirring youth ours seemed pale and empty. Now we, too, had passed behind the scenes; we, too, had been initiated into the jumble of glory and calamity, war, and had been acting history. In one step we had passed from civilisation and luxury, such as

177

our fathers knew not, to a campaign of uncommon privation.

We, too, knew of the marshalling of hosts, the licensed devastation, the ghastly burden of the battlefield, and the sensation of fronting death; and, henceforth, the pages of military history, hitherto somewhat dim and oracular, were for us illuminated by the red light of experience.

The Letters

1856

15 February	Balaklava	Father
7 April	Balaklava	Mother
16 April	Balaklava	Father
14 May	Balaklava	Mother
End May	Balaklava	– —

Balaklava
15 February 1856
My dearest Father,

I sit down to write this letter but what to put in it, except to thank you for all you have sent me and are going to send, I don't know. Peace, as at home, is the topic here.

Everybody is well, comfortable, in good spirits and ready for everything. I believe the continuance of the war would please the majority. There are two parties, the peace and the war, and they amuse themselves concocting shaves, and a great deal of chaff goes on, sometimes bitter, but most often good-natured. Theatricals seem the order of the evening. I am going on Monday to dine, sleep and see the performance of the 23rd Foot R.W.F.[Royal Welch Fusiliers] at the hospital.

I, as I told you some time ago, have finished the hutting and was complimented by the present Quartermaster-General, who told me I might go and live in idleness at Balaklava for a month, as he said he was sure I wanted rest, which I do not.

But I was very glad of the opportunity, as I am learning surveying with a very good kind friend, Mr Wakefield,[9] who made the public roads in Australia. He is the chief of the Butcher and Baker Corps, attached to the Commissariat. He is one of the best-informed men I have met. I hope in a mail or two to send you properly surveyed a plan of my establishment in the Crimea, and which I believe I may say is second to none in the Crimea, General's not excepted.

I enclose a copy of a poem written by Arthur Hardinge, who is a great friend of mine, on Lord Winchester's marriage. It is very clever.

Should peace be established, I will be one of the last to come home, as I will have to superintend the embarkation of stores, troops etc, this, bore as it is, I do not in the least grudge, as I must take the rough with the smooth.

My horses are well. I had a pointer from Kertch, given me yesterday, which I will try to bring home, or send. He is a good shaped young dog, a little sleek across the loins, but otherwise well made.

A man of the 77th was hung today or is to be hung in a day or two for killing a man. If they had hung a few more it would have been advantageous for the army.

Many thanks for the papers, which I get pretty regularly on the whole. I am going to write to Bob a business letter. With best love to Mother and with every good wish and many thanks for all you have done for my welfare.

>Believe me,
>Your affectionate son,
>Gerald L. Goodlake.

Balaklava
7 April 1856

My dearest Mother

I think it is your turn by several letters for one now, not that I have a word to say.

Peace has been known some time here. The place is swarming with Russian officers, and men's passes are to be given out by the Commander-in-Chief of both armies. I suppose I will visit like the rest, Simferopol and Bachesonai[10] etc.

I long to see you again, I shall be very glad to come home for that, but the war being over is a sad sore blow for me; one more year for me would have done. I must not, I suppose, be selfish; I have got through it all and ought to be satisfied, but I cannot feel so, the war has not done me much good. I have made the acquaintance of young Nightingale[11] and Dr Roebuck, 39th Regiment.

Not a word is known who is to go away first. I think, myself, the Sardinians and then the Guards. I shall not be able to go with them, I could of course resign, but it would not be the thing, and therefore I shall not do so. I shall finish the embarkation of my Brigade, and then I do not expect to be home before July or August. I hope Sir

James Dunlop's gun will turn up. There are some satin towels embroidered for you in the box, they went in the *Oneida*. You received one box, for it contained blankets and flags, it went in the same ship, a long thin box *comme ca*.

Marshal Pélissier has given £60 to be run for. I shall run my mare Bathsheba. I got £10 in money last races. I may enter one for the pony race. Horses are worth nothing, I shall be obliged to bring them home. The dear old Cob is quite well, I nearly live on him by day, nothing can trot near him in the Crimea.

I have sent home a Russian gun, which must be kept dark, also a gravestone of beautiful marble; also two Russian shells, ditto lots of shells and Malakoff roses, which I hope you will soon receive, the latter for you, particularly for you.

I am glad old Webb [Groom] likes Bobby, as he is a good judge, and that he carries the Gov. well in the Park.

I am so grieved to hear about poor old Cook; everyone I have told feels the same for him. I had great respect for him. I never saw a better style of tradesman. There are not many of his class left, I fear. The place swarms with Travelling Gentlemen [Civilian Visitors]. I hear that there are crowds at Malta and Constantinople. I am sorry Harry Vane never came out. It is not too late now; he would have seen five armies equipped and all but at war and as well, Constantinople, Kursk, Bachmut,[12] Sevastopol; he could do it all in two months and never regret it.

You must remember me to all my friends and tell Bob to do so. I suppose the London Season has hardly commenced.

When you write again just let Bob find out what clothes I have that are fit to wear, shirts, boots, socks, trousers, and to make a sort of inventory. I expect I will have to get a great many new things. The mails have been very irregular, five to six days behind time. I have not always got my papers lately.

I must now conclude, my dearest Mother, this very stupid epistle. My spirits not being very high. With best love to the Gov., Bob etc.
        Believe me,
                Your very affectionate son,
                  G. L. Goodlake

Balaklava
16 April 1856
My dearest Father,

The *Peninsular* has been in harbour for the last three days, but has not yet landed her cargo. I will let you know the moment I get my box.

Yesterday there were some French races. I send a programme, a good day's sport. You will see from the bill of fare all about them, Grand Dukes and I don't know how many Russian big-wigs besides. The first race was won by Paddy, a bay, belonging to Bertie Taylor [not identified]; his horse won last time. Rose, my mare, was nowhere, bad start and could not get up to her competitors.

I was dining with a lot of fellows at the front, and I stated that I did not believe the Turkish or Arab ponies were very good, they spurted along, but if anything English was put against them they would be licked. I said I firmly believed my dear old Cob would lick their heads off. Everybody roared, so I quietly entered him for the 14.2 steeple-chase, under the name of 'Toy', my favourite plaything. When he went into the square, which was railed off in front of the grandstand, everyone roared with laughter, Russian, French and English. I was told I was making a fool of myself before everybody, and the crowd commenced chaffing about 'Where is his cart? Where was his waggon?' Off they started, he never was baulked and to the mortification and astonishment of the gaping idiots around, my beloved 'Toy' came in first, hard held and would have taken the hurdles at the off point, and he is no worse. The stakes are worth £34 and a very handsome cup made out of a Russian hand grenade with an inscription on it. It caused the greatest laughter and amusement.

With best love to Mother, Bob and Olive, and with many thanks for the 'Peninsular' box.

Believe me ever,
Your very affectionate son,
G. L. Goodlake

Balaklava
14 May 1856
My dearest Mother

I am so much obliged for all the things that you have sent me. I have just seen Colonel Napier[13] who said he saw you. I hope you saw the letter from Colonel McMurdo;[14] he has been so kind and civil.

Never mind, Mother, about the Brevet Major. I received a message

181

from the Duke of Cambridge.[15] I feel confident that everything that has been done that can be done. The Colonel is quite well. I was with him today and he is going to have the Cob, himself and myself done in a photograph for you. We will try and get it done tomorrow.

Beloved Bob was good enough to send me a knife, fork and spoon, but they are rather too slight for rough work, so could you send me a leather roll of knife, fork and spoon, three of each. The Gov. gave me one when I started last year.

You need not direct to me naming my official capacity, as it may not last long and until I am regularly put in that position (I mean for a continuance). I do not mean to wear staff uniform or anything of that sort. I am on special duty for the present.

It is very late so I must now conclude this short epistle. With best love and a thousand thanks.

> Believe me ever,
> Your very affectionate son,
> G. L. Goodlake.

P.S. Astley[16] begs to be remembered and has just come in and made me go back with him to look at a horse that is very ill.

Balaklava
About the end of May 1856

There is to be a review of the British Army tomorrow. We shall turn out 27,000 bayonets, and a good show of Artillery, Lancers, etc, will be present.

Do you know Lord Methuen?[17] He sleeps *chez moi* tomorrow. He commands the militia at Corfu.

I have finished a plan of my domain, and am happy to say I am able to survey any wood, country or river sufficiently for military purposes. The compass is not a good one.

General Windham, Colonel Morris, A.Harding,[18] St George Foley[19] dine with me.

I am wonderfully well, though I daresay you will say that I look very old. My beard is not a very good one. It comes out very much now. I shall not trim it off until you have had one sight.

I am afraid there is not the slightest chance of procuring a rifle for Bathurst.[20] You cannot buy one, and almost anything that has been taken has gone home long ago. I have sent a magnificent block of marble and a Russian cannon by the *Chester* transport to Dalgety [Shipping Agents]. I am also sending home some shell hand grenades, grape and canister, also four Russian 13 inch shells, also specimens of Balaclava marble, Malakoff roses and bulbs.

I got the £10 second prize money for the last race, as 'Muster Role' was disqualified. Then came a really serious business. It was a very windy day, very hot and dusty. Blundell rode for me.

There was a review of 25,000 Russians on the Mackenzie Heights at night. Well, they looked, healthy, well dressed and clean. A peculiar smell they had. There are parties going all over the Crimea, Bessarabia, Simferopol, Alma, Yalta etc.

I have not had a moment to myself lately, we are all so busy at Balaklava. About 6,000 Sardines embarked today. I expect the Guards to go the latter end of next week. I shall be last with the others of the Independent Brigades. I cannot go home with my Regiment, as I should very much like to do, people say such things nowadays. If I went, some would say: 'Look at that Guardsman, the moment he has anything to do off he goes and cuts the Staff'. I have never, to my knowledge, given anybody a chance of a remark on my not doing my duty, and will not now! It will only be for a couple of months or so.

There has been the deuce of a row at Kazatch[21] about a French piquet shooting some of our men who were out rat hunting. The *Stromboli*[22] sent off some marines to see what was the matter. They shot the staff adjutant's horse, killed the marine left with the butt ends of their muskets and shot the officer, and a report has just reached me that he is dead. The marines took the piquet and their arms without firing a shot. The French Admiral said he was sorry but French sailors were regular <u>devils</u> when they smelt powder (their own I suppose). There will be some hanging, I hope, in this matter.

★ ★ ★ ★ ★ ★ ★ ★

Here the letters abruptly end. – Margaret Goodlake

[Editor's Note:Index According to Regimental Records, Captain Goodlake left the Crimea in the same boat as Lieutenant-General Lord Rokeby, who commanded the 1st Division, on 6 June 1856. The Grenadier Guards left on 3 June, the Coldstream Guards on 4 June and the Scots Fusilier Guards on 11 June 1856.

Captain Goodlake is listed in the Adjutant-General's Return on Officers in the Army Crimea, dated 17 March 1857, as Deputy Assistant Quartermaster General at 1st Division, despite the fact that he was working for the Quartermaster-General at Headquarters.

Notes

1 *The Coldstream Guards in the Crimea*, p.285, Lieutenant-Colonel Ross-of-Bladensburg

2 *Crimea*, p.501,Trevor Royle.

3 *The Coldstream Guards in the Crimea*, pp. 285–7, Lieutenant-Colonel Ross-of-Bladensburg.

4 Ibid, pp. 295–6.

5 Commissary-General William Henry Drake writes in his letters that he met Mr Wakefield, who had been appointed Army Works Corps Superintendent Commissariat Branch on 2 December 1854. Each formation had a Commissariat Branch attached to them to organize supplies.

6 Military drawing was taught at Sandhurst, as before the existence of photography and before the availability of accurate maps, drawing was a necessary skill for an officer to possess. He could be required to reconnoitre an area and prepare maps and topographical drawings of enemy positions and other natural features that his general had to take into account when deciding on a line of advance.

7 *Invasion of the Crimea*, Vol.VIII, pp. 67–72, Kinglake. See also *The Crimean War,* plate 16, R.L.V.ffrench Blake, which has a picture from the *Illustrated London News*, showing both the raft and the gig, equipped with a rocket launcher.

8 *The Story of the Campaigns of Sebastopol*, p.325, Lieutenant-Colonel E. Bruce Hamley RA, William Blackwood, London. Reprinted 2003 by the Naval & Military Press.

9 See fn. 5.

10 Simferopol, a major town in the Crimea, north-east of Sevastopol and east of Kalamita Bay. Bachesonai, Bakhchi Serai, a town on the Simferopol to Balaclava road.

11 See p.164, fn. 35.

12 Kursk: a town in Russia. Bachmut: There is no town of this name in the Crimea. It is almost certainly Bakhchi Serai, which was the Russian headquarters. The ancient Palace of the Khans is there.

13 Brevet Lieutenant-Colonel W.E.Napier, Assistant Quartermaster General and Assistant Director, Land Transport Corps.

14 Director, Land Transport Corps.

15 Lord Hardinge resigned as Commander-in-Chief on 9 July 1856, after suffering a stroke. On 13 July 1856 the Duke of Cambridge was appointed Commander-in-Chief in his place.

16 See p.42, fn. 8.

17 Lord Methuen, born 1779, Member of Parliament for Wiltshire in several parliaments. Colonel of the Wiltshire Militia. Created a Baron in July 1838.

18 Chief of Staff to General Codrington. Colonel C.H. Morris, Royal Artillery, Assistant Adjutant-General at Headquarters and attached to General Windham. Lieutenant-Colonel Hon Arthur Hardinge, see p.124, fn. 3.

19 Colonel Hon St George Foley CB, The Queen's Assistant-Commissioner at the Headquarters of the French Army in the Crimea from the first landing to the end of the war.

20 See p.44, fn. 37.

21 The Royal Navy's anchorage.

22 *HMS Stromboli*, a paddle gunboat of shallow draught, with 6 guns used in the Sea of Azov on 3 June 1855, after the capture of Kertch, to bombard Russian coastal traffic and thus cut off Russian supplies coming from that area and from Taganrog, at the NE of the Sea of Azov, near the estuary of the river Don. This was a major supply base where stores were stacked on the beach, but the port could only be approached through shoals. *Stromboli*, commanded by Commander Cowper Coles, constructed a raft, which would pass over the shoals, carrying a 42-cwt gun. Lieutenant Horton, of *Ardent*, equipped his pinnace with a 32-pounder to bombard the Russians. There was also a division of light boats, carrying rockets and one gun.

The British and French forces destroyed all the stores, vessels and Government buildings at Taganrog without loss of any of their men or vessels.

Chapter Nine

General Goodlake's Post-war Career, Retirement and Death

1856 to 1890

Military Career.

On the 14 June Captain Goodlake was appointed Brevet Major for service in the field, having served for six years in the Army.

On 24 February 1857 his award of the Victoria Cross was published in the *London Gazette* for gallant conduct in command of the Sharpshooters during the Siege of Sevastopol. He received the Victoria Cross from HM Queen Victoria at the First Victoria Cross Investiture on 26 June 1857 in Hyde Park.

On 29 November 1859 he became a Captain and Lieutenant-Colonel by Purchase and on 30 April 1869 he was promoted to Colonel by Brevet.

On 5 November 1870 he married Margaret, daughter of Ewen Curwen of Grosvenor Place, London S.W.1. There were no children from this marriage.

From 30 April 1869 to 10 August 1879 he was Aide-de-Camp to HM Queen Victoria.

On being appointed a Regimental Major on 14 August he became Commanding Officer of the 2nd Battalion until 20 July 1875, when he commanded the 1st Battalion, until he retired on half-pay on 7 August 1875.

On 11 August 1879 he was appointed Major-General to the Land Forces and retired from the Army with the honorary rank of Lieutenant-General on 1 July 1881.

Retirement

The article below in the *Sporting Mirror* shows that, in his retirement, he carried on his interests in shooting, horses and racing, and then added to this coursing and fishing.

THE SPORTING MIRROR.

No. 12.]   JANUARY, 1882.   VOL. II.

MAJOR-GENERAL GERALD GOODLAKE, V.C.

T is always pleasurable to be able to chronicle the doings of a sportsman, and more especially when he is popular, and a staunch and representative member of the tried and true brigade. In this wide world there are sportsmen belonging to many classes, sportsmen who indulge in the various fancies and in the different pastimes for many distinctive reasons, but to find a sportsman who is immersed in sport heart and soul for itself alone, is really becoming something of a rarity. The old school are gradually dying off and filthy lucre is becoming such a fascination and attraction amongst the present that it is a difficulty to select any one gentleman who is a fit and proper representative to fill up the blanks in sporting circles which each year become more numerous. There are very few at the present moment who can equal General Goodlake in his sincere love for all matters relating to sport. He is endeared to it in a far greater degree than the majority of followers who call themselves sportsmen at the present time, and unlike the majority he is not only competent in the theory of all the branches but has also evidenced his proficiency in all matters appertaining to the practice thereof.

General Gerald Goodlake belongs to an ancient family whose members have distinguished themselves in many a contest in flood and field, and who have figured prominently in the sporting history of the neighbourhood of the Vale of White Horse. He was born at Wadley in the month of May, 1833; thus at the present time he is in his forty-eighth year. From earliest boyhood Gerald Goodlake always displayed great activity and a remarkable fondness

187

for anything relating to sport. Horses and dogs seemed to possess a fascination for him, and consequently it is not surprising that he is held in the highest esteem amongst those who love these animals for themselves alone, and not as the mediums for speculation upon their efforts. Like many hundreds of our good sportsmen, Gerald Goodlake was educated at Eton, and when there he proved his proficiency in athletics by winning prizes for running and for swimming. Although some five years younger than Sir J. D. Astley, their careers have been identical to a certain extent. Both were at Eton, both were particularly fond of sport, and proved their ability at pedestrianism, and both fought manfully for their country during the Crimean War. Whilst Sir John was gazetted to the Scots – then called the Fusilier Guards, his schoolfellow joined the Coldstream, and with them he went through the whole of the Crimean campaign, gaining honour and glory, and was one of the earliest recipients of the Victoria Cross.

Before General Goodlake went to the East he was one of the best amateur runners of his day, and, under the tuition of Jimmy Paterson, who was then known by the nickname of "the Flying Tailor", he proved a formidable opponent to the rivals who contended against him on the running track. His love for pedestrianism has not forsaken him at the present time, and his stalwart figure was generally seen alongside of the burlier form of Sir J. D. Astley at the start of one of the long distance competitions at the Agricultural Hall at Islington. During the time that Weston competed in their midst General Goodlake took great interest in the proceedings, and he was generally to be found there. It is perhaps with the coursing world that he is most intimately associated. As a genuine lover of the leash, few men are more popular, and he always takes great interest in the doings of the leading long-tails of the season. In 1874 he was elected to the chair at the Waterloo banquet for the first time on the evening previous to the commencement of the Derby of the Leash, and since that time he has generally occupied a like position. As an owner of greyhounds he has not done particularly well, though some good animals have at times emanated from his kennel. As far back as 1865 Mr. Carruther's Meg ran in his nomination and proved successful, beating Mr. Kennedy's King Tom, who figured in Mr. Knowles's nomination, in the final course.

Years ago, before he filled out to the extent he has done, he was very proficient with the gloves, and was, in addition, a capital rider across country. He is also fond of fishing, and is an excellent shot. He is also a most noted pisciculturist, and breeds a large number of trout every season. Altogether General Goodlake can fairly be styled one of the best all-round sportsmen of the present age, and although he does not participate largely in the pleasures

of the turf, his figure is as well known at Newmarket, Ascot and Goodwood
as everywhere else where the most enthusiastic sportsmen always congregate.

General Goodlake died on 5 April 1890 at his house Denham Fishery. The obituary notice, which appeared in the *Journal of the Household Brigade* that year, is shown below:

> We regret to record the death of Lieutenant-General Gerald Littlehales Goodlake, V.C., late Coldstream Guards, and A.D.C. to the Queen, which occurred at his place Denham Fishery near Uxbridge, on the 5th of April last, in the 58th year of his age. The funeral took place at Harefield Church on Wednesday April 9th, and the ceremony was of itself striking evidence of the deep respect and esteem in which the General was held by all classes. Amongst those present were many Guardsmen, past and present, Sir John Astley, Lieutenant-Generals Hon. R. Monck, Sir R. Gipps, K.C.B., Major-General Lord W. Seymour, Colonel P. Crawley, Sir Seymour Blane, Sir Reginald Cathcart, Colonel the Hon. H. Corry, Captains Falkener and Birch, Lieutenant Monck, Sergeant Major J. Brace, Quarter Master Sergeants Johnson, Brownlow, and Austin, Sergeants Smith, Farrow, and Snelling, and Privates Clark and Page, Coldstream Guards. A very large number of wreaths and crosses were sent.
>
> He was mentioned in Despatches, holds the Crimean War Medal with four clasps, the Victoria Cross, is a Knight of Legion of Honour, and holds the Turkish medal of Medjidie, 5th Class.
>
> General Goodlake was famous as a sportsman, and in 1865 nominated the winner of the Waterloo Cup.

He is buried in the Churchyard of St Mary the Virgin, Harefield Parish Church, Harefield, Middlesex.

NULLI SECUNDUS*

* *Second to None,* the Motto of the Coldstream Guards.

Officers of 1st Battalion Coldstream Guards Serving in the Crimean War

Name in Bold Type: Present at the Battle of Inkerman. **Date of Arrival in Bold Type:** Sailed with the Battalion from Portsmouth.

Medals: A–Alma, B–Balaklava, I–Inkerman, S–Siege of Sebastopol.

*Received Medals on 16 May 1855 from Her Majesty Queen Victoria on Horse Guards.

KIA: Killed in Action; DOW: Died of Wounds; DOD: Died of Disease; W: Wounded; SW: Severely Wounded; POW: Prisoner of War; FBU: Force Broken Up.

Brevet Rank: Dates of Appointment are shown in italics. R: Retired; D: Died; H: Half Pay; E: Exchanged into another Regiment.

1 Coldstream

Name	Arrive	Leave	Medals	Wounds/Death	Ensign Lieut.	Lieut Capt.	Capt Lt-Col.	Major	Col	Maj-Gen	Retired
	Crimea										
Adair, A. W.	1. 5.55	– –	S		17. 1.55	18. 5.59					1860E
Amherst, Hon W. A. (Viscount Holmesdale.)	18.10.54 -. 5.55	24.12.54 4. 6.56	B I S*	SW–Inkerman Home–FBU	3. 3.54	4. 3.55					1862R
Armytage, H.	**14. 9.54** 2.56	12.10.55 4. 6.56	A B I S	Private Affairs Home–FBU	30. 7.47	13.12.53	26.10.58	12.12.54			1870R
Baring, C.[1]	14. 9.54 -. 6.55	-.12.54 -.10.55	A S*	Alma-arm Amputated Medical Cert.	2. 7.47	29. 4.53	21.12.55	12.12.54	2. 9.68	23. 8.78	1890D
Bouverie, H.M.	**14. 9.54**	-. -. -	B I	KIA–Inkerman	13. 7.47	27. 5.53					1854D
Boyle, Hon. R.E.	-. -. -	-. -. -		DOD–Varna	-. -.29	-. -.33	-. -.46				1854D
Burdett, C.S. (*Ex 60th Foot.*)	9.12.54	4. 6.56	S	Home–FBU	25. 6.41	29.10.47	22. 8.54				1859R
Burton, F. A. P.	11.12.54	8. 4.55	S	Home–2 Bn	8. 5.46	27. 6.51					1855R
Carleton, D. W. (Lord Dorchester)	18.10.54	3.10 55	B I S	Medical Cert.	11. 6.41	13. 7.47	14. 7.54	9.11.62	22. 6.56		1868E 1897D
Caulfield, J. A. (Viscount Charlemont)	2.55	4.9.55	S	Home–2 Bn	?	?					1858R

Name	Arrive Crimea	Leave	Medals	Wounds/Death	Ensign Lieut.	Lieut Capt.	Capt Lt-Col.	Major	Col	Maj-Gen	Retired
Cocks, C. L. (Ex 54th Foot)	2. 5.55 / 2.55	20.6.55 / 3.56	S	Leave / Leave	24. 1.40	7. 8.46	20. 6.54				???
Cowell, J. C. M.	14. 9.54	-. -. -	B I S	KIA–Inkerman	25. 9.40	11. 6.47	20. 6.54				1854D
Crawley, P. S. (Ex 74th Foot.)	14. 9.54 / 3.56	26.11.55 / 4. 6.56	A B I S	Private Affairs / Home–FBU	23. 6.48	14. 7.54	?	12.12.54			1867R
Crombie, T.[2]	14. 9.54	?			12. 8.24	18. 4.26	8. 5.32	16.11.41	20.10.48		1855H
Cumming, H. W.	14. 9.54	?	?		6. 3.38	30.12.42	27. 5.53				1854R
Daniell, H.	2. 5.55	9.10.55	S	Medical Cert.	13. 8.29	27. 3.35	29.10.47	9.11.56			1856R
Dawkins, W. G. (Ex 49th Foot.)	? 54	?	A B S	Home–2nd Bn	6. 9.44	25. 4.58	6.11.64				1865H
Dawson, Hon T. V.	14. 9.54	-. -. -	A B I S	KIA–Inkerman	11. 8.37	30. 5.43	22. 8.51				1854D
Disbrowe, E. A. (Ex 85th Foot.)	28. 6.54	-. -. -	A B I S	KIA–Inkerman	12. 3.52	18. 2.53					1854D
Drummond, G. D.	2. 5.55	4. 6.56	A B S	Home–FBU	10. 6.26	3. 8.30	29. 4.44	20. 6.54			1856D
Drummond, Hon H. R.	14. 9.54	-. -. -	A	DOD–1.10.55	?	?	?				1855D
Dunkellin, Lord	14. 9.54 / 22.10.54 / 9.12.54 / 8 10.55	22.10.54 / 8.12.54 / 8.10.55 / 4. 6.56	A S*	POW / To 2 Bn / Home–FBU	27. 3.46	27. 4.49	3.11.54				1860R
Dunlop, Sir James Bt	14. 9.54	26.11.54	A B I S	Private Affairs	22.11.54	27. 4.59	14. 7.54	2. 4.55			1858D
Eliot, Hon G. C. C. (Adjutant)	14. 9.54	-. -. -	A B I S	KIA–Inkerman	11. 6.47	31.10.51					1854D
Fitzroy, Lord A. C. L.[3]	18.10.54 / 14. 6.55	7.11.54 / 14. 9.55	B I-S*	SW–Inkerman / Medical Cert.	17. 5.39	24. 8.41	30. 7.47				1855H / 1918D
Fremantle, A. J. L.				Invalided–Varna	29. 4.53	6.11.54					??
Goodlake, G. L. VC[4] (DAQMG–1st Div Ex-Rifle Bde.)	14. 9.54	4. 6.56	A B I S	Home–FBU	27. 6.51	27. 8.54	29.11.59	14. 6.66	30. 8.69	11. 8.79	1890D
Greville, C.	26. 9.54	-. -. -	B I S	KIA–Inkerman	10. 6.53						1854D
Halkett, J. (Ex 29th Foot.)	18.10.54	7.11.54	B I S	SW–Inkerman	23. 4.41	1. 7.47	20. 6.54				1870D

Name	Arrive Crimea	Leave	Medals	Wounds/Death	Ensign Lieut.	Lieut Capt.	Capt Lt-Col.	Major	Col	Maj-Gen	Retired
Heneage, M. W.	18.10.54 / -. 5.55	24.12.54 / 15. 3.56	B I S	Home–2 Bn / Medical Cert.	13.12.53	23.12.54	21.12.60				1866R
Ives, G. M.	11.12.54	6. 8.55	S	Medical Cert.	2. 8.54						1855R
Jolliffe, Hylton	**14. 9.54**	-.10.54	A S	DOD 4.10.54	15.12.48	9. 5.51					1854D
Lambton, A.	11.12.54	15. 3.56	S	Home 2 Bn.	4. 8.54	15. 2.56					1886H
Lane-Fox, Hon C. P. L.	6. 3.55	30. 8.55	S	Med. Cert.	19.12.50	8. 4.53					1856R
Lane, H J B	2. 5.55	4. 6.56	S	Home–FBU	16. 1.55	26.10.58					1867R
MacKinnon, L. D.	**14. 9.54**	-. -. -	B I S	DOW–Inkerman	30. 5.43	25. 2.48					1854D
Markham, W. T. (Ex 62nd Foot.)	**14. 9.54**	1. 7.55	S	Home–2 Bn.	?	?					1886D
Newton, W. S.	18.10.54	8. 4.55	B I S*	Home–2.Bn.	5.12.34	31.12.39	25. 2.48	18.11.56	28.11.54		1861H
Paulet, Lord Frederick (Comd. Bn, Nov.54)	**14. 9.54**	26. 5.55	A B I S	Home–2.Bn.	11. 6.26	21. 9.30	8. 5.46	20. 2.55	20. 6.54	13.12.60	1871D
Perceval, S.	8. 4.55	4. 6.56	S	Home–FBU	13. 1.57	15.10.41	23. 6.48	26.10.58	28.11.54		????
Ramsden, F. H. (*Ex Rifle Bde.*)	**14. 9.54**	-. -. -	A B I S	KIA–Inkerman	11. 7.51	28. 7.54					1854D
Rose, G. E. (*Into Rifle Bde.*)	11.12.54	4. 6.56	S	Home–FBU	24. 8.54						1857E
Stepney, A. St G. H.	-. 1.55	???	S		16. 5.34	10.11.37	15. 7.54	3. 4.48 / 9. 7.50	26.10.58		1866R
Strong, C. W.	**14. 9.54**	1. 1.55 / 6. 5.55	A B I S	Medical Cert. / Home–2 Bn	6. 5.42	1. 9.48	6.11.54				1869D
Tierney, M. E.	**14. 9.54**	13.11.54		Retired Regt.	10. 3.37	27. 1.43	27. 4.49				1854R
Tower, H. (*Ex 48th Foot.*)	**14. 9.54**	26.11.55	A B I S	Private Affrs.	21.11.51	4. 9.54	9. 3.60				1870D
Trevelyan, W.	28. 6.54	-. -. -		DOD. 21. 9.54 Varna	18.11.17	25. 9.25	19. 9.26	28.12.32	10. 8.41		1854D
Upton, Hon. G.[5]	**14. 9.54**	15.11.54	A B I S*	Sev.wounded							1854D

Name	Arrive (Crimea)	Leave	Medals	Wounds/Death	Ensign Lieut.	Lieut. Capt.	Capt. Lt-Col.	Major	Col	Maj-Gen	Retired
GCB											
Viscount Templetown (Comdr. Bn. Feb 1954)	5. 1.55	–. 3.55		Inkerman Home–Regt–Lt-Col	24. 4.23	29.10.25	2.12.26	16. 6.37	11.11.51	26.10.58	1890D
Whitshed, Sir St V. B. H.	23.11.54	15. 3.56	S	Home–2 Bn.	1. 8.54	2 10.55					1859R
Wigram.G. J. CB	11.12.54	15. 3.56	S	Home–2 Bn	3. 8.54	14. 2.56					1885H
Wilson, C. T. *(Ex 59th Foot.)*	14. 9.54 ????	22.11.54 8. 4.55	A B I S*	Medical Cert. Home–2 Bn	30.12.42	1. 5.46	?				1855R
Wood, W. M.[6] *(Ex 60th Foot.)*	18.10.54	5. 5.55	B I S	Home–2 Bn	22. 7.36	24. 5.41	13.12.53	28.11.54			1866H

Officers who landed in the Crimea after the Fall of Sebastopol

Name	Arrive (Crimea)	Leave	Medals	Wounds/Death	Ensign Lieut.	Lieut. Capt.	Capt. Lt-Col.	Major	Col	Maj-Gen	Retired
Cecil, Lord E.	8.10.55	4. 6.56		Home–FBU	13. 1.51	20.12.54					1863R
Edwardes, Hon W.	8.10.55	4. 6.56		Home–FBU	24.11.54	5. 2.58					1870R
Feilding, Hon W. H. A.	8.10.55	4. 6.56		Home–FBU	26. 7.53	15.12.54					1904D
Forbes, Sir W.	10. 2.56	4. 6.56		Home–FBU	???	???					1857R
Hall, J. H. H. Sir	27.10.54	20. 6.55		?	2. 8.54	15. 2.56					1882H
Legge, Hon.E.	9. 3.56	4. 6.56		Home–FBU	12. 2.55	29.11.59	?				1875R
Mainwaring, Sir S. T.	9. 3.56	4. 6.56		Home–FBU	?	?					1858R.
Newdegate, F. *(Ex 66th Foot.)*	8.10.55	4. 6.56		Home–FBU	?	?					1859R
Reeve, W.	8.10.55	4. 6.56		Home–FBU	29.12.46	21. 8.51	30.11.55				1866R
Seymour, Lord W. F. E.[7]	9. 3.56	4. 6.56		Home–FBU	18. 1.55	13. 5.59					1884R

Officers who served in the Crimea with Other Regiments.

Name	Arrive Crimea	Leave	Medals	Wounds/Death	Ensign Lieut.	Lieut Capt.	Capt Lt-Col.	Major	Col	Maj-Gen	Retired
Blackett, C. E.[8]	14. 9.54	15. 3.56	A B S	Home–2 Bn.	-.10.47	4. 2.54					1875R
Egerton, P. L. B.[9]	14. 9.54	13. 4.55	A S		11. 8.54	23. 3.55					
Fitzroy, G. R.[10]	14. 9.54	??	A I S*	SW–Inkerman							1885E
Fremantle, F. W.[11]	11.54	6.55	S	SW–Redan	14.11.51	22.12.54	24.11.57				
Gordon,R.H[12]. (ADC-Gen. Sir J Simpson.)	14. 9.54	8. 4.55	A I S	Private Affairs	?	?	?				1855E
Joliffe, Hedworth (Ex 4th Light Dragoons)	14. 9.54	?	A B I S		8.12.48	9. 5.51	?				1855R 1899D

Quartermasters, Paymasters & Surgeons

Name	Arrive Crimea	Leave	Medals	Wounds/Death	Ensign Lieut.	Lieut Capt.	Capt Lt-Col.	Major	Col	Maj-Gen	Retired
Falconer, A. (QM)	14. 9.54	4. 6.56	A B I S	Home–FBU	4. 6.56						
Rogers, T. L. (Asst.Surg)	12. 6.55	4. 6.56	S	Home–FBU	4. 6.56						
Skelton, J. (Bn.Surg.)	14. 9.54 -.10.55	1.11.54 4. 6.56	A S*	Sick Leave Home–FBU	20. 3.53 4. 6.56						1857D
Trotter, W. (Asst.Surg)	14. 9.54	15. 3.56	S	Home–2 Bn.	26. 5.54 ?						
Wildbore, F. (Asst.Surg)	14. 9.54 12.54 7.55 8.55	1. 2.54 10.55 8.55 6. 6.56	?????	Sick Leave Sick Leave Home FBU	4. 6.56						
Wyatt, J. (Asst.Surg)	14. 9.54 ? 10. 8.55	21.12.54 10. 7.55 4. 6.56	A B I S	Sick Leave Home–FBU	17. 6.51 4. 6.56						
(Bn. Surg.)					9. 4.57						
Bowen, F. (Asst. Surg.)	20. 5.55	4. 6.56		Home–FBU	4. 6.56						
Cay, C. W. (Asst.Surg.)	30.11.54	20.11.55	S	Home–2 Bn.	12. 6.46						

Notes

1 Lieutenant-General, 1881.

2 Served in Bulgaria

3 Equerry to HM The Queen Victoria.

4 Present at the battles of Alma, Balaklava, Inkerman, Tchernaya and the Siege and Fall of Sebastopol. He volunteered for the Sharpshooters of the Brigade of Guards, commanded them for 42 days, was engaged at the repulse of the sortie of 26 October 1854 and served on the Quartermaster-General's staff from February 1855. *Hart's Army List 1860*, p.165.

5 Gazetted Regimental Lieutenant-Colonel, 28 February 1855. *Coldstream Guards in the Crimea*, p.223; General 1873, Colonel, 2nd Life Guards,1876.

6 Lieutenant-Colonel Commanding, 1863.

7 Midshipman, Baltic Fleet, 1854.

8 Served entire Eastern Campaign with 93rd Highlanders, Alma, Balaklava and Siege of Sevastopol.

9 Served entire Eastern Campaign with 2nd Battalion Rifle Brigade up to 13 April 1855, Alma and Siege of Sevastopol.

10 Served in the Eastern Campaign of 1854 with 41st Foot, Alma, Inkerman (severely wounded) and Siege of Sevastopol.

11 Served in the Eastern Campaign of 1854–55 with the Rifle Brigade; Redan 18 June 1855 (severely wounded).

12 Served with 38th Regiment throughout the Eastern Campaign, Alma, Inkerman and Siege of Sevastopol. He commanded a party, which repulsed the sortie on 20 December, for which he was honourably mentioned by Lord Raglan and promoted into the Coldstream Guards. He exchanged into 42nd Highlanders. *Hart's Army List, 1860*, pages 255–6. He did not serve with the Battalion.

Generals and Staff Officers, Coldstream Guards Serving in the Crimean War

Name in Bold Type: Present at the Battle of Inkerman. **Date of Arrival in Bold Type:** Sailed with the Battalion from Portsmouth.

Medals: A—Alma, B—Balaklava, I—Inkerman, S–Siege of Sebastopol.

*Received Medals on 16 May 1855 from Her Majesty Queen Victoria on Horse Guards.

KIA: Killed in Action; DOW: Died of Wounds; DOD: Died of Disease; W: Wounded; SW: Severely Wounded; POW: Prisoner of War; FBU: Force Broken Up.

Brevet Rank: Dates of Appointment are shown in italics. R: Retired; D: Died; H: Half Pay; E: Exchanged into another Regiment.

Name	Arrive Crimea	Leave Crimea	Medals	Wounds/Death	Ensign Lieut.	Lieut Capt.	Capt Lt-Col.	Major	Col	Maj-Gen	Retired
Airey, Sir J. T. (*AQMG-Light Div. Ex 22nd Foot*).	6.10.55 28. 3.56	6.10.55 15. 6.56	A I S	Private Affairs Home–FBU	11. 2.30	3. 5.33	15. 7.54	11.11.61	26.10.58	?	1867R
Bentinck, Sir H. (*Comdr.Gds.Bde; Comdr. 4th Div.*)	**14. 9.54** 3. 6.55	2.12.54 9.10.55	A B I S	Wounded Inkerman Private Affairs	25. 3.13	18. 1.20	16. 5.29		23.11.41	11.11.51	1878D
Bingham, Lord (*Extra ADC to Earl of Lucan–Ex 21st and 89th Foot*).	**14. 9.54** 3.10.55	17. 2.55 4. 6.56	A B I S*	Eng.+ Gen. Home–FBU	14.10.51	22. 8.54	20.12.59	17. 7.55			1860R
Boyle,Hon. R.E.				DOD–Varna	–. –.26	–. –.29	–. –.33	–. –.46			1854D
Boyle, Hon W. G. (*ADC-Gen Evans. Ex 21st and 89th Foot*)	14. 9.54	3.11.54	A I S* *de*	Eng.+ Gen.	16. 9.51	13. 1.54 *Lacy*		12.12.54	?		1887R 1908D
Byng, Hon H.W. (*Earl of Strafford*) (*ADC-Brig-Gen Bentinck*)	10.11.55	4. 6.56		Home–FBU	27. 8.47	3. 3.54	2. 5.56				1899D

Name	Arrive Crimea	Leave	Medals	Wounds/Death	Ensign Lieut.	Lieut Capt.	Capt Lt-Col.	Major	Col	Maj-Gen	Retired
Burghersh, Lord CB (*ADC-Lord Raglan*) (*Later Earl of Westmorland*)	14. **9.54**	3. 7.55	A B I	Home–2 Bn	24. 2.43	26. 7.44	20. 9.54 / 22. 4.53	7. 6.59			
Campbell, Hon H. W. (*ADC-Gen.Sir W. Codrington.*)	14. **9.54** / 1.10.55 / 1.12.55 / 8. 5.56	1.10.55 / 25.10.55 / 8. 5.56 / 25. 6.56	A I S	Medical Cert. / Medical Cert. / Home +C-in-C.	21.11.54	19. 6.55	?				
Clarke-Jervoise, H. (*ADC-Maj.Gen.Airey –DAQMG-1st Div Ex 42nd Foot.*)	14. **9.54**	2. 6.56	A I S	Home–FBU	8. 4.53	6. 4.55	?				1873R
Codrington, Sir W. J.[1] (*C-in-C*)	14. **9.54**	25. 6.56	A B I S	Home–FBU	22. 2.21	24. 4.23	20. 7.26		9.11.46	20. 6.54	1884D
Conolly, J. A. VC[2] (*DAAG Cavalry Div/ ADC-Gen.Bentinck*)	4. 9.54 / 29. 8.55	2.11.54 / 22.12.55	A I S	SW–Inkerman / Private Affairs	26. 8.50	22.12.54		17. 7.55			1870R
Cust, H. (*ADC-Gen Bentinck*)	14. **9.54**	–. –. –	A	KIA–Alma	7. 8.48	?					1854D
Feilding, Hon P. R. B.[3] (*Brigade Major–Alma*) (*DAQMG-1st Div.*)	14. **9.54** / 8.55	7.11.54 / 4. 6.56	A B I S*	SW–Inkerman / Home–FBU	7 8.46	21. 8.51	23.11.55	12.12.54			1904R
Hardinge, Hon A.[4] (*DAQMG-1st Div. AQMG-HQ.*)	14. **9.54**	26. 6.56	A B I S	Home–FBU	22.12.45	1. 6.49	20. 2.55	12.12.54	25. 5.58	6. 3.68	1892D
Hay, C. M.[5] (*CO–ICG.*)	–. –. –	20. 6.54		Promoted Maj-Gen.–Varna	20. 4.20	1.11.21	24.12.25	22. 6.31	9.11.46	20. 6.54	?
Le Couteur, J. H. (*Musketry Instructor Turkish Contingent.*)	11.12.54	4. 6.56	S	Home–FBU	27. 3.46	15. 3.53	18.11.56	2.11.55			1868R
Maxse, H. F. B.[6] (*ADC-Lord Cardigan*) *Ex 21st Foot*	14. **9.54**	28.11.54	A B S*	W–Balaklava	–. –. –	1. 6.49	29.12.54	17. 7.55			1858H / 1883D

Name	Arrive Crimea	Leave	Medals	Wounds/Death	Ensign Lieut.	Lieut Capt.	Capt Lt-Col.	Major	Col	Maj-Gen	Retired
Somerset, P. G. H. (*ADC-Lord Raglan. Ex 33rd Foot.*)	14. 9.54	3. 7.55	A B I S	Home–2 Bn.	1. 5.40	28.12.46	3. 3.52	2. 2.58			1855E 1875D
Steele, T. M.[7] (*Military Secretary– Lord Raglan*)	14. 9.54	27.11.55	A B I S	Home–2 .Bn.	20. 7.38	29. 3.44	31.10.51	28.11.54			1863H 1890D
Thellusson, A. G. B. (*ADC-Col.Drummond*)	2. 5.55	6. 6.56	S	Home–FBU	10.12.47	26. 6.54		2.11.55		?	1859R
Wellesley, Hon. W. H. Viscount Dangan (*ADC-Lord Rokeby*)	17. 7.55	24. 5.56	S	Home–FBU	23. 7.52	21. 9.54		20. 4.59			1863R

Notes

1 Lieutenant-General 6 June 1856
2 Served in the Eastern Campaign of 1854 with 49th Regt. VC–Little Inkerman, dangerously wounded. Present at Alma and Siege of Sevastopol.
3 Served as Brigade Major, Guards Brigade at the Battle of the Alma and as DAQMG on the staff of the 1st Division for the Battles of Balaklava and Inkerman, and for the Siege of Sevastopol. Lieutenant-General, 1886; General, 1891; KCB, 1893.
4 AQMG-HQ from Spring 1855; Colonel of Regiment, 1890; Lieutenant-General, 1877; General, 1883; KCB, 1886.
5 Commanding Officer, 1st Coldstream, did not serve in the Crimea, as he was promoted to Major-General by the Brevet of 20 June 1854, when the Battalion was at Varna.
6 He rode with Lord Cardigan in the Charge of the Light Brigade at Balaklava and was wounded. Present at the Battle of the Alma and the Siege of Sevastopol.
7 General, 1877; GCB, 1887. Regimental Lieutenant-Colonel, 1884.

Appendix C

Military Terms

ABATTIS   A rampart of trees, felled and laid side by side with the branches towards the enemy

ADJUTANT-GENERAL   The Adjutant-General is responsible for discipline & administration. During and after the Crimean War, the Quartermaster-General reported to and was junior to the Adjutant-General. Staff officers junior to this post were :-

Deputy Adjutant-General	DAG
Assistant Adjutant-General	AAG
Deputy Assistant Adjutant-General	DAAG

ARMY WORKS CORPS   Sir Joseph Paxton had proposed, and with the agreement of the Government had organized the formation of this civilian-based organization, a forerunner of the Pioneer Corps of the Second World War. It provided navvies to work on construction projects, such as maintaining the railway track, road building and digging trenches. Its Superintendent, William Doyne, ex Resident Engineer of the Rugby & Leamington Railway from 1847–50, landed in the Crimea around 10 Aug. 1855, with the 720 men of his Corps landing a week later. Their main tasks were to maintain the railway and to build a new all-weather road from Balaklava to Kadikoi, up to Headquarters and then up the northeast valley. This road was completed in six weeks. See *The Grand Crimean Central Railway,* pp.100-101,121–3, Brian Cooke, Cavalier House, 2nd Edition 1997.

AUGMENTATION   An increase in the establishment of officers and men in a battalion or regiment. Normally these additional officer posts were non-purchase posts.

BATTALION   An infantry regiment would have a number of battalions. At the time of the Crimean War, the Grenadiers had three battalions and the Coldstream and Scots Fusilier Guards each had two battalions. The Foot Guards battalions, which took part in the war, each had an initial overall strength of 1000 men in the field.

BATTERIES & TROOPS   Field Artillery Batteries each had four 9 pounder guns and two 24 pounder howitzers.

Royal Horse Artillery, I Troop supported the Cavalry Division and was equipped with four 6 pounder guns and two 12 pounder howitzers. C Troop, armed like the field batteries, supported the Light Division, which also had another field battery. The 1st, 2nd & 3rd Divisions were supported by two field batteries, while the 4th Division had one field battery. Horse Artillery Troops were able to move faster than Field Batteries, as all the gunners were mounted on horses instead of being seated on limbers.

BEARSKIN CAP   In 1678 Grenadier Companies were first formed in the three Regiments of Foot Guards and in other Regiments to go forward and throw grenades to clear away the enemy.

In 1768 it was decreed that the caps worn by Grenadier Companies and by Fusilier Regiments were to be made of black bearskin.

The First Guards defeated the Grenadiers of the Imperial Guard at Waterloo. In recognition of this, the Prince Regent ordered that the Regiment should be called henceforth the First or Grenadier Regiment of Foot Guards and that all ranks should wear the bearskin cap.

In 1831 William IV decided that all his Guards should be dressed in a similar fashion. By renaming the two other Regiments, the Coldstream and Scots, as Fusilier Guards, they would both be entitled to wear fusilier bearskin caps. However, the Coldstream decided not to change their name and only the Scots Fusilier Guards adopted this name.

Each cap has a socket on each side to take the relevant Regimental plume: Grenadiers, a white plume worn on the left side of the cap; Coldstream, a red plume worn on the right side of the

200

cap. The Scots Fusilier Guards wore no plume. In battle the Grenadiers took the right of the line, the Coldstream the left and the Scots Fusilier Guards were in the centre. *The History of the Bearskin Cap,* Capt. D .D. Horn, Curator, The Guards Museum.

Positions on the flanks of a formation were allocated according to the seniority of the regiment or company, with the most senior unit on the right flank, the next most senior on the left flank and other units placed alternatively right and left inside the more senior units.

BLUE COAT   The undress uniform of the Brigade of Guards, a frogged blue frock-coat, worn instead of a red or scarlet full dress coatee with tails.

BLUE LIGHTS   Fireworks, fired by a gun, rather like a flare, used for signalling, made from saltpetre, sulphur, and a little red orpiment.

BOUQUET   "These consist of a number of small shells or grenades enclosed in a large one, which, on exploding, scatters not only destruction in its vicinity, but the small shells like so many serpents, with the impetus imparted from the parent shell, insidiously go on bursting at uncertain intervals, some on the ground, some in the air, rendering all calculations erroneous, and no locality except a bombproof (shelter) safe." *The Sebastopol Trenches,* Vol III page 108–9, Colonel Reynell Pack, Kerby & Endean, London 1878. Republished by Pallas Armata.

BREVET   An Army rank which was held at the same time as regimental rank. It decided army seniority, while regimental rank governed regimental seniority (cf.Double Rank in the Brigade of Guards.) Only Brevet Lieutenant-Colonels or Brevet Majors were appointed. The term was also used for the annual list of promotions, such as that of June 1854 while the army was in Bulgaria.

BRIGADE FIRING   Almost certainly Brigade Minie firing exercises, to get the troops used to estimating ranges and firing the new rifle musket.

BUTCHER & BAKER CORPS   Another name for the Commissariat.

BUTCHER'S BILL   The list of killed and wounded.

CAMPAIGN MEDALS CRIMEA 1854–56   Awarded by HM Queen Victoria by an order dated 15 December 1854.The medal is made of silver, with on the obverse the head of Queen Victoria with the words *VICTORIA REGINA* & below *1854*. The reverse has a winged figure of Victory crowning, with a wreath of laurel, a Roman soldier who holds a sword in the right hand and bears on his left arm a shield on which is the figure of a lion. On the left *CRIMEA*. Ribbon, light blue with narrow yellow borders. This medal was awarded to troops landing in the Crimea up to 9 September 1855, the day on which Sevastopol fell.

Clasps, in the shape of oak leaves, ornamented with acorns; ALMA, BALAKLAVA, INKERMANN, SEBASTOPOL were awarded to those troops present at those battles. *Encyclopaedia Britannica,* Campaign Medals, 1911.

CANISTERS   A form of shell used by artillery of all nations, consisting of a light container full of small lead shot. The container burst at the muzzle and the shot was dispersed, like the shot from a shot-gun. It was only effective at short range but was deadly against troops. Also known as case-shot. Fired from cannon only.

CARCASSES   A special sort of shell fired from guns, howitzers and mortars. The carcass shell was spherical, hollow and was pierced by three or four holes. It could be filled with various compounds, but was most commonly used with an incendiary composition of saltpetre, sulphur, rosin, antimony, tallow and turpentine. The flame was extremely powerful, and nearly inextinguishable. They were much used for the bombardment of towns, setting fire to shipping, etc.

CHASSEURS   Elite French infantry, originally formed at Vincennes, who were very famous for their high standard of musketry and for their *elan* on the battlefield.

COLONELS.   The Sovereign is Colonel-in-Chief of each Regiment of Foot Guards. There are also Colonels for each Regiment, who at the time of the Crimean War were:-

Grenadiers, Field Marshal HRH Prince Albert.
Coldstream, Field Marshal the Earl of Strafford.
Scots Fusilier Guards, General HRH George,
Duke of Cambridge.

Each regiment of Foot Guards has a full Colonel, referred to as the Lieutenant-Colonel, commanding the Regiment.

COLOUR SERGEANT   A General Order of 6 July 1813 established the rank of Colour Sergeant, with the establishment of one per company. *Redcoat,* p.125, Richard Holmes.

COLOURS   Each battalion of the Brigade of Guards has two colours, the Queen's Colour and the Regimental Colour. The Queen's Colour is carried on parades, at which the Sovereign, a Head of State or Member of the Royal Family are present. The Regimental Colour is carried on other occasions. In the Crimean War both Colours were carried on the battlefield of the Alma by all three battalions of Foot Guards. However, at Inkerman only the Grenadier Colours were carried on the battlefield.

The Colours acted as a rallying point on a battlefield and for this reason it was very important that soldiers would know their battalion colours well and be able to recognize them in the smoke of battle. For this reason colours were regularly trooped through the ranks.

COMMISSIARIAT DEPARTMENT OR COMMISSIONAIRE   This department, which handled supply and transport for the Army, was controlled by the Treasury. James Fiddler, a civilian aged 66, was brought back from retirement and appointed to run this department. It was quite unable to handle the supplying of an army of 30,000 men, as the Land Transport Corps, established by Wellington, had been disbanded in peacetime. Furthermore, it had no reserve of competent staff to handle this expansion.

COMPANY   Normally there were eight companies in a Foot Guards battalion, each commanded by a Captain, with a Lieutenant and an Ensign, with two sergeants, three corporals and a drummer, with around a hundred rank and file. However, at the beginning of the war two additional companies were added to the three overseas battalions, with these additional companies remaining in England as reserves.

COX   Cox & Co were the Army's paying agents for officers' pay and allowances. All officers had bank accounts with the Pall Mall branch, which also acted as their bankers. The bank then became Cox & Kings, and was subsequently acquired by Lloyds Bank.

DISTINGUISHED CONDUCT MEDAL   Instituted by Royal Warrant on 30 September 1862. It replaced the Meritorious Service Medal or Silver Medal and was awarded to Non-Commissioned Officers and Privates for gallantry in the field. Obverse side, the Head of Queen Victoria. Reverse side, a military trophy, with, in the centre, the Royal Arms and the inscription, For Distinguished Conduct in the Field. Ribbon, three stripes of equal width, outsides red and centre blue. *Encyclopaedia Britannica,* Medals,1911.

DOUBLE RANK   Up to 1871 officers in the Brigade of Guards below the rank of Colonel held a rank in their Regiment and a higher one in the army:-

> Captain and Lieutenant-Colonel.
> Lieutenant and Captain.
> Ensign and Lieutenant.

They always used and were referred to by their higher rank. The first rank determined their regimental seniority and the second their army seniority.

DOUBLE-SHOTTED WITH GRAPE   Double shotting was loading a gun with two projectiles. Grape was fired from a shell made up of nine or so smaller balls on a frame that held them together for loading and storing. On firing, the frame would work loose leaving the separate round-shot flying free. It was not much used by British artillery and never from brass guns as it scored the barrel. See entry for 'Grape' below.

DRILL SERGEANT   A senior warrant officer responsible for maintaining a high standard of drill in the battalion. At the time of the Crimean War the Regimental Sergeant-Major, the Regimental Quartermaster-Sergeant and the Drill Sergeants were classified as Battalion Staff Sergeants.

ELECTRIC TELEGRAPH   The British and French Governments wanted to establish telegraphic communication with their armies in the Crimea. The French laid a line from the cable's furthest easternmost point, located on the Austrian and Hungarian border with the Turkish Empire, via Bucharest to a point near Varna in Bulgaria on the Black Sea coast. The British laid a 300-mile submarine cable to a point near to St George's Monastery near Balaklava. This work was completed by the end of April 1855 by the Sunderland firm of R.S.Newall without any serious problems. It was by far the most ambitious telegraph project ever undertaken till then. It was used alternately by the British and the French. British messages were sent by six specially trained NCOs, forming a rudimentary Royal Corps of Signals. *The Grand Crimean Central Railway,* pp. 103–4, Brian Cooke.

EMBRASURE An opening in a wall to enable a cannon to be fired at the enemy.

ENSIGN A Second Lieutenant. In an infantry battalion the Queen's Colour and the Regimental Colour were each carried by an Ensign.

FASCINES Bundles of sticks bound together, used for reinforcing the walls of trenches.

FATIGUES Manual duties, such as barrack or camp cleaning, or cookhouse duties, assigned to soldiers often as a punishment for an offence.

FILE FIRING File firing from right or left of companies or from any particular part of the line, as may be directed.

'On the order being given, the most left-hand flank file makes ready, adjusts sights for distance and comes to the present. The front man fires first, immediately followed by the rear man, both load in quick time and at the same time. In file and volley firing the front man must remain perfectly steady after giving their fire, otherwise the aim of the rear man will be deranged.

'When the flank file is bringing the rifle to the present, the next file makes ready, coming to the present and firing; the next file proceeds likewise and so continue by files in succession to the first round, after which each file, as soon as loaded, will fire independently; i.e. without reference to the files either to right or left. On the order to cease firing, each file, as it completes its loading, will shoulder arms'. *Field Exercises and Evolutions of Infantry as revised by Her Majesty's Command,* 1859.

FORLORN HOPE The advance guard of a hazardous attack.

FOUGASSE 'A square or oblong case, made of metal or stout timber bound with iron hoops; in either case it is filled with gunpowder or gunpowder enclosed in bottles, grenades or shells, or a mixture of both, or of all three. The case is buried from an inch to a foot below the soil. Gutta-percha or other pipes, filled with gunpowder, spring from each end; these rise above the surface and are connected together by a few inches of glass tubing, containing at one end some phosphoric preparation, and at the other a few drops of powerful acid, or perhaps altogether loaded with detonating powder. This glass tube, when broken by the foot getting entangled in it, or by direct pressure of the foot, ignites the charge, and an unexpected mine is fired'. *The Sebastopol Trenches,* p.154, Colonel Reynell Pack.

FUSILIERS   In a Foot Guards context, the Scots Fusilier Guards, the name of the 3rd Guards until 4 April 1877, when they became known simply as the Scots Guards. The name was originally given to them to allow them to wear the bearskin cap. Fusilier Regiments wore a similar but smaller bearskin cap.

In a general sense the word meant certain elite line regiments, which had historically been used to guard the artillery train and had been armed with fusils, which were less likely to ignite powder. Although now armed and employed like the rest of the line infantry, the Fusilier regiments jealously guarded their traditions and dress customs and still do to this day.

GABIONS   Cylindrical wicker baskets, filled with earth and stones and used to build fortifications.

GRAPE   See 'Double-Shotted' above. Could be used as a term by the Infantry when they meant ' Canister or Case Shot'.

HOWITZER   A cannon with a barrel longer than a mortar that delivers shells with medium velocities, either by a low or, more usually, by a high trajectory against targets that cannot be reached by flat trajectories.

L.S. CORPS   Land Service Corps, a misnomer for the Land Transport Corps.

LAND TRANSPORT CORPS   From 1794–1833 army transport was provided by the Royal Waggon Train. It was then disbanded on the grounds of saving money, promoted largely by Gladstone, the Chancellor of the Exchequer, and the Treasury. Although Lord Raglan had asked for the re-establishment of the Waggon Train, the Land Transport Corps was not set up until March 1855 to provide transport, when it became clear that the idea, promoted by the Treasury, of using local transport was impossible, as none was available. Furthermore there was no single organization in charge of all transport, as the French Army did with its *Train des Equipages*. This remedy had the disadvantage that the LTC was a military organization, while the Commissariat was a civilian body. Furthermore, transport and supply were two separate organizations, which did not promote efficiency.

Colonel William McMurdo, the new Superintendant of this Corps, arrived in the Crimea in early March, 1855, and his 258 men arrived at the end of March. Their task was to take charge of both road and rail transport, with the added responsibility of maintaining the rail track and its equipment. *The Grand Crimean Central Railway*, pp.75–80, Brian Cooke.

In 1856 the LTC was renamed the Military Train until 1869, when it was merged with the Commissariat to become the Commissariat and the Army Service Corps. From 1888 it became known as the Army Service Corps until 1918, when the Corps added the prefix Royal. In 1965 the name was changed to the Royal Corps of Transport. In 1993, after incorporating the Royal Ordnance Corps, it became the Royal Logistics Corps.

MINIE A muzzle-loading rifled long-arm rifle-musket, properly called the Pattern '51 Rifle Musket. It successfully overcame the problem of the easy loading of a 'ball' or 'bullet' which would, when fired, expand and take up the rifling of the barrel, leading to hugely increased ranges and accuracy. It was a British-made rifle, which fired the Minie bullet, named after a French Captain Minie who had perfected the invention of the expanding bullet. On its introduction, the infantry could engage the enemy at ranges of up 900–1000 yards. It had a high muzzle velocity and a bullet fired at a formation of men could penetrate 3 or 4 persons in a packed body of troops, and sometimes more.

The sights had to be set correctly to the appropriate range of the target, which had to be estimated by the rifleman; so troops had to be taught to judge distance, a new skill. The drill for loading was significantly different from that of the 1842 pattern musket, the Brown Bess, which it replaced.

According to Colonel Ross-of-Bladensburg, 'On 31 August 1855 the Guards Brigade exchanged the whole of their arms and ammunition for the new Enfield rifle – the Pattern '53, then introduced, and, at that time, there were two patterns in use by the troops of the British Army standing before Sevastopol. The

Coldstream Guards in the Crimea, p.246 Note p 247, 'The bore of the new rifle was .577, while the Minie's bore was .702'.

MISFIRES & HANG FIRES   The Russian muskets and rifles had leather caps to put over the nipple to prevent it getting wet. The nipple or inverted cone is pierced with a touch hole upon which the hammer exploded the cap. Minie rifles, piled outside a tent which got wet, did not fire the first time. Then caps were fired to dry out the cone. For this reason 75 caps were carried for 60 cartridges. Small charges of powder were also fired to dry out the barrels. British muskets used to have leather caps to cover the striker to allow 'dry firing' without damaging the nipple; the issue of these leather caps was discontinued, as a matter of economy, by the Treasury. (See also Squibbing.)

MORTARS   Short-barrelled weapons, which were used for firing 8 inch, 10 inch or 13 inch shells. The ranges of these shells were, respectively, 1720, 2530 & 2700 yards.

MOUNTED OFFICERS   There were four Mounted Officers in a Foot Guards battalion, the Commanding Officer, the two Colonels commanding the two Wings, each with four companies, and the Adjutant. All General Officers and Staff Officers were Mounted Officers. All Mounted Officers rode horses on the battlefield, which resulted in a number horses and officers being killed in action, as they were easy targets for the enemy to shoot at.

MUFTI   Civilian or plain clothes worn by a military person, who normally wears uniform.

NAVAL BRIGADE   A force of around 1000 sailors from the ships of the Black Sea Fleet. They returned to their ship's companies when a ship was transferred to another station and therefore served for a shorter time in the Crimea, around three months, than the Army. They were used to man naval gun batteries and also sometimes carried ladders in an assault on an objective, such as the Redan.

PATROL   A body of men, normally commanded by a subaltern, sent out to reconnoitre the country and to report on the strength of any enemy present and on any enemy activity.

PIQUET, PICQUET, PICKET   A body of men placed in front of an army to warn the main body of the approach of the enemy. They engaged the enemy and gradually fell back to the front-line troops.

'An Outlying Picquet is a body of 30–40 men, who go about five miles out, in front or in rear of an army, to give an alarm of any approach of the enemy, and if driven in to keep the enemy in check as long as possible to give the main body time to get under arms. From this body, detached men are again placed forward to give notice of anyone coming from the enemy These are scouts [infantry] or vedettes [cavalry].

'It is normally commanded by a captain or lieutenant and remains in position for 24 hours and must always be on the alert.'

'An Inlying Picquet is a body which remains within the lines, ready, under arms, to turn out at a moment's notice in support of the outlying picquet'. *The Crimean War, a Reappraisal, from the Letters of Captain Temple Godman, 5th Dragoon Guards.* p.90, Philip Warner.

PRICE'S CANDLE STOVES   Before Christmas 1854 Price's Patent Candle Company proposed lighter 'candle stoves for the troops' use. Lord Grey asked in the Lords why by 22 January the Company had received no reply after the matter had been considered by three officers in the Commissariat Department. *War & Administration.(Hansard- 29 January 1855 cxxxvi-c1073)*, pp. 67–68, John Sweetman, Scottish Academic Press, 1972.

QUEEN'S BIRTHDAY PARADE   Trooping the Colour.

QMG   Quartermaster-General: in charge of all supplies, food clothing, arms & ammunition, as well as the transport required for the Army. The following staff officers are junior to the QMG.

> Deputy Quartermaster-General DQMG
> Assistant Quartermaster-General AQMG
> Deputy Assistant Quartermaster-General DAQMG

RAILWAY   The Grand Crimean Central Railway. The building of this railway was suggested to the Government by Sir Morton Peto MP, of Peto, Brassey & Betts, railway engineers, to solve the Army's supply problems. He promised to build a railway and have it operating in three weeks, which the Government accepted. James Beatty, the Project Manager, arrived on 19 January 1855, the 530 navvies arrived on 3 February and started work on 8 February. By 23 February a load of stores had been carried to Kadikoi, a distance of 2¾ miles. By 26 March the track, including a double line of tracks to Kadikoi, was operational up to the British HQ, a further distance of 4 miles, which needed the installation of a stationary engine to pull the trucks up the steep gradient outside Kadikoi; in all 7 miles of track had been built in 7 weeks. Later on the track was extended another 3 miles up the north-east valley to the Woronzoff Road, to supply the 3rd and 4th Divisions on the Heights. Later a spur was connected to supply the Sardinians. During the height of the siege between 250 to 300 tons were carried daily to supply the divisions with ammunition, food, clothing, guns, huts, etc.

RED COAT Red or scarlet full dress coatee with tails, worn by officers in the Brigade of Guards.

REGULATION Up to 1871, when the purchase of commissions in the cavalry and infantry was abolished, the regulation price, fixed by the War Office, had to be paid to the present holder of a rank in a regiment for promotion to this rank by the officer wishing to be promoted. In addition to this amount, there was an extra payment, which was dependent on where the unit was to be located. It was higher if the unit was home-based and low or even non-existent if it was due for overseas or active service.

ROCKETS Rockets were fired from a tube, which could deliver shot, shells or carcasses. The range of a 6-pounder rocket was around 600 yards and for a 12-pounder rocket 1000 yards.

ROUND SHOT Solid iron cannon balls, which bounced over the ground and therefore could be avoided by observant soldiers. Used mainly against massed ranks of troops and to destroy fortifications.

SAP A narrow trench, dug for protection against enemy fire, while approaching an enemy position, prior to an attack. Also used for the technique of digging forward under the enemy's fortifications, and then exploding a mine to blow up these fortifications and kill troops.

SERGEANT-MAJOR In the Brigade of Guards, the Regimental Sergeant-Major, the most senior battalion warrant officer, is always called 'The Sergeant-Major'.

SHARPSHOOTERS Each battalion in the Army in the Crimea, selected around 10 of their best shots, who were equipped with

Minie rifles. They found concealed positions from which they could pick off Russian officers and artillerymen. This tactic was introduced as a result of the increased accuracy of the Minie rifle. The Guards Brigade took this to great lengths under Captain Goodlake and his detachment of 30 men, 10 from each of the three battalions. Their efforts at Little Inkerman were very largely responsible for stopping the attack by Russian sailors on the British left flank, for which Goodlake was awarded the VC. [See Chapter 3 The Development of Sharpshooting and Captain Goodlake's VC].

SHELLS Hollow round spheres, filled with a charge of powder and fitted with a fuse which could be set to explode the charge after a given number of seconds.

SOLDIER SERVANT A soldier detailed to look after an officer, keeping his kit clean, making his bed and sometimes cooking his ration for him. To be distinguished from the batman, who looked after the bat pony to which a company commander or a higher officer was entitled to in order to carry his kit.

SQUIBBING The practice of firing off small blank charges to dry out the barrel of a musket or rifle and to clear the nipple of moisture in order to prevent misfires and hang fires. This is why an excess of caps was carried in relation to the number of cartridges. Seventy-five caps were issued for sixty cartridges.

STAFF UNIFORM Properly a blue frock coat and a cocked hat with white cocks' feathers. In the Crimea officers appointed to the staff were often without the approved uniform and remained in their 'regimentals'. The cocked hat was soon replaced by the forage cap except on very formal occasions. General Scarlett, who led the Heavy Cavalry Brigade on 25 October 1854 in their brilliant charge, was a stickler for observing dress regulations. Although he wore a non-regulation helmet of leather made to his design, he ordered his ADC, Lieutenant Elliott, who paraded that day wearing a forage cap, to go and put on his cocked hat for the battle, which was clearly coming. The result was that the enemy largely overlooked General Scarlett himself, wearing his non-regulation leather-helmet, and concentrated on attacking Elliot who they assumed must be the most important officer. He had put a silk scarf inside his hat to prevent it falling off. This gave him some protection, as he was repeatedly cut about the head, but he survived to paint the scene, in which very reasonably he placed himself and not Scarlett, at the centre of the melee. *The Destruction of Lord Raglan*, pp. 137–9, C. Hibbert.

STOCK   A leather 'kerchief' worn by the infantry to protect the neck and to force the soldier to keep his head up. It was very uncomfortable to wear and was discarded by the soldiers as soon as they could do so, to the fury of, for example, General Sir George Brown, commanding the Light Division, who was a stickler for such things.

SUBALTERNS   Officers with the regimental rank of Lieutenant and Ensign, which are below the regimental rank of Captain.

VICTORIA CROSS   This medal was established by HM Queen Victoria by Royal Warrant on 29 January 1856. It was awarded both to officers and men in the Naval and Military Services, who had distinguished themselves before the enemy 'for valour'. The first Investiture for this medal was held on 26 June 1857, after all the claims for this medal had been investigated. A review was held in Hyde Park before Her Majesty the Queen, who pinned to the breast of each man the bronze cross he had won in the field for personal bravery. Initially it could not be awarded posthumously.

The awards of this medal, during this campaign, to the Foot Guards Regiments were:-
Grenadiers 4
Coldstream 4
Scots Fusiliers 5

VOLLEY-FIRING   Units, either battalions or companies which fired all their rifles at the same time, as opposed to file firing which gave a continuous fire at a target such as the defences of Sebastopol, to prevent the Russians from repairing damage to their fortifications from shell fire. A company was not normally subdivided into platoons, but this could be done to carry out specific tasks, as part of a battalion's sequence of volley-firing. See *Redcoat*, p.125, Richard Holmes.

WILKINSON'S   Henry Nock was a long-established gunmaker, established in business around 1770. He employed James Wilkinson [born 1758] as his foreman. James married Nock's daughter and on his death in 1804 succeeded to the business. Appointed Gunmaker-in-Ordinary to King George III in 1805, he continued to work until at least 1839, when he was contracted to make guns for the East India Company; he died in 1848. James's son Henry (born 1794), who joined his father as a gunsmith in 1818, then took over to the business. Henry was a highly skilled and inquiring technician, who undertook extensive studies into the nature of steels, from which he became an expert in the construction of swords. However, the making of swords took second place to that of guns until several years had passed. His inventions and technical improvements were many and various in number. Henry wrote a series of books, which included *Engines of War* in 1841 and then *Observations (Theoretical & Practical) on Muskets, Rifles and Projectiles* in 1852. His last work, written sometime later, was *Observations on Swords*. He died in 1861, the Company then becoming James Wilkinson & Son, which then evolved into Wilkinson Sword. Until the beginning of the Great War, they remained noted gunsmiths, while increasingly being in the forefront of sword development and marketing. (W.S.Curtis, Chairman, Crimean War Research Society).

WING There were two Wings, each with four companies, in a battalion. In the Brigade of Guards, they were usually commanded by a Regimental Major with an Army rank of Colonel or senior Lieutenant-Colonel. They were called Mounted Officers.

ZOUAVE French Colonial troops, recruited initially from North Africa.

Appendix D

Bibliography

Coldstream Guards

Published Books

Coldstream Guards RHQ, *Regimental Records*.

Coldstream Guards RHQ, *A History of the Coldstream Guards*, Leo Cooper, London, 2000.

Coldstream Guards RHQ, *Sergeant William McMillan's Diary*, Published by the Coldstream Guards.

Coldstream Guards RHQ, *A Short History of the Regiment's Victoria Cross Holders*, Lance-Sergeant L. Pearce.

Marker R., *Record of the Coldstream Guards, 1650–1918*, Published 1923. British Infantry, Acc.no.25758.

Ross-of-Bladensburg, Lieutenant-Colonel, *A History of the Coldstream Guards from 1815 to 1895.* (A Continuation of Daniel MacKinnon's *Origin & Services of the Coldstream Guards*, 2 vols, Richard Bentley, London, 1835). A.D.Innes & Co, London, 1896.

Ross-of-Bladensburg, Lieutenant-Colonel, *The Coldstream Guards in the Crimea*, Innes, London, 1896.

Wilson, Colonel C.T., Coldstream Guards, *A Regimental Officer, Our Veterans of 1854 In Camp & before the Enemy*, Street, London, 1859.

Windham, Lieutenant-General Sir Charles, *Diary & Letters*, Edited by Major Hugh Pearse, Keegan Paul, 1897.

Wyatt, Battalion Surgeon John, *A History of the 1ˢᵗ Battalion Coldstream Guards during the Eastern Campaign from February 1854 to June 1856*, 1858, London.

Diaries & Mss

Amherst Wm, Letters 23–24 Oct. 1854. Colonel Lord F. Paulet letter on his being wounded, National Army Museum,7305–75.

Chadburn, Sergeant, Crimean Letters, Mrs Alma Chadburn.

Clarke Jervoise, Henry, 42 Highlanders, ADC to Lieutenant-General Airey, Transferred Coldstream Guards. Letters 1854–56; vol 1–310 pages; vol.2–375 pages, Regimental Headquarters Coldstream Guards.

Cocks, Captain and Lieutenant-Colonel C.L., Coldstream Guards, Diary, February 22 to 15 July 1854, and Letters on the Crimean War; photostat copy; National Army Museum-Archives- 8111-13.Original at Regimental Headquarters Coldstream Guards.

Codrington, Major-General Sir William, Coldstream Guards, Letters, 1851–55, National Army Museum, Archives, 7808-90.

Goodlake, Captain Gerald, V.C., Coldstream Guards, Crimean War Letters, March 1854 to May 1856; typescript bound volume, Regimental Headquarters Coldstream Guards.

Heneage, Lieutenant Michael, Coldstream Guards, Crimean War Letters, RHQ, Coldstream Guards.

Ricketts, Asst Surgeon, Crimean Diary, *United Services Magazine,* March 1855.

Skelton, Dr Joseph, Surgeon, Coldstream Guards, Crimean Letters, Mrs Diana Drummond, Great-Great-Great Niece.

Tower, Captain H, Coldstream Guards, Crimean Diary, 1854–56; Alma, Balaclava, Inkerman, 218 pages. National Army Museum, Archives,Acc.no-8202-18.

Diaries-Grenadier Guards

Tipping, Captain Alfred, Letters from the East during the Campaign of 1854, Egerton Skipwith.

General

Published Books

Adkin, Mark, *The Waterloo Companion,* Aurum Press, London 2001.

Airlie, Mabell, Countess of, *With the Guards We Shall Go,* Hodder & Stoughton, 1933.

Anonymous, *Russian Account of the Battle of Inkerman from the German,* John Murray, 1856.

Aubrey-Fletcher, H.L, *A History of the Foot Guards to 1856,* Constable, London 1927.

Barthorp, M, *Heroes of the Crimea*, Blandford,1991.

Benson, A.C.and Esher, Viscount, (Editors), *The Letters of Queen Victoria*, Vol. III 1854–1861, John Murray, London, 1908.

Bentley, Nicolas, *Russell's Despatches from the Crimea*, London, 1970.

Bonham Carter, Victor, (Editor), *Surgeon in the Crimea. The Experiences of George Lawson, 1854–1855*, Military Book Society, London, 1968.

Caldwell, George and Robert Cooper, *Rifle Green in the Crimea*, Bugle Horn Publications, 1994.

Calthorpe, Colonel S, *Letters from Headquarters, by an Officer on the Staff*, John Murray, London, 1856.

Cavendish-Taylor, G, *Journal of Adventures with the British Army in the Crimea*, Hurst & Blackett, London. 1856.

Churchill, Sir Winston, *Marlborough. His Life and Times*, vol.I, George G.Harrap, London, 1933.

Clifford, Major Henry, VC *His Letters & Sketches from the Crimea*, Michael Joseph, 1956.

Cooke, Brian, *The Grand Crimean Central Railway*, Cavaliers House, 2nd Edition, 1997.

Creagh, Sir O'Moore V.C. and E.M.Humphreys, *The Victoria Cross-1856–1920*. Reprinted by J.B.Hayward & Son, 1985.

Danchev, Alex and Daniel Todman, *War Diaries 1939–45. Field Marshal Lord Alanbrooke*. Weidenfeld & Nicolson, London, 2001.

Dictionary of National Biography

Encyclopaedia Britannica, 1911 Edition.

ffrench-Blake, R.L.V, *The Crimean War*, Leo Cooper, London, 1971.

Fortescue, Sir John, *History of the British Army*, vol. X111, Macmillan, London, 1930.

Hamilton, Lieutenant-General Sir J.F., *History of the Grenadier Guards*, vol. III, John Murray, 1871.

Hamley, General Sir Edward, *War in the Crimea*, Seeley, London, 1896. *The Story of the Campaign of Sevastopol*, Blackwood, 1855. Reprinted by the Naval & Military Press, 2003.

Hargrave Mawson,Michael, *Eyewitness in the Crimea, The Crimean War Letters of Lieutenant Colonel George Frederick Dallas*, Greenhill Books, London, 2001.

Harries Jenkins, G, *The Army in Victorian Society*, London, 1977.

Hart, Lieutenant-Colonel H.G, *Annual Army Lists-1853–60*.

Her Majesty's Government, War Office, *Field Exercises & Evolutions of Infantry, as revised by Her Majesty's Command*, 1859.

Hibbert, C, *The Destruction of Lord Raglan*, Viking, London,1984. *Wellington-A Personal History*, HarperCollins, London, 1977.

Holmes, Richard, *Redcoat. The British Soldier in the Age of Horse & Musket,* HarperCollins, London, 2001.

Kerr, Sir David Lindsay, *The Constitutional History of Modern Britain-1485–1937,* A & C Black London, 1948.

Kinglake A.W, *The Invasion of the Crimea,* vol.111 (1866), vol. 1V (1868), vol. V (1875), vol. V1 (1880), vol.V11 (1882), vol. VIII (1887), Blackwood, Edinburgh and London.

Knollys, J & Major V.J.Elliott, *The Victoria Cross in the Crimea,* Dean, London, 1877.

Lambert, Andrew & Stephen Badsey, *The War Correspondents. The Crimean War,* Bramley,1994.

London Gazette, Captain Goodlake's VC, 24 February 1857.

Longford, Elizabeth, *Wellington, Pillar of State,* Weidenfeld & Nicolson, London, 1972. *Wellington, The Years of the Sword,* HarperCollins, London, 1985.

Lysons, Sir D, *The Crimean War from First to Last,* Murray, 1895.

McGuigan, Ron, *Into Battle-The British Order of Battle for the Crimean War 1854–56,* Withycut House, Bowden, 2001.

Mansfield, H.O. *Charles Ashe Windham, A Norfolk Soldier (1810–1970),* Terence Dalton, Lavenham, Suffolk, 1973.

Massie, Alistair, *The Crimean War. The Untold Stories,* Sidgwick & Jackson, London, 2004.

Maurice, Major-General Sir F, *The History of the Scots Guards,* vol. II, Chatto & Windus, London, 1934.

Mercer, Patrick, *Give them a Volley & Charge. The Battle of Inkerman-1854,* Spellmount, Staplehurst, Kent 1998. *Inkerman 1854-The Soldiers' Battle,* Campaign Series, Osprey, 1998.

Nightingale, Florence, *Notes on matters affecting the Health, Efficiency, and Hospital Administration of the British Army,* London, 1858.

Nolan,E.H, *The Illustrated History of the War against Russia,* vols 1 & II, London, 1857.

Pack, Colonel Reynell, *Sebastopol Trenches and Five Months in Them,* Kerry & Endeen, 1878. (Republished by Pallas Armata–2001).

Paget, Colonel Sir Julian, *The Story of the Guards,* Osprey, London, 1976.

Parry, Douglas H, *Britain's Roll of Glory,* Cassell, 1895. Renamed 1913, *VC- Its Heroes & Their Valour.*

Pemberton, W Baring, *Battles of the Crimean War,* B.T.Batsford, London, 1962.

Pillinger, Dennis & Anthony Staunton, *Victoria Cross Presentations & Locations,* Published by the Authors, 2000.

Reeve, Henry, *The Greville Memoirs, Queen Victoria's Reign,* vol.5,

1841–46; vol. 6, 1846–52; vol.7, 1852–55; vol.8, 1855–60; Longmans Green, London, 1888.

Robins, Major Colin, *Captain Dunscombe's Diary*, Withycut House, Bowdon, 2003.

Royle, Trevor,*The Crimea- The Great Crimean War-1854–1856*, Little Brown, London, 1999.

Russell, Sir William Howard, *The British Expedition to the Crimea*, Routledge, London, 1858.

Ryan, George, *The Lives of Our Heroes of the Crimea*, James Field & Co, London, 1855.

Sayer, Captain, *Despatches & Papers relative to the Campaign in Turkey, Asia Minor & the Crimea*, Harrison, London, 1857.Reprinted by Pallas Armata, 2001.

Schama, Simon. *A History of Britain–3000 BC to AD 1603*, BBC, London, 2000. *A History of Britain- The British Wars-1603- 1776*, BBC, London, 2001.

Seaton, Albert, *The Crimean War-A Russian Chronicle*, London, 1977.

Selby, J, *The Thin Red Line of Balaklava*, Hamish Hamilton, London 1970.

Small, Hugh, *Florence Nightingale-Avenging Angel*, Constable, London, 1998.

Stephenson, Sir F.C.A, *At Home & on the Battlefield*, John Murray, 1915.

Strachan, Hew, *From Waterloo to Balaklava-Tactics, Technology & the British Army 1815–54*, Cambridge University Press, 1985.

—— *Wellington's Legacy, Reform of the British Army 1830–54*, Manchester University Press, 1984.

St Aubyn, Giles, *The Royal George. The Life of Prince George, Duke of Cambridge*, Constable, London, 1963.

Steevens, Lieutenant-Colonel Nathaniel, *The Crimean Campaign with The Connaught Rangers 1854–55–56*, Griffith & Farran, London, 1858. Reprinted 2002, Naval & Military Press.

Todleben, General F.E.L., *La Defense de Sebastopol*, 1863–70.

Trevelyan, G.M, *England Under the Stuarts*, Methuen, London, 1904.

Twiston Davies, David, *The Daily Telegraph Book of Military Obituaries*, Grub Street, London, 2003.

Tyrrell, Henry, *History of the War with Russia*, vols. I-VI, London Printing & Publishing Company, 1856.

Warner, Philip, *The Crimean War: An Appraisal*, Wordsworth Editions, Ware, Herts, 2001.

Wetherall, G.A, *Returns Relating to Officers in the Army (Crimea.)*, The House of Commons, London 1857.

Wedgwood, C.V, *The Great Rebellion-The King's Peace 1637–1641*, Collins, London, 1955.

Weintraub, Stanley, *Albert-Uncrowned King,* John Murray, London 1997.

Wilkinson, Philip, *A History of the Victoria Cross,* Constable, 1894.

Windham,. Major-General C.A, *Crimean Diaries & Letters,* London, 1897.

Wolseley, Field Marshal Viscount, *The Story of a Soldier's Life,* vols 1 & 2, Constable, London, 1903.

Wood, Field Marshal Sir Evelyn, *The Crimea in 1854 & 1894,* Chapman & Hall, London 1895. *From Midshipman to Field Marshal,* Methuen, 1906.

Woodham Smith, C, *The Reason Why,* Constable & Co, 1953. *Florence Nightingale,* Constable & Co, 1950.

Woodward, E.L., *The Age of Reform 1815–70,* Clarendon Press, Oxford, 1938.

Army Organization & Administration

Gordon, Hampden, *The War Office,* Putnam, London, 1935.

Spiers, Edward M, *The Late Victorian Army-1868–1902,* Manchester University Press,1992.

Sweetman, John, *War And Administration-The Significance of the Crimean War for the British Army,* Scottish Academic Press, Edinburgh, 1984.

Stevens, Megan, *Thesis on the Crimean Letters of Commissary-General W.H.Drake,* Royal Logistics Museum, Deepcut, Camberley, Surrey.

Journals

Edinburgh Review, 1854-Report of the Commissioners on Promotion in the Army Speech by Rt.Hon Sidney Herbert on Moving Army Estimates. Republished by Pallas Armata-May 1998.

Guards Museum History of the Bearskin Cap by Capt.D.D.Horn-Curator

Military History Society-"Victoria Cross Biography on Capt.Gerald Goodlake VC" By Canon W.M.Lummis MC.

*Royal Statistical Society-*1980-"The Purchase System in the British Army-1660–1871" by Anthony Bruce.

Society for Army Historical Research Journal for-Vol.XII page 221-"The Era of Army Purchase" by Brig-Gen.H Biddulph.

Royal United Services Institution, Journal of the -1858 -Lane Fox,Lt.Col.A, Grenadier Guards, "On the Improvement of the Rifle, as A Weapon of General Use" Republished by Pallas Armata March 2000.

Victorian Military Society, Journal of the -Issue no 69. June 1992.
   "Crimean Sharpshooters" by Michael Barthrop
War Correspondent (Journal of the Crimean War Research Society) Vol.14
   No 1-April 1996-"Infantry Shoulder Arms of the Crimean War-Part
   Five-Great Britain-Minie Rifle Pattern 51 by W.S.Curtis.
—— Vol 14 No. 1-April 1996 " Double Rank in the Guards" by Major
   Colin Robins.
—— Vol. 21 No. 1-April 2003. The Naval Hospital at Therapia -Pt 1 by
   Prof. Richard Huntsman, Mary Bruin & Deborah Holttum. Reprinted
   from the *Journal of the Royal Naval Medical Service*-Vol. 88, No. 1,
   2002. pp 5–27.

Periodicals
The Journal of the Household Brigade.
Illustrated London News (July-September 1854)
Punch. Vols XXV-XXV11 1853–54
Colbourne's United Services Magazine

Appendix E

1st Battalion Coldstream Guards – Effective Strength and Casualties – Crimean War 1854–56*

Effective Strength	Officers		NCOs & Men		Total	
Battalion Feb. 1854	35		919		954	
Reinforcements	56		1141		1197	
Total	91		2060		2151	
Losses		%		%		%
Killed in action	9	9.8	81	3.9	90	4.2
Died of wounds	1	1.1	54	2.6	55	2.6
Died of disease	3	3.3	564	27.4	567	26.4
	13	14.2	699	33.9	712	33.2
Admissions to Hospital Regt. & General.						
Disease	17	18.7	2785	135.2	2802	130.3
Wounds	7	7.7	243	11.8	250	11.6
Accidents	–		73	3.5	73	3.4
Total	24	26.4	3101	150.5	3125	145.3
Invalided & Discharged						
Disease	7	7.7	52	2.5	59	2.7
Wounds	–		59	2.9	59	2.7
Total	7	7.7	111	5.4	118	5.5
Total Loss	20	22.0	810	39.3	830	38.6

* *The Coldstream Guards in the Crimea* Appendix E, pp. 306–7, Lieutenant-Colonel Ross-of-Bladensburg.

Index

PEOPLE
(a) British Military Forces
Notes –
*(i)   Military ranks shown below are those
      borne by officers at the time of the
      Crimean War.*
*(ii) Only those officers referred to in text and
      footnotes are indexed – for other officers
      serving in the Crimea, see Appendix A.*
*(iii) Goodlake refers in his letters to some
      officers and men for whom no
      subsequent identification has been
      possible; these men are denoted in the
      index by (U) after their name.*

**Generals & Staff Officers serving
in Crimea – Coldstream Guards**
Airey, Lieut-General Sir J.T. – 11,
      102, 108, 116, 149, 158, 169.
Bentinck, Lieut-General Sir H.
      George – 7, 20, 29, 32, 34, 39,
      45, 70, 77, 79, 96, 115.
Bingham, Captain & :Lieut-Colonel
      Lord – 25, 26, 30, 36, 44, 45.
Boyle, Lieut-Colonel The Hon R.E.,
      MP – 21.
Byng, Captain The Hon H.W. . Earl
      of Strafford – 95, 98.
Codrington, General Sir William –
      11, 23, 31, 45, 46, 59, 81, 137,
      138, 146, 152, 153, 155, 157,
      166.
Hardinge, Lieut-Colonel The Hon

Arthur – 120, 128, 179, 182,
      185.
Steele, Colonel Sir Thomas (Tom) –
      107, 151, 154.
Wellesley, Captain The Hon W.H.,
      Viscount Dangan – 36.

**Officers & men serving in Crimea
– 1st Bn. Coldstream Guards**
Adair, Lieut A.W. – 120, 128.
Amherst, Lieut The Hon W.A. – 78.
Armytage, Lieut & Captain Henry –
      26, 27, 45, 95, 98.
Ashton, Sgt-Major Joseph (Later
      Lieut – Rifle Brigade) – 55, 64,
      77.
Bouverie, Captain H.M. – 78, 151,
      154.
Burton, Captain & Lieut-Colonel
      F.A.P. – 43, 120, 128.
Cowell, Lieut-Colonel J.C.M. – 78.
Crawley, Brevet Major Peter (&
      family) – 25–27, 30, 32, 34, 42,
      44, 45, 47, 70, 81, 91, 94, 104,
      106, 111, 118, 126, 151, 163,
      169, 189.
Cumming, Lieut H.W. – 33, 46.
Dawkins, Captain & Lieut-Colonel
      W.G. – 26, 44, 70.
Dawson, Captain & Lieut-Colonel
      The Hon T.V. – 25, 44, 70, 78.
Disbrowe, Captain E.A. – 78.

Drummond, Lieut & Captain The Hon H.R. – 169.
Dunkellin, Captain & Lieut-Colonel Lord – 78, 162, 169.
Dunlop, Lieut & Captain Sir James, Bt – 27, 33, 42, 45, 47, 91, 165, 180.
Eliot, Lieut & Captain The Hon. G.C.C. – 25, 45, 70, 78.
Falconer, QM A. – 89, 97, 116.
Fielding, Captain The Hon W.H.A. – 78.
Fitzroy, Lieut-Colonel Lord A.C.L. – 78.
Fremantle, Captain AJ.L.. – 95, 98.
Goodlake, Captain Littlehales, VC – family & ancestry, 6; education, 6; overall military career, 6, 7; career summary during period of letters, Feb–Aug 1854, 22, 23; Sep 1854–Feb 1855, 51, 53–64, 69–72, 74, 75; Mar–June 1855, 99–103; June–Aug 1855, 131–132; Sep 1855–Jan 1856,155–158; Jan–May 1856, 174–176; personality, 176–178; post-war career, 186; retirement,187–188; death,188.
Greville, Lieut C. – 78.
Halkett, Lieut-Colonel J. – 78.
Jolliffe, Captain Hylton – 33, 46.
Lane, Lieut H.J. Bagot – 120, 128.
Larcombe, Soldier-Servant – 80, 91, 110, 116, 119, 121, 123, 138, 144.
Mackinnon, Captain L.D. – 78.
Markham, Lieut W.T. – 91, 97.
Newton, Colonel W.S. – 25, 45, 70.
Paulet, Colonel Lord Frederick. – 7, 69, 70, 109.
Ramsden. Lieut & Captain F. Henry – 35, 36, 42, 46, 47, 78.
Skelton, Sgt J. – 45.
Strong, Captan & Lieut-Colonel C.W. – 70.
Tierny, Captain & Lieut-Colonel C.G. – 44, 48.

Tower, Captain & Lieut-Colonel H. – 70.
Trevelyan, Captain & Lieut-Colonel – 21, 42, 47.
Upton, Lieut-Colonel The Hon George – 7, 40, 42, 47, 70, 78, 104, 105, 109, 111, 115–117, 119, 126, 127.
Whitshed, Captain & Lieut Sir St V.B.H. – 91, 97.
Wildbore, A/Surgeon F. – 25, 44.
Willison (U) – 27.
Wilson, Captain & Lieut-Colonel C.T. – 58, 64, 65, 70, 96, 121, 128, 146.

Officers & men serving in Crimea – 3rd Bn. Grenadier Guards
Anstruther, Lieut-Colonel Sir Robert, Bt – 37, 44, 45.
Bathurst, Lieut & Captain W. (Bill) – 35, 46, 94, 120, 182.
Blenkins, Surgeon G. – 44, 48.
Bruce, Lieut-Colonel The Hon R. – 111, 127.
Cameron, Lieut & Captain W.G. – 53, 78, 96.
Davies, Lieut F.B. – 78, 96.
Foley, Colonel The Hon St George, CB – 154, 182, 185.
Fergusson, Lieut & Captain Sir James, Bt – 94, 98, 120, 128.
Hogge, Captain N. – 111, 127.
Hood, Colonel Grosvenor – 78, 96.
Lewis, Colonel C. – 147, 154.
Neville, Captain The Hon, H. – 78.
Newman, Captain Sir R., Bt – 78, 96.
Pakenham, Lieut-Colonel R. – 78, 96.
Percy, Lieut-Colonel Lord Her.ry, VC – 96.
Rowley, Captain – 78, 96.
Sturt, Captain Napier – 78, 89, 90, 96, 97.
Tipping, Captain Alfred – 73, 78, 95, 96.

Officers & men serving in Crimea – 1st Bn. Scots Fusilier Guards

Astley, Lieut & Captain Sir John – 29, 44, 45, 165, 182, 188, 189.

Baring, Lieut & Captain Francis – 53, 78, 96.

Blane, Lieut & Captain Sir Seymour – 165, 170, 189.

Buckley, Lieut & Captain D.F. – 161, 169.

Campbell, Lieut & Captain A.C., Baron Blythswood – 90, 97, 114.

Craig, Sgt James, VC – 169.

Dalrymple, Captain & Lieut-Colonel J.H. – 36, 46.

Drummond, Captain Hugh (Harry) – 78, 96, 159.

Farquharson, Captain & Lieut-Colonel James – 159. 168.

Hunter Blair, Lieut-Colonel J. – 96, 98.

Scarlett, Captain & Lieut-Colonel The Hon W.F. – 138, 153.

Shuckburgh, Captain G.H. – 78, 96.

Smith, Drummer, VC – 169.

Stephenson, Captain & Lieut-Colonel F. (Ben) – 32, 45.

Walker, Colonel Edward F. – 159, 168.

Wallace, Captain – 34.

Other officers & men serving in Crimea

Adams, Brig-General Henry (49th Foot Rgt) – 46, 79, 96.

Blundell (U) – 183.

Bourchier, Major Claude Thomas, VC (Rifle Brigade) – 62, 118, 127.

Briton, Captain (U) – 84, 85.

Brock, Soldier-Servant (7th Fusiliers) – 107, 137, 143.

Brown, Lieut-General Sir George – 11, 30, 45, 69, 131, 137, 138, 152, 153.

Browne, Captain The Hon C. (7th Fusiliers) – 111, 127.

Cambridge, Major-General, Duke of – 7, 33, 47, 95, 115, 116, 119, 121, 182, 184.

Campbell, General Sir Colin, Baron Clyde – 11, 97, 106, 166, 170.

Campbell, Major-General Sir John – 136, 140, 152.

Cartwright, Captain (Rifle Brigade) – 58.

Cathcart, Lieut-General Sir Reginald – 77, 96, 189.

Clifford, Captain Henry, VC (Rifle Brigade) – 63, 65, 157.

Cooksley, DA/Commissionary-General A.F. – 26, 45.

Cowper Coles, Commander (Royal Navy) – 175.

Dallas, Captain & Brevet Major George Frederick (46th South Devonshire Rgt) – 47.

De Lacy Evans, Lieut-General Sir George – 152.

Dixon, Capt (7th Fusiliers) – 143, 145, 153.

Doyne, William (Army Works Corps) – 157.

Duckworth, Major (5th Dragoon Guards) – – 43.

Dundas, Rear-Admiral Sir Richard (Royal Navy) – 16, 43, 156.

Egerton, Colonel P,I.B, (77th Rgt) – 114, 127.

Elliott, Lieut A.J.H. (5th Dragoon Guards) – 43, 48.

Estcourt, Major-General Sir James – 137, 138, 152.

Eyre, Lieut-General William – 137, 153.

Fox, Charley – 106.

Gifford, Captain (Royal Navy) – 34, 45.

Gordon, Captain R.H. (38th Rgt; later Coldstream) – 112, 162, 169.

Gregory, Captain George (Royal Marines) – 86, 97.

Hamley, Captain F.B. – 132, 177.

Hardinge, General Lord – 12, 50, 116, 121, 127, 128, 179, 184.

Hay, Captain Lord John (Naval Brigade) – 113, 127.

Herbert, Brevet-Colonel The Hon Percy – 164, 169, 170, 175.

Horton, Lieut (Royal Navy) – 185.

Jones, Lieut-General H. (Royal Engineers) – 95, 98.

Le Marchant, Colonel Thomas (5th Dragoon Guards) – 43, 48.

Lempriere, Captain (77th Rgt) – 114, 127, 150.

Lyons, Rear-Admiral Sir E. (Royal Navy) – 23, 43, 152.

Lysons, Lieut-Colonel Daniel (23rd Foot Rgt) – 135.

Macdonald, Major The Hon James, W.R. ('Jemmy') – 39, 47.

McMurdo, Colonel William (Land Transport Corps) – 112, 116, 127, 162, 163, 169, 181.

Macnish (93rd Highlanders) – 31.

Markham, Captain (2nd Rifle Bn.) – 56, 57.

Michell, Lieut-General John (Royal Artilery) & family – 123, 128.

Morris, Colonel C.H. (Royal Artillery) – 182, 185.

Napier, Vice-Admiral Sir Charles (Royal Navy) – 156, 158.

Napier, Brevet Lieut-Colonel W.E. (Land Transport Corps) – 181, 184.

Nightingale, Lieut Arthur C. (93rd Foot Rgt – Sutherland Highlanders) – 167, 179.

Norton, Majpr (88th Rgt) – 121.

Paget, Colonel Lord George (4th Light Dragoons) – 47.

Paulet Somerset, Lieut-Colonel – 145, 153.

Pearson, Brevet Major R.L.O. (7th Fusiliers) – 137, 138, 143, 152.

Pennyfather, Lieut-General – 137, 138, 152.

Raglan, Field Marshal Lord – 7, 8, 19–22, 28, 33, 34, 40, 45, 50, 68, 69, 71, 72, 76, 80–82, 88–90, 93, 94, 97, 100, 104–107, 115, 116, 119, 121, 130, 131, 134–136, 138–140, 143, 153, 169.

Roebuck, Surgeon (39th Regt) – 179.

Rokeby, Lieut-General Lord – 68, 110, 112, 115–117, 121, 171, 183.

Scarlett, Lieut-General Sir James – 43, 45, 48, 131, 138, 143, 145.

Shadforth, Lieut-Colonel (57th Foot Rgt) – 135.

Shirley, Colonel (28th Rgt) – 124.

Simpson, General Sir James – 8, 11, 130, 131, 133, 141, 142,149, 153, 155, 157, 166.

Stanlake (Stanlock), Private William, VC, DCM – 57.

Taylor, Bertie (U) – 181.

Thompson, Major (5th Dragoon Guards) – 43.

Torrens, Brig-General A. – 79, 96.

Tryon, Lieut (Rifle Brigade) – 62, 127.

Turner (Surgeon (U) – 81.

Vane. Captain Freddy (7th Fusiliers – & family) – 23, 29, 33, 34, 81, 85, 89, 90, 92, 94, 105, 107, 111, 112, 114, 121, 124, 125, 127, 135, 136, 142, 144, 147, 160.

Vivian, Captain R.H. (14th Rgt) – 80, 97.

Wakefield (Army Works Corps) – 175, 178, 184.

Webb, Lieut (88th Rgt) – 58.

Wetherall, Colonel Sir Edward (Land Transport Corps) – 164, 169.

Windham, Lieut-General – 146, 153, 182.

Woodford, Colonel C.J. (Rifle Brigade) – 104, 126.

Yea, Brevet Colonel (7th Fusiliers – & family) – 29, 45, 81, 85, 87, 90, 92, 107, 111, 119, 121, 122, 128, 131, 133–138, 140, 143, 145, 146.

(b) Other Military Forces
French
Canrobert, Marshal – 67, 69, 70, 72, 94, 100, 101, 107, 114.
Napoleon III, Emperor – 16, 120, 151, 166.
Neil, General H. – 94, 96.
Pélissier, Marshal – 100, 131, 134, 180.
St Arnaud, Marshal – 43, 47, 70, 97.

Sardinian
Marmora, General – 122.

Turkish
Omar Pasha – 37, 87, 166.

Russian
Constantine, Grand Duke – 77.
Dannenberg, General – 65.
Gortzakoff, Prince Michael – 120, 128.
Federoff, Colonel – 56, 64.
Liprandi, Lieut-General Pavel – 67, 94, 98, 131, 132, 146.
Nicholas I, Tsar – 15, 16, 20, 106.
Pauloff, General – 65.
Soimonoff, General – 59, 65.
Todleben, General F.E.I. – 59, 65.

(c) Other Personalities
Note – authors of credited works are included in this section only when they are specifically referred to in the main text.
Aberdeen, Prime Minister, Lord – 68, 97, 173.
Albert, Prince (Prince Consort) – 8, 23, 128.
Anstruther, Henry (23rd Foot Rgt) – 45.
Barthrop, Michael – 54, 63–65.
Birch, Captain – 189.
Brace, Sgt-Major – 189.
Brownlow, QM Sgt – 189.
Byng, Field Marshal Sir John, Lord Strafford (Coldstream Guards) – 91, 95, 97, 111, 115,121, 128.

Calthorpe, Captain S.J.G. (Coldstream Guards) – 50, 61, 62, 64.
Clark, Private – 189.
Cook (tradesman) – 180.
Corry, Colonel The Hon H. – 189.
Curtis, W.S. – 50, 61.
Derby, Lord – 94.
Falkener, Captain – 189.
Farrow, Sgt – 189.
George, Prince Regent – 11.
Gipps, Lieut-General Sir R., KCB – 189.
Goodlake family (specific references in letters to Goodlake's parents) – Emilia Jane ('Bob' – sister), 30, 32, 33, 35, 41, 44, 79, 84, 85, 88–90, 94, 105, 108, 110, 114, 115, 119, 121, 123, 138, 141, 142, 144, 146, 147, 150, 152, 160, 163, 164, 179–182; Margaret (wife), 186; Harry (brother), 33; Tom (brother),146, 147, 152, 163.
Hamilton, Lieut-General Sir F.W. (GG) – 50.
Hamley, Lieut-Colonel E. Bruce (Royal Artillery) – 177, 184.
Herbert, Sidney (Lord Herbert of Lea), Secretary-at-War – 12, 74, 87, 95, 98.
Hodkiss (family cook) – 106.
James II, King – 11.
Johnson, QM Sgt – 189.
Kinglake, A.W. – 53–55, 57, 59, 64.
Methuen, Colonel Lord, MP (Wiltshire Rgt) – 182, 184.
Monck, Lieut-General The Hon R. – 189.
Monck – Lieut – 189.
Newcastle, Duke of, Secretary of State for War – 21, 22, 45, 79, 95, 96, 98, 100, 173.
Nightingale, Florence – 74, 101, 173, 174.
Page, Private – 189.
Palmerston, Lord, Prime Minister – 68, 97.

Panmure, Lord, Secretary of State for War – 97, 141, 166.
Pringle, Sir John – 75.
Pusey, Lady E. – 164.
Ross-of-Bladensburg, Lieut-Colonel – 21, 44, 64, 92, 174.
Russell, Lord John – 106, 126.
Russell, William – 23, 72.
Seymour, Major-General Lord W.F.E. (Coldstream Guards) – 189.
Smith – Sgt – 189.
Snelling – Sgt – 189.
Soyer, Alexis – 157, 160.
Shaftesbury, Lord – 101.
Stuart De Decies, Colonel Baron (Waterford Militia) – 147, 154.
Sutherland, Dr – 101.
Victoria, Queen – 31, 172, 176, 186.
Ward, Baron William – 122, 128.
Webb (family groom) – 180.
Wellington, Duke of – 7, 8, 9, 12, 73, 127, 177.
Wilkinson, James (& family) – 165, 170.
William III, King – 11.

PLACES
(a) The Crimean War Zone
Azov, Sea of (general references) – 100, 101, 125, 128, 129, 151, 175, 185.
Black Sea, The (general references) – 32, 46, 153, 154, 170.
Bulgaria – Aladyn, 19, 20, 39; Balchik Bay, 66; Constanza, 46; Dobruja, The, 42, 46, 101; Dschaseli, 19; Galata Serai, 19; Gevreclek, 19; Pera, 35; Shumla, 20, 31; Silistra, 20; Stambool, 35; Trajan's Wall, 46; Varna (& Plain of), 19, 20, 22, 24, 25, 31, 34, 36, 37, 41–43, 47, 50, 66, 69, 85, 133, 134, 170.
Crimea – general references, 6–9, 12; 36, 45, 46, 48, 50, 51, 58, 65, 69, 72, 74, 75, 79, 89, 90, 98–100, 113, 128, 132–134,

140, 147, 152–154, 169, 170, 172, 173, 175, 177, 178, 180, 183, 184, 188, 189; Alma, The (& River), 6, 11, 47, 50, 66, 67, 73, 76, 92, 141, 152, 155–159, 162, 169, 183; Arabat, 122, 128; Bachesonai (Bakhchi Serai / Bachmut), 179, 180, 184; Baidar, (& Valley of), 153, 164, 165, 169; Balaklava, 7, 11, 45, 48, 54, 67, 68, 70, 73–76, 81, 82, 84, 86, 87, 92, 94, 99–101, 103, 104, 118, 132, 133, 135, 139, 147, 153, 155–159, 165, 168, 169, 175, 178, 183; Belbek, River (& Valley), 67, 139, 151, 153; Bulganak, River, 66; Careenage Ravine, 54–56, 64, 65; Chersonese, Cape, 97; Eupatoria, 66, 151; Fediukine Heights, 67; Inkerman, 6, 7; 46, 47, 50, 51, 53, 59, 62, 68, 70, 71, 74, 76, 77, 92, 104, 118, 125, 145, 152–154, 156, 169; Kadikoi, 67, 68, 74, 100, 153; Kaffa (& Gulf of), 164, 166, 170; Kalamita Bay (Old Fort), 66, 69, 154, 184; Kamiesch Bay, 143, 153, 171, 176; Kazatch, 171; Katcha, River, 67, 69; Kazatch anchorage, 182; Kertch (& Straits of), 100, 101, 118–120, 122, 152, 154, 169, 170, 175, 185; Lancaster Battery, 64; Mackenzie Heights, 60, 154, 166, 170, 183; Mackenzie's Farm, 67; Malakoff, The (& Tower), 102, 124, 130, 131, 134, 135, 150, 155, 156, 160, 161, 180, 185; Mamelon, The, 57, 101, 110, 112, 123–125, 130, 131, 143, 159; Perekop, 147, 151, 153, 154; Redan, The (Batteries / Quarries), 59, 62, 101, 102, 114, 124, 127, 130, 131, 134–136, 155,156, 169;

Crimea – general references
(continued)
Redoubt, The, 62; St George,
Monastery of, 153, 170;
Sandbag Battery, The, 70, 96;
Sapoune Heights, The, 74, 93,
131; Sevastopol (& Harbour), 7,
21, 22, 25, 28; 40–44, 47, 54,
57; 59, 60, 62, 65, 67, 72; 74,
76–79, 81, 84–86, 89, 91, 93,
95, 97, 99–101, 107, 113–115,
118, 123, 125, 130, 134, 148,
150–157, 159, 161, 169, 177,
180, 184, 186; Simferopol, 179,
183, 184; Taganrog, 176;
Tchernaya, The (& Bridge /
River / Valley), 7, 60, 61, 67,
130–133, 148, 149, 153, 170,
177;. Traktir, 67; Windmill
Ravine, 54; Woronzoff Road, 99,
100, 169; Yenikale (Yeni Kale),
100, 101, 122, 128; Yalta – 183.
Danube, River – 46.
Don, River & Estuary – general
references, 100, 101, 128, 129,
175, 185; Taguerot, 125, 129.
Russia – Anapa, 40; Bessarabia, 183;
Kursk, 180; Odessa, 23, 28, 40,
45, 77, 96, 97, 125; Rostov,
100, 101.
Silistria (Rumania) – general
references, 31, 34, 37.
Turkish Empire – Beicos Bay, 34, 37,
46; Besika Bay, 16;
Constantinople (& suburbs), 15,
16, 20, 21, 28, 45, 151, 180;
Dardanelles, The,15, 16, 19, 27;
Gallipoli, 27, 28; Mountain, 34;
Scutari, 19, 20, 22–24, 28; 36,
74, 84, 172, 173; Sweet Waters
(Golden Horn), 32; Terek, 34;
Troy, Plains of – 22, 27.

(b) Europe
Austria – Vienna, 126, 170.
Biscay, Bay of – 26.
Corfu – 182.
Finland & The Baltic – general
reference, 156; Helsinki, 156;
Sveaborg, 156, 158.
France – Paris, 171, 172.
Gibraltar – 25.
Great Britain & Ireland – Aldershot
Camp, 172, 176; Ascot
Racecourse, 188; Chobham,
Surrey, 8, 23; Cowes, Isle of
Wight, 25; Denham Fishery
(Uxbridge), Middlesex, 188,
189; Devon, County of, 57;
Edinburgh, 31; Eton College, 6,
26, 39, 112, 187, 188;
Goodwood Racecourse, 188;
Hamworth, Middlesex (Manor
of), 6; Harefield, Middlesex,
189; Letcombe Regis, Berkshire
– 6; London (various locations),
111, 121, 143, 153, 167, 170,
172, 176, 186, 188; Portsmouth,
172; Ryde, Isle of Wight, 147;
Shellingford, Berkshire, 6;
Southampton, 18, 20; Spithead,
47, 172, 176; Waterford,
Ireland, 154; White Horse, Vale
of, 187; Woxendon (Uxonden),
Middlesex (Manor of), 6;
Windsor Castle, 172.
India – 11, 173.
Malta – general references, 18–20, 22,
24, 25, 28, 30, 50, 172, 180;
Lazeretto, The, 18, 25, 26; Fort
Manuel, 25; Fort Tigne, 25;
Valetta, 26.
Mediterranean Sea – 173.